Generation

Generation is both an introduction to and a comparative study of contemporary psychoanalytic clinical theory. It provides the reader with a comprehensive overview of how new ways of thinking about the psycho-analytic process have evolved and are still in development today.

Jean White presents a detailed study of contemporary Independent, Lacanian and post-Kleinian theory, set within the wider context of the international expansion of psychoanalysis. Contemporary clinical practice is discussed in relation to concepts of psychopathology, transference and countertransference and innovations in technique. Each school's explicit and implicit models of psychic growth and their view of the aims of the psychoanalytic process are explored. Written in clear, accessible language and interwoven throughout with clinical vignettes, *Generation* provides an invaluable initiation into the work of notoriously difficult authors such as Lacan and Bion.

This stimulating presentation of contemporary psychoanalytic theory will be of great interest to psychoanalytic psychotherapists, psychodynamic counsellors and psychoanalysts of all theoretical orientations.

Jean White is a psychoanalytic psychotherapist in private practice in London. Since 1986, she has consulted to many public sector organisations and lectured for a range of psychoanalytic psychotherapy trainings. She is a member of the Guild of Psychotherapists and the Forum for Independent Psychotherapists.

Generation

Preoccupations and Conflicts in Contemporary Psychoanalysis

Jean White

Routledge
Taylor & Francis Group

LONDON AND NEW YORK

First published 2006 by Routledge
27 Church Road, Hove, East Sussex BN3 2FA

Simultaneously published in the USA and Canada
by Taylor & Francis Inc
270 Madison Avenue, New York, NY 10016

Routledge is an imprint of the Taylor & Francis Group, an informa business

Typeset in Times by Garfield Morgan, Mumbles, Swansea
Printed and bound in Great Britain by MPG Books, Bodmin, Cornwall
Cover design by Richard Massing

This publication has been produced with paper manufactured to strict
environmental standards and with pulp derived from sustainable forests.

British Library Cataloguing in Publication Data
A catalogue record for this book is available from the British Library

Library of Congress Cataloging-in-Publication Data
White, Jean, 1950–
    Generation : preoccupations and conflicts in contemporary psychoanalysis
/ Jean White.
        p. ; cm.
    Includes bibliographical references and index.
    ISBN13 978-1-58391-961-3 (hbk.)
    ISBN10 1-58391-961-9 (hbk.)
    ISBN13 978-1-58391-962-0 (pbk.)
    ISBN10 1-58391-962-7 (pbk.)
1. Psychoanalysis. I. Title.
    [DNLM: 1. Psychoanalytic Theory–Case Reports. 2. Cross-Cultural
Comparison–Case Reports. 3. Psychoanalytic Therapy–Case Reports.
WM 460 W585g 2006]
RC506.W4744 2006
616.89'17–dc22

                                                        2006010018

ISBN13 978-1-58391-961-3 (hbk)
ISBN13 978-1-58391-962-0 (pbk)

ISBN10 1-58391-961-9 (hbk)
ISBN10 1-58391-962-7 (pbk)

This is an extraordinary work. The author and her work evoke the image of a human global position satellite who (which) surveys the entire landscape, microscopically and globally, of the Zeitgeist of psychoanalytic theory and practice. The author has an astonishing in-depth understanding of all the psychoanalytic schools, their cross-influencing of each other and detailed discussions of how each school approximates a wide range of psychopathology and how each deals with therapeutic approaches to confront them. I cannot think of any major analyst or theory that has been left out. Moreover, the author, who pleads for analytic pluralism, has masterfully proved her point. This is an exceptional work that should find itself in every psychoanalyst's and psychotherapist's library.

James S. Grotstein, Clinical Professor of Psychiatry David Geffen School of Medicine, UCLA, Training and Supervising Analyst Los Angeles Psychoanalytic Society/Institute and The Psychoanalytic Center of California

This is quite simply the most intelligent book on contemporary psychoanalysis to be found. White's discussion of the many different schools of thought is accurate, astute, and above all, fair. Her integration of clinical material from her own practice to illuminate different theoretical perspectives is more than helpful—it is the best integration of theory and practice I have read.

Christopher Bollas

At a time when clinical psychoanalysis is more likely to perish because of the relentless infighting amongst the members of its numerous factions and orthodoxies, than owing to the rise of cognitive-behavioural therapy, Jean White courageously shows how contemporary psychoanalytic practice can benefit from the concurrent application of insights developed separately within the Lacanian, the post-Kleinian and the Independent tradition. In a brilliant exploration of the similarities and differences between these traditions, White is not concerned with developing an eclectic, unified or integrated model of psychoanalytic practice, but with arguing in favour of a less myopic, more diversified and more effective type of clinical work. As such, this book will not only contribute to theoretical discussions about divergent techniques, but will effectively constitute a milestone for the preservation of clinical psychoanalysis as a non-dogmatic, dynamic form of therapy, whose predicates are perennially open to revision.

Dany Nobus
Brunel University

Be not afeard; the isle is full of noises,
Sounds and sweet airs, that give delight,
                              and hurt not.
Sometimes a thousand twangling instruments
Will hum about mine ears; and sometime voices,
That, if I then had wak'd after long sleep,
Will make me sleep again; and then, in dreaming,
The clouds methought would open,
                              and show riches
Ready to drop upon me; that, when I wak'd,
I cried to dream again.

Caliban in *The Tempest*
(Act III, Scene II)
William Shakespeare

[W]hat is there in the activity that characterises the baby's aliveness
starts off as a unit or unity . . . [O]ne could profitably use the idea of the
fire from the dragon's mouth. I quote from Pliny who (in paying
tribute to fire) writes, "Who can say whether in essence fire is
constructive or destructive?"

Winnicott 1968 [1989]: 239

*C'est quand vous avez trouvé le mot qui concentre autour de lui le plus
grand nombre de fils de ce mycélium que vous savez que c'est là le centre
de gravité caché du désir dont il s'agit.*

[It is when you have found the word which condenses around itself the
greatest number of strands of this mycelium that you know that there is
the hidden centre of gravity of the desire it is about.]

Lacan (1967 [2005]: 40)

[R]eality is not something which lends itself to being known. It is
impossible to know reality for the same reason that makes it impossible
to sing potatoes . . . Reality has to be "been".

Bion (1965 [1984]: 148)

Contents

PART III
The future?   201

Acknowledgements

A number of colleagues and friends sustained me in this enterprise. I should especially like to thank Laurence Spurling for bearing the whole book in mind and Julia Vellacott for her detailed editorial comments. I should also like to give particular thanks to Nina Farhi, Philip Hill and Dale Mathers for their critical engagement with the text. Vivien Burgoyne, Berthe Ficarra, Dany Nobus, Eileen Smith and Meredith Yates also read chapters or parts of the book and made invaluable comments. I am deeply indebted to all these people. My mistakes, of course, remain my own. I should also like to thank Kate Hawes at Routledge for commissioning this book, and Helen Pritt and Claire Lipscomb for their unfailing courtesy and patience.

My greatest debt is to my patients from whom I have learnt so much over the last 25 years, and to my students and supervisees for stimulating my desire to learn.

Permissions

Chapter 1

Introduction

At the beginning of the third millennium, we are witnessing a renaissance in psychoanalytic theory and practice. Important and new developments began to emerge in the decades after Freud's death, and are now gathering clinical momentum. Recent advances in psychoanalytic theory use the understandings uncovered by Freud and Klein in ways more in tune with paradigm shifts in physics and the human sciences.[1]

Sigmund Freud's extraordinary achievement brought the personal, the subjective and the irrational into the rational scientism of his day, when Newtonian mechanical models still held sway. Although he trained as a neurologist at a time when a biological medical model predominated, Freud (1856–1939) dared to explore the uncharted and indomitable unconscious. He brought to the fore the contradictions inherent in adult sexuality and the dangerous subject of child sexuality, the intricacies of gender acquisition, the drives which transmute our animal nature, the perilous regions of transference and transference love, and the problem of human destructiveness. A complex, contradictory model of human development emerged in which we were no longer masters in our own houses. Controversial arenas Freud opened are still under question today. Some excellent new translations of Freud's work under the general editorship of Adam Phillips show us how relevant his thought remains (see bibliography). Melanie Klein (1882–1960) pioneered the investigation of pre-Oedipal and pre-verbal states of mind and, in so doing, made psychoanalytic work with psychotic and inaccessibly defended patients possible. Her revolutionary ideas are still being developed by today's Kleinians—and some of these are explored later in the book.

WINNICOTT, LACAN AND BION

Recent psychoanalytic theory builds on and sometimes transcends Freud's investigations and discoveries, and owes much to some other key theorists. André Green (2005a) cites the work of Winnicott, Lacan and Bion as the conceptual precursors of twenty-first-century psychoanalysis. Michael Eigen (1981) invokes the same three theorists as opening hitherto unknown aspects of human experience and unprecedented possibilities for human evolution.

Winnicott (1896–1971), Lacan (1901–81) and Bion (1897–1979) all unlocked the potential of the Freudian paradigm into a new dimension of meaning. Winnicott used the insights gained from more than forty years as a paediatrician to put forward a fresh model of child and human development and an expanded version of the psychoanalytic process, based more closely on early mothering. He introduced new conceptual areas such as 'intermediate', 'potential' and 'transitional' space (Winnicott 1971). Lacan revitalized the Freudian paradigm with insights gained from modern linguistic theory, and re-affirmed the fundamental importance of sexuality, the drives, the symbolic father and the radical and subversive power of the unconscious. Bion transformed the Freudian and Kleinian metapsychologies with a new theory of mind and human growth.

The style and ways of thinking of these three theorists have something in common. There is no longer a unified, closed model of human development. All three share a refusal to be pinned to rigid systematic explanation. At the same time, different but powerful systematic elements in each of their modes of thinking lend changed perspectives from which to view the analytic process. I believe the tensions and dialectic between the systematic and the multiple and ambiguous in these discourses sustain the possibility of fresh perspectives and advances in psychoanalytic theory.

All three viewed the birth of the human subject as profoundly intersubjective. Winnicott's (1947) axiom, 'There is no such thing as a baby . . .,' refers to the illusion of omnipotence sustained if a baby is sufficiently held within 'primary maternal preoccupation', from which she can be 'disillusioned' at a pace necessary for the gradual emergence of an authentic self (Winnicott 1951, 1956). Lacan (1960) believed that a child is born into the desire and language of an Other,[2] whose claims dominate her subjectivity until put into question in analysis. Bion's (1962) 'maternal reverie', through which a mother contains her baby's projected 'nameless dread' (or anxiety about annihilation) until such time as the child can bear and express their own feelings, demonstrates how a capacity for thought is not a one-person activity.

At the same time, the body cannot be put out of the question: '. . . the ego is above all a *corporeal* entity: it . . . is itself the *projection* of a surface (Freud 1923 [2003]: 117, translator's emphases). Winnicott's 'primitive emotional development' and view of aggression as a driving force in ordinary development show how physical predispositions cannot be separated from the psychological (Winnicott 1945, 1950). Lacan's re-emphasis on the drives after Seminar XI (1964a), albeit mediated through language and the symbolic order, affirms the 'real' body as a generative force although inevitably overwritten with signifiers. Bion's (1965, 1967) traditionally Kleinian emphasis on constitutional excess of destructive aggression and envy as factors in the aetiology of serious disturbance reveal the body as potentially problematic and disruptive of psychological development. These areas of psychoanalytic theory explode the dualism between nature and nurture (cf. Shepherdson 2000).

The style of Winnicott, Lacan and Bion is, in varying forms and degrees, elliptical: there is no reductive explanation; meaning is deliberately fluid. Their form reflects the direction of their thought. Although structural elements remain (both Winnicott and Lacan make use of a concept of the ego, albeit mainly as a problem in Lacan's case), all three shift the Freudian structural and topographical models towards differing forms of subjectivity constantly in evolution and a process model of mind and self.[3]

All three conceive of psychic growth as emanating from states of mind which are not predetermined and cannot be entirely defined: Bion's (1965, 1970) 'O', Winnicott's (1951, 1971) 'transitional space' and Lacan's (1953) 'subjectification', which begins its elusive life in non-existence, like a spark flashing between two signifiers. Bion's theory of thinking and his later work on transformations and 'O' introduce the possibility of a mind which is potentially in limitless development. Lacan's situation of the construction of the subject and the unconscious with the entry into language and the symbolic order, and their evolution through the 'precipitation' of subjectivity, the opening of the space of desire and, in his later work, the *jouissance* of the drive, can also take us we know not where.[4] Winnicott's concepts of 'intermediate' and 'potential' space, with transitional areas between self and not-self, and also some of his thinking about the uses of aggression, ego orgasm and the role of aesthetics in human development again emphasize a self in progress, a being in the process of becoming, and the creative potential of encounters with difference if they can be 'used' fearlessly (see Chapter 2).

CONTEMPORARY DEVELOPMENTS

These fresh perspectives on what being human might involve—and how people grow—have multiple implications for psychoanalytic technique. The unexpected, new and unknown are now valued as much as any predetermined representation of development, although as Phillips (1993) points out, it is impossible to have one without the other. The 'classical' psychoanalytic paradigm, as it had become, has changed from a model in which the analyst interprets the transference and the patient's pathology from an elevated state of knowledge, to a shared venture into the unknown, one in which the analyst may be changed as much as the patient.

The range of significant and mutative clinical interventions has expanded from the hegemony of the transference interpretation to include the intersubjective moment, the unconscious dynamism of the 'analytic third' (Ogden 1994a), and a renewed interest in the polyvalence of language, and humour and surprise in many forms. This evolution of clinical praxis renders a version of psychoanalysis that is potentially livelier, more relevant to a wider range of people and more tolerant of the myriad possibilities inherent in subjectivity.

We now have the tools to reveal the construction of racial, sexual and social identities as operative in the transference/countertransference matrix, although a great deal of work remains to be done in these areas. It is arguable, and I hope this book will demonstrate, that these recent theoretical revelations expand the potential scope of human subjectivity, and render it more fluid, more puzzling, more complex but also more exciting and generative of the unanticipated.

THE SCOPE AND LIMITATIONS OF THIS BOOK

The idea for this book grew out of a series of postgraduate lectures I gave in 2000 and 2001, based at Birkbeck College, University of London. I became aware of a dearth of comparative accounts of contemporary psychoanalysis and keen interest in the subject. *Generation*, although primarily a work of theory, maintains a clinical perspective throughout. The prioritization of theoretical developments has been problematic for me. While all theories of knowledge are partial and incomplete, and what they exclude is as significant as what they reveal, I have had to omit hugely important areas of contemporary psychoanalytic theory. I will focus primarily on the contemporary Independent school, Lacanian and post-Lacanian theory and post-Kleinian developments in Britain, the United States and France and, to a lesser extent, in some other European countries, Australia and South America.

In so doing, I reveal my personal clinical preoccupations. These areas of theoretical extension and application are still very much alive, growing through their capacity to encompass debate and disagreement. One marker of the vitality of a theoretical paradigm, in my view, is its ability to contain and generate difference, which in turn facilitates further thinking and new developments. These three paradigms are also in widespread global use.

There is a necessary debate and tension between those who argue for the possibility of synthesizing psychoanalytic theories (Bateman and Holmes 1995: 48; Britton 2003: xi) and those, like myself, who view divergence as stimulating and potentially creative. Green suggests one can no longer refer to psychoanalytic theory in the singular (Green 1986 [1997]: 13). Phillips can see no reason why psychoanalysts should agree with each other (Phillips 1993: xvi), whilst Lacan declared 'It is in no way necessary that the tree of science should have a single trunk' (Lacan 1964a [2004]: 8). Although, as we shall see, some surprising areas of commonality and overlap emerge from the three contemporary paradigms discussed here, their incorporation of difference serves their continuing vigour, so long as dissent is used in the service of dialogue and not in a factional or paranoid way.

I aim to be academically accurate but not exhaustive. *Generation* is not intended to be an encyclopaedia. Nonetheless, I hope to capture (not tame, but represent) something of the spirit of contemporary theory.

Chronology is inevitably a difficult area in the history of ideas. I outline some originative concepts from Winnicott, Lacan and Bion and then focus on more recent innovations in theory. Both Bion and Lacan made paradigmatic shifts during the 1960s and 1970s, the last decades of both their lives, and Winnicott's (1969) revolutionary concept of 'object usage' also emerged towards the end of his life.

A necessary and useful tension exists between the ideas of the paradigmatic generators and those of subsequent writers who change some concepts almost out of recognition. One example is Winnicott's 'true self' (1960), which, in the hands of two contemporary Independents, Christopher Bollas (1992) and Thomas Ogden (1994a), becomes a post-modern concept (see Chapter 2). Another is Lacan's account of the formation of the human subject and the unconscious through language, which is used by Luce Irigaray (1985) to reveal psychoanalytic discourse as a patriarchal construct, unaware of its own monolithic assumptions (see Chapter 3).

Ownership of ideas can be a tricky area. Sometimes a number of theorists are at work in the same conceptual field at the same time, especially some post-Kleinian theorists who work as a team (for example Steiner and Britton 1994). Occasionally, there is apparent synchronicity: two contemporary Independent theorists, Jessica Benjamin and Thomas Ogden, both develop the concept of intersubjectivity in the 1990s, and pursue parallel paths with slightly different emphases whilst making little reference to each other's work.

The psychoanalysts whose work primarily informs this book from the Independent school are Donald Winnicott, Marion Milner, Masud Khan and Christopher Bollas in Britain; Thomas Ogden and Jessica Benjamin in the USA; and André Green and Joyce McDougall in France. From the Lacanians, I focus particularly on the work of Jacques Lacan, Julia Kristeva and Luce Irigaray, but also discuss the input of Joël Dor and Juan-David Nasio in France and Bruce Fink in the USA. From the post-Kleinians, I select Wilfred Bion, Donald Meltzer, J. Henri Rey, Herbert Rosenfeld, John Steiner and Ron Britton who were or are all based in Britain. I also discuss the work of many others, whose approach, sensibility or ideas have influenced this analytic generation.

PSYCHOANALYTIC INTERNATIONALISM

Generation's international focus is in keeping with the history of psycho-analysis as an immigrant discipline. Nonetheless, national intellectual mores, education and traditions do impact on psychoanalytic theory. As Green states:

> French psychoanalysts belong to a different cultural tradition from that of the Anglo-Saxon world, where empiricism and pragmatism are considered to be qualities; where intellectualism and abstraction count as vices rather than as virtues.
>
> (Green 1986 [1997]: 4)

Where necessary, I highlight national and regional influences on the thought of the theorists I discuss whilst retaining a global perspective. However, many of these theorists do not fit neatly into either a national or an intellectual category. Some examples are: Green, a French Independent whose work owes as much or more to the influence of London Independents and post-Kleinians as to Lacan; McDougall, a New Zealander who trained in both London and Paris, and whose work incorporates insights from all three contemporary schools; and Kristeva, Bulgarian by birth and practising in Paris, who is a Lacanian much influenced by Independents and some post-Kleinians. Other internationalists are Bollas, American by birth but an Independent in London combining theoretical sources from all three schools; and Rosenfeld (originally German), Rey (French) and Meltzer (American), all post-Kleinians who were based in London but whose impact has been global. Neville Symington (originally British) is an Australian Independent influenced by post-Kleinian thinking. The interweaving between national and international influence and impact is another necessary tension sustaining this book.

Some hugely significant areas of psychoanalytic theory have had to be omitted and some are mentioned in relation to the three paradigms I prioritize. I cannot include the Jungians as a separate grouping because of my ignorance. Excellent introductions to contemporary Jungian thought have already been written (Samuels 1985; Astor 1995). Some clinical Jungian developments are predicated on Winnicottian and post-Kleinian insights (for example, see Fordham 1995).

Nor do I discuss the 'ego psychologists' in any detail. Outstanding introductions to ego psychology already exist (for example Black and Mitchell 1995), but there is an additional factor. The focus of the three schools discussed here is on the unconscious and on the unexpected developments it can generate. Ego psychology can have a tendency towards adaptational or normalizing concepts of development, whilst the theorists I review have moved on to more fluid and open models of subjectivity with no predetermined end point. One of the several shared perspectives in Bion and Lacan's work is that they both relegate the ego to '. . . a figment of psychoanalysts' imagination' (Bion Talamo 1997: 52) or '. . . the sum of the identifications of the subject . . . like the superimposition of various coats borrowed from what I would call the bric-a-brac of its props department' (Lacan 1954–5 [1991]: 155).

Other significant omissions from Britain and North America include neo-Freudian and attachment-based theorists who are clinically innovative but do not, in my view, represent completely separate psychoanalytic paradigms. Their work contributes to the thinking of contemporary Independents in particular. In Britain and North America, the relational school of psychoanalysis (Aron and Mitchell 1999), emergent from the work of Bowlby and the 'intersubjectivists',[5] exerts a powerful reciprocal influence on Independent theory and is discussed in that context. The 'hermeneutic' school of psychoanalysis, expounded by Roy Schafer (1981, 1983, 1992, 1997a) and Donald Spence (1982), which focuses on the importance of developing a personal narrative, is mentioned in the discussion of psychosis and borderlinity in Chapter 6. As a theory of creation of meaning, 'hermeneutics' in psychoanalysis bears affinity with the symbolizing aspect of subjectification in Lacanian theory (see Chapter 3). 'Modern' or 'New' psychoanalysis has, as its theorists acknowledge, not been developed into a separate metapsychology (Spotnitz 1976, 1985; Meadow 2003). Some of its insights are mentioned in relation to severe disturbance in Chapter 6 and its incorporation of Lacanian theory in the conclusion.

THE GLOBAL SPREAD OF INDEPENDENT, LACANIAN AND POST-KLEINIAN PSYCHOANALYSIS

One factor in the schools of psychoanalysis I select as paradigmatic generators is their capacity, like great rivers, to include, subsume and make use of vast hinterlands of feeding intellectual tributaries, some of whom could also make justifiable claim to 'great river' status. These three paradigms are all now in near-universal usage, and their influence continues to grow. Their advances in theory and clinical practice are still evolving. Despite all these factors, they maintain distinct and identifiable clinical approaches, cohesive metapsychologies and consistent inherent values. All these components will emerge in the course of this book.

To put the three paradigms in context, I will give a brief history of the global spread of psychoanalysis since the Second World War. When Freud died in 1939, many refugee psychoanalysts from Austria and Germany were settling in Britain and the USA. In London, the Psychoanalytic Society was riven by the 'Controversial Discussions' between Melanie Klein and Anna Freud and their respective followers (1942–4). These centred on whether the psychoanalysis of children should be modified by educational and advisory input (Anna Freud) or a more purist concentration on the vicissitudes of internal object relations and a recognition of the transferential bond from the beginning of analysis (Melanie Klein) (Bateman and Holmes 1995). Klein's position was closer to that at which Lacan would shortly arrive (Roudinesco 1993). Despite Winnicott's courageous denunciation of the controversial discussions as '. . . this disaster which will be a clumping based not on science but on personalities' (Roudinesco 1993 [1997]: 193), the British Society remained divided into Kleinian and neo-Freudian (or Anna Freudian) schools, with the Independent group maintaining a position of intellectual and clinical autonomy. This cohabitation, as Green points out with very British understatement, was not always easy (Green 2005a: 11). In 2005, the group system was disbanded in the British Society.

The Paris Psychoanalytic Society (SPP), inaugurated in 1926, has always been riven by factionalism (Roudinesco 1982). In 1953, the SPP split over the question of 'lay' analysis and Lacan joined the *Société Française de Psychanalyse* (SFP). In 1963, Lacan was finally refused re-admittance to the IPA mainly because of his 'innovations' in technique, in particular his use of shortened analytic sessions (Roudinesco 1993). Despite this 'excommunication' (Lacan 1964a), Lacan became and has remained the most influential psychoanalytic theorist in France since his *Écrits* were first published in 1966, and France has the highest per capita number of psychoanalysts in the world (Rabaté 2003a). It is easy to forget now what a breath of fresh air Lacanian theory brought to an analytic world beginning to ossify under the weight of more normalizing versions of psychoanalysis. Although his iconoclasm and refusal to be pinned down to easily intelligible meanings are still being criticized (Pierrakos 2004), Lacan and his re-vision and re-awakening of Freudian theory shook up the analytic world and continues to do so. His cultural and intellectual influence remains pervasive in Europe, and is now becoming so in North and South America and some Asian countries, especially China (Rabaté 2003a). As Robert Young says: '. . . looking at the history of psychoanalytic criticism, of Marxism, and of feminism, it is obvious that the shift came with Lacan. Lacan's re-reading of Freud effectively changed the whole terrain of the use of psychoanalysis in contemporary cultural theory' (Young, in Donald (ed.) 1991: 140).

Lacan's clinical influence is now spreading in North and South America, Britain and other parts of Europe, including the German-speaking world (Haber 1992; Fink 1995, 1997, 2004; Gurewich *et al.* 1999b; Harari 2004). In France, meanwhile, innovative recent psychoanalytic thinking has come from 'French feminists', in particular Kristeva and Irigaray.[6] France is also the professional home of some creative and original Independent theorists, whose ranks include Janine Chasseguet-Smirgel as well as Green and McDougall.

Green considers that at the end of the Second World War, the 'European space' was divided between the influence of the English (Northern Europe, from Holland to Scandinavia) and the French (the French-speaking nations and Southern Europe, Belgium, Spain, Italy, Portugal and Switzerland). These days, deems Green, the British influence is predominant (Green 2005a: 10). The authors in Kutter's (1992, 1995) edited two-volume collection on psychoanalysis across the world support his views, but with significant exceptions. In Italy, for example, interest in post-Kleinian theory is huge (Meltzer 1986; Bion Talamo *et al.* 2000), whilst attention to Independent thought is also widespread, in particular the work of Winnicott, Khan, Kohut and Matte-Blanco (Novelletto 1992). In Spain, the Madrid Psychoanalytic Association was inaugurated by León and Rebeca Grinberg, Argentinians of post-Kleinian persuasion (Muñoz and Grinberg 1992). The Israel Psychoanalytic Society is largely Freudian and neo-Freudian in orientation (Lowental and Cohen 1992).

North America represents an increasingly large proportion of the psychoanalytic community (Bateman and Holmes 1995). Ego psychology, as practised and disseminated by Hartmann, Loewenstein and Kris, became the predominant metapsychology until the Kohutian revolution in the early 1970s. At this point, the psychology of the 'Self' began to succeed that of the 'Ego', and the developmental vicissitudes of narcissism came to replace those of drive theory. Kleinian influence in the United States escalated after Bion's arrival in Los Angeles in 1968, although it has remained relatively confined to the West coast (Grotstein 1981; Caper 1999). The ingress of Lacanian theory in cultural studies in the United States was spearheaded by Wilden's (1968) translation of Lacan's (1953) 'Rome Discourse'. Muller and Richardson (1982) and Schneiderman (1980) introduced Lacan as a clinical presence. Fink's (1995, 1997, 2004) clarity of exposition initiated a more widespread circulation of Lacanian theory, although he initially met with massive resistance (Fink 1995). More recently, an open debate between some American psychoanalysts and French Lacanians resulted in a series of Lacanian publications (Dor 1997, 1998, 2001; Nasio 1997; Gurewich *et al.* 1999b; Van Haute 2002). Lacanian ideas are now beginning to filter into mainstream American psychoanalysis and to contribute to the break-up of the hegemony of the ego psychologists begun by Kohut in 1971.

Psychoanalysis as a treatment modality is now very widespread, particularly in the Americas. Psychoanalytic societies in Mexico, Argentina, Brazil, Peru, Uruguay, Colombia, Chile and Venezuela incorporate Kleinian and post-Kleinian influences (Racker 1968; Langer 1989, 2000). More recently, interest in Lacanian theory, especially its drive-related aspects, has increased in South America (Harari 2004), and Winnicott, Green, Balint and Kohut are cited as catalysts of Independent thinking (Filho 1995). The Canadian Psychoanalytic Society is influenced by attachment theory and also Independent theory (Green, McDougall and Chasseguet-Smirgel are mentioned), although their predominant orientation is French classical psychoanalysis (Hanly 1995).

Australia hosts a significant psychoanalytic community, strongly influenced by the Independents (Balint, Fairbairn, Winnicott, Neville and Joan Symington), but also some Kleinians (Martin 1995) and a growing Lacanian population (Glowinski, Marks & Murphy 2001).

It has been more difficult for psychoanalysis to flourish in nations where there have been totalitarian regimes, whether of the extreme right or left. During its fascist military junta, Chile lost several important theorists: Ignacio Matte-Blanco emigrated to Italy, León and Rebeca Grinberg to Rome and Otto Kernberg to the USA (Muñoz and Grinberg 1992; Novelletto 1992; Arrué 1995), but in spite of this damage, the Chilean Psychoanalytic Society today remains unsplit and closely linked to clinical and academic institutions (Arrué 1995). The early history of psychoanalysis had many Russian connections. The Bolsheviks considered it a progressive development of radical social thought, but the Communist regime was antipathetic. Hence, the Russian Psychoanalytic Society was not established until 1989 and does not as yet have a training (Fischer and Fischer 1995). In the former 'Eastern Bloc' of Europe, psychoanalysis was also suppressed by Communism. Nonetheless, small, recently instated psychoanalytic societies exist in Bulgaria, Hungary, Romania, Slovenia and Poland, primarily influenced by Freud, Klein and some Independent and Lacanian theorists (Harmatta and Szönyi 1992; Pawlak and Sokolik 1992; Lunacek 1995; Sandor 1995; Tomov and Atanassov 1995).

A notable engagement of psychoanalysis with the political arena began with Marie Langer's pioneering work in Mexico and Nicaragua (Langer 1989). In Cuba, the University of La Habana sponsored exchanges of ideas between left-wing psychoanalysts from Latin America and Europe and Cuban Marxist psychologists in 1986, 1988, 1990 and 1992 (Danneberg 1995).

The institution of psychoanalysis as a treatment modality is more problematic where the culture is different from a Western intellectual model and this may be part of the reason why it is largely absent in Africa and the Arab world (Kutter 1995). In India, an actively didactic form of psychoanalysis was encouraged by Girindrashekhar Bose until the 1950s, whilst today Kleinian influence is predominant. Indian psychoanalysis has not yet engaged with Indian culture, mythology or social mores (Kakar 1995). There is as yet no psychoanalytical society in China, but interest in psychoanalytic ideas increased after a visit from H.C. Halberstadt-Freud to the Chinese Medical Association in 1991 (Gerlach 1995), and M.L. Ng explored the relevance of psychoanalytic theory to the Chinese way of thinking (Ng 1985). Japan, on the other hand, has a small psychoanalytic society, with interests in Klein, Winnicott and Bion predominant (Okonogi 1995). This notable exception may be partly because there has been a real attempt to engage with Japanese culture. Joan Raphael-Leff (1992) explored the implications of a prevalent ancient Buddhist myth in Japan: the 'Ajase' legend. In this legend a queen, fearing that she is losing her beauty and her husband's love with age, consults a soothsayer who forecasts that a sage will be reborn as her son. The queen kills the sage, who curses her and prophesies that her son will kill the king, whereupon the queen tries to kill her son too. Ajase, the son, sustains a broken finger from his fall from a high tower and tries to kill his mother. All are eventually reconciled with the help of the Buddha, and Ajase goes on to become a respected ruler (Okonogi 1995). More optimistic than the Oedipus myth, this ancient story encapsulates maternal ambivalence, matricidal desire, the stage of concern and forgiveness. Engagement with cultures other than those with which it is already familiar remains a challenge for psychoanalysis. Japan may be ahead of us in this respect.

THE AIMS AND OUTLINE OF *GENERATION*

My aim throughout this book is to identify the cutting edge of psycho-analytic theory today. As Stephen Mitchell pointed out, psychoanalytic theory is sometimes still presented as though it were confined to a regressive Freudian orthodoxy (Black and Mitchell 1995). Without denying either Freud's brilliance or his continuing inspiration for many theorists, this is really no longer the case.

Generation is written and organized in such a way that chapters may be read individually if need be. I hope the reader will forgive any slight repetition incurred by this method. The three chapters in Part I introduce the traditions, the theorists and the major concepts. Part II is a comparative discussion of contemporary praxis. The whole book is cross-referenced.

The need both to think comparatively and to discover areas of commonality and difference within and between psychoanalytic theories is urgent (Green 2005b; Wallerstein 2005). I will explore some of the concepts introduced by Winnicott, Lacan and Bion, and then concentrate on the ways in which the clinical thought of the three paradigms is developing. Clinical illustrations of the concepts are used throughout, but more extensively in Part II than in Part I.

In Part II I begin with narcissism, for two reasons. First, the concept of narcissism represents a metapsychological watershed for all three traditions. Secondly, for the post-Kleinian and Independent groups it serves as a foundational clinical concept. Lacanians make use of the concept developmentally: inaugurated through the 'mirror stage', the ego is conceived as a narcissistic structure (Lacan 1949). For post-Kleinians, as for Freud, narcissism forms the divide between neurotic or potentially psychotic structures of self. Within the Independent tradition, a critical debate waged around clinical technique and approaches to narcissism between Kohut and Kernberg in the 1970s, and a resurgence of interest in the meanings of this concept followed Symington's (1993) *Narcissism – A New Theory*.

Chapter 6, 'Structures of psychopathology', outlines, contextualizes, compares, contrasts and, where applicable, highlights shared attitudes and assumptions about the five major categories of forms of disturbance or structures of subjectivity in current usage: psychosis, psychosomatosis, borderlinity, perversion and neurosis. Psychosis, perversion and neurosis were the three metapsychological categories introduced by Freud (1924a). Lacanians still adhere to these demarcations, although borderlinity is beginning to be discussed cross-paradigmatically (Gurewich *et al.* 1999b). In this chapter, I discuss all three contemporary schools' concepts of psychosis, perversion and neurosis, and where applicable, the sub-categories inherent within them, such as the Lacanian distinction between hysteria, obsessionality and phobia as sub-structures of neurosis. Psychosomatosis, as differentiated from hysteria, is beginning to be used as a clinical concept by the Independents after McDougall's (1989) *Theatres of the Body*. Some post-Kleinians also work with a model of psychosomatosis, or 'soma-psychotic' mechanisms, consequent from Bion's thinking about the evacuation of beta elements, one route of which may be through the body, an idea subsequently developed by Meltzer (1986).

Chapter 7, 'Motivational echoes: Transference and countertransference in contemporary theory', explores the three schools' developments in thinking about these central clinical concepts. In this chapter the mutual interrelation and influence of the contemporary Independent and post-Kleinian schools become clear although, paradoxically, they also serve to sharpen their differences in technique, particularly in relation to regression, timing and interpretation or non-interpretation. Refinements in the analyst's use of herself as a clinical instrument are of critical importance here, articulated and applied in interestingly different ways by both Independents and post-Kleinians. These clinical advances may arguably enlarge the scope of personal subjectivity itself, and the ways in which we extend ourselves through relating to others, or intersubjectivity. Here, the Lacanian group's approach is dramatically different.

Chapter 8, 'Surprise, humour and non-interpretation: A new look at psychoanalytic technique', focuses on innovations in psychoanalytic practice resulting from these new ideas about human subjectivity, growth and development. All three contemporary schools have theorized their technique extensively. Relative strengths and weaknesses are discussed.

Chapter 9, 'The aims of analysis and psychic growth', is in many ways the most significant chapter of the book. Here, the underlying assumptions and value systems of the three paradigms are drawn out. Of course, each psychoanalytic school has a different version of what it means to be a human being, what is precious about human life and what is essential about how we live it. Prospective clients, as well as clinicians who refer, may want to take these considerations into account when choosing an analyst or therapist. This chapter is also primary because recent theorizations of growth and development from these three contemporary schools constitute some radical concepts of ontology. At their best, some of these theories expand what it means to be human, and what is possible within human experience.

The short conclusion summarizes some ideas put forward in other parts of the book and explores putative areas of theoretical advance for the future. Chapter 10 also highlights areas of conflict and lack of articulation which remain, and points the way tentatively to what these three schools could learn from each other. I have tried to be as impartial and objective as is humanly (im)possible, but inevitably my biases and values pervade this book.

Although each chapter can be read singly as an introduction to one paradigm (Part I) or recent theoretical developments around a particular issue (Part II), I intend *Generation* to constitute more than the sum of its parts. As well as presenting and discussing contemporary theory, the book advances a particular view of psychoanalysis and clinical practice. My aim is to set as a standard an open, process-based, undogmatic and mutual model of analysis, with analyst and analysand cooperating as partners of equal authority in a shared exploratory endeavour.

Of paramount importance to this way of thinking is the opening up of different perspectives or, in Bion's (1970) term, 'multiple vertices' on the same issue or problem. The capacity to hold in mind or consider a variety of perspectives at the same time constitutes, *in and of itself*, a therapeutic instrument of equivalent significance to, for example, the notion of deep containment articulated by Caper (1999) (outlined in Chapter 8). For the ability to think pluralistically, without forced synthesis, is one of the most potent weapons against ideological fundamentalism and its clinical equivalent, certainty. More abuses have been perpetrated in the name of being 'right' than ever with knowing maleficence.

But, even more essential to the therapist's armoury, pluralistic perspectives are one route out of those transference/countertransference gridlocks that are the relational manifestation of internal stasis and pathology. Pluralistic thinking and the ability to shift perspective are indissoluble from the process of psychoanalytic psychotherapy itself, just as theoretical certainty is pathological. Imagine how different our psychoanalytic institutions and organizations would be if this insight were applied universally.

A NOTE ON STYLE

I have used the pronouns he, she and they, and his, her and their, inter-changeably throughout the text. I have also used 'patient', 'client' and 'analysand': no one of these terms conveys sufficiently fully what is involved in being engaged in a psychoanalytic process. 'Patient' and 'analysand' are too passive, 'client' too market-oriented.

Where no translator is cited, the translation from the French is my own.

NOTES

1. See, for example, Capra (1975, 1982, 1996), Gell-Mann (1994), Waldrop (1992), Stacey (1996) and Penrose (2004), and within cultural theory, Elliott and Frosh (1995) and Elliott (1999, 2001).
2. The term 'Other' (*le grand Autre*) in Lacanian theory as it is used here refers to the 'Other' of the social and interpersonal context of the symbolic order into which a child is born. This 'Other' also refers to the Other of the unconscious. 'other' or '*objet petit a*', on the other hand, refers to the other experienced in imaginary fantasy. These distinctions are explained and explored in Chapters 3, 6 and 7 and in Evans (1996) and Gurewich (1999a). Although Lacan later revised his theory of intersubjectivity and the Other took on different resonances after 1964, he retained the symbolic constitution of the human subject.
3. Both Freud and Klein introduced process models of mind with the vicissitudes of drive-related development (Freud 1915c) and internal object relationships (Klein 1975a, 1975b). However, both Freud's structural and topographical models (ego, id and superego) and Klein's (1960) introjection of a benign parental couple in mental health do set, at least theoretical, limits to development.
4. Bion's late work is explored in Chapter 9. Lacan's 'precipitation of subjectivity' is discussed in Chapter 3 and the *jouissance* of the drive in Chapter 9.
5. The American 'Relational' school of psychoanalysis grew out of work on the uses of intersubjectivity, or the capacity to grow through the recognition of the differences inherent in the subjectivity of another person, developed further by Ogden and Benjamin during the 1990s. Its major discussion forum is the journal *Psychoanalytic Dialogues*.
6. For a discussion of Kristeva and Irigaray's work, see Chapters 3, 7 and 9.

Part I

Introducing the three paradigms

Chapter 2

Contemporary Independents

The term 'contemporary Independent' should, by definition, defy classification. The Independent school in Britain originated from the tripartite division of the psychoanalytic society after the 'Controversial Discussions' between the followers of Melanie Klein and those of Anna Freud during 1942–4.[1] At first, the Independents were termed the 'middle group', but from 1973 on they officially became 'the Independent Group' (Kohon 1986: 49), thereby staking out a claim for intellectual and clinical autonomy. The disbanding of the group system in London in no way diminishes their theoretical stature.

Rayner (1990) argues that the Independents inherited something of the philosophical romanticism of the European tradition after Kant and the idealist tradition of Schopenhauer and Nietzsche. Hence, they prioritize emotion, passion even, the quality of subjective experience, intuition, and cultural and aesthetic experience. As a consequence of these implicit ideals, throughout contemporary Independent writing there is a powerful emphasis on creativity.

Their stress on opening inherent potential exists in a dialectical tension with several different ways of looking at the uses of intersubjectivity, or the capacity to grow through the recognition of another's subjectivity. At the same time their streak of British pragmatism means that Independents are prepared to learn from mistakes and consider the applicability of ideas from a range of sources. Today, the influence of Independent theory and practice can be found in many parts of the world, including Australia, South America and throughout Europe. In the United States, Independent analysts are mounting a serious challenge to the intellectual and clinical hegemony of the ego psychologists and self psychologists in a resurgence of theoretical innovation.

The hallmarks of an Independent analyst include theoretical eclecticism and/or pluralism,[2] with Winnicott and Freud as the most frequent underlying influences. Independents share a belief in the importance of external reality, in particular the early maternal environment, in the evolution of self. Their centralization of affect results in a sensitivity to nuances of feeling and mood and subtle shifts in emotional register in every analytic session. Independents respect their patients' strengths whatever their level of psychopathology and allow for privacy as well as exposure in the course of analysis. Their recognition of the formative uses and value of the aesthetic dimension of experience shades, at times, into a celebration of the epiphanic moment, and almost always results in a literary quality of writing.

Independents rarely use 'jargon' unless it is unavoidable and frequently draw from literature, art, poetry and music to illustrate concepts. They almost universally share a particular sensibility—hard to put one's finger on without destroying its subtlety—marked by humility, tentativeness, a certain grace and lightness of touch (not levity), an understated use of irony and humour, and a delicate sense of what might, in a secular way, be termed the sacred in human experience.

The theorists whose work primarily informs this chapter, Marion Milner, Masud Khan and Christopher Bollas (from the British Society), Thomas Ogden and Jessica Benjamin (from the United States, Ogden in San Francisco and Benjamin in New York), and André Green and Joyce McDougall (in Paris), are all original and independent theorists in their own right as well as being part of an Independent tradition. Both here and throughout the book, I shall also discuss the input of many others, including Harold Searles and Michael Eigen in the United States, Patrick Casement, Nina Coltart, Adam Phillips and Harold Stewart in Britain, Janine Chasseguet-Smirgel in France and Neville Symington in Australia, who have also contributed original ideas and whose way of thinking about their work has inspired this analytic generation and is likely to continue to influence generations to come.

Independents have been enriched by dialogue with and openness to the ideas of other contemporary psychoanalytic schools. The influence of attachment theory (Bowlby 1969, 1973, 1980) is evident in what has been termed the 'relational' school of psychoanalysis (Aron and Mitchell 1999) which, as its name suggests, takes as its fundamental premise that we are formed, develop and are changed through significant relationships with others. Relationists see the psychoanalytic process as '. . . requiring the transformation of two people in their engagement with each other' (Mitchell 1997: 35). One of its extensions, the concept of intersubjectivity, or the developmental potential inherent in the acknowledgement of the difference of another person's perspective, has its roots in both infant psychology (Trevarthen 1980; Stern 1985), philosophy (Hegel 1807; Husserl 1935) and sociology (Habermas 1970),[3] and was introduced to psycho-analysis by Stolorow, Brandschaft and Attwood (1987). A shift from uni-fied concepts of self to complex, multiple and evolving self-states bespeaks the (at least indirect) influence of postmodernism, and is part of a gradual change from a structural model of mind to one in which processes enabling powerful formative subjective experiences are seen as more important.

Some Independent theorists, especially Green, Bollas and McDougall, have been influenced by post-Kleinian theory, particularly Bion. To a limited degree, some knowledge and usage of Lacanian and post-Lacanian theory is becoming one of the distinguishing features of a truly Independent analyst. Many of the theorists I discuss make partial but significant use of Lacanian concepts. In contradistinction, therefore, to the bulk of Lacanian and post-Kleinian theory, the Independent tradition is inclusive of other perspectives, both historically and currently, although not to the extent that it could ever be subsumed by them.

Independents have been termed 'object relations' by some (Kohon 1986). This appellation has some historical and theoretical applicability in revealing the influence of Fairbairn, Balint and Guntrip. Contemporary Independents, like most post-Kleinians, do use to varying extents models of an internal world with inner interrelationships between different parts of the self and internal objects. However, I shall not use the term 'object relations' here because of its suggestion of a less open model of the self and its evolution than is being reached towards by today's Independents.

The primary influence on the thinking of most Independent theorists remains Winnicott, the Independent analyst *par excellence*, who robustly and slightly ruthlessly insisted on culling his influences from everywhere though not necessarily acknowledging their origins. The powerful hold exerted by Winnicott's thinking over the Independents goes deeper than a heuristic affinity though. It belongs in the nature of certain concepts, not necessarily developed to a huge extent by Winnicott himself, which have been taken up by these theorists and both mined for their potential and re-worked in a way which is more in tune with the shift from structural to process-based concepts of self.

These Winnicottian concepts require a reassessment of the psychoanalytic frame of reference, and provide a starting point for a version of psychoanalysis slightly different from the classical one—one which is more artistic than scientific (and explodes that dualism) and which privileges deep unconscious processes as the route to development. This constitutes a radical departure from a view that a dynamic unconscious can be brought under control to reinforce the ego. Here, psychoanalysts emphasize the future as much as the past, and new and unexpected developments are seen as far more significant than arrival at any preconceived or adaptive belief in 'normalcy'. These concepts open the possibility of new vistas in the practice of psychoanalysis and in human development, and require a revision of the interrelationship between internal and external reality, and objectivity and subjectivity. These concepts describe (but not absolutely—they cannot be pinned down) areas of experience that by their very nature push the shift away from Western empirical science and positivism, which was begun by Freud, much further towards a self in process with few fixed points along the journey. Above all Winnicott emphasized the quality of subjective experience, and contemporary developments of his theories posit a less radical rupture between infant development and adult experience. They aim to keep it all on board.

Particularly fruitful concepts in all of these respects include 'regression to dependence' (Winnicott 1954b); the developmental potential inherent in certain forms of aggression (1950); the use of an object (1969); the true self (1960); the 'third area' or 'intermediate' or 'transitional' space (1971); 'ego orgasm' (1958b); and, above all, the value of both uncertainty and non-interpretation, which today's Independents all consider vital to practice.[4]

True to form, Independent theorists make use of these concepts in original and unpredictable ways. Powerful trends in Independent thinking, which emerged in the 1980s and 1990s and which are still gathering intellectual and clinical momentum, include Benjamin's expansion of the concept of intersubjectivity drawing from Winnicott's 'use of an object'; Ogden's 'analytic third' which extends Winnicott's 'transitional space' into the analytic relationship; the questioning and breaking open of gender identifications (primarily Benjamin, but also Ogden); necessary ruthlessness (Bollas and Benjamin);[5] and multiple extensions and elaborations of object usage (Bollas). I shall explore the meanings and implications of all these concepts in this chapter.

REGRESSION TO DEPENDENCE

> The setting of analysis reproduces the early and earliest mothering techniques. It invites regression by reason of its reliability.
>
> (Winnicott 1954b: 286)

Winnicott reconstituted the template of the analytic relationship conceived by Freud and made it more akin to that of the mother/infant relationship, perhaps as a result of working as both a paediatrician and a psychoanalyst for over forty years. His revolutionary views on analytic technique have inspired the ways in which today's Independents think about the setting, or the containing and facilitating environment, and timing in the different stages of analysis. In a very different fashion from post-Kleinian or Lacanian technique, Independents emphasize the therapeutic potential of a period of regression to dependence in which the patient can be contained in the analytic setting as if it were a maternal environment. With patients with disturbances of the self,[6] this can provide a deeply reparative experience, in that the patient can regress to very early, unorganized states of mind and have experiences which may have been missed or may have been disturbed at an early stage of life, or to repair a 'basic fault' (Balint 1968). But as Khan points out: 'The analyst's task is not to *be* or *become* the mother. We cannot, even if we try . . . What we do provide are some of the functions of the mother as a protective shield and auxiliary ego' (Khan 1964 [1996]: 67, his emphases).

Winnicott believed in the possibility of regression to a state of fusion with the object, or to a stage at which boundaries between self and other are not yet properly differentiated. He thought that the analytic attitude needed to approximate to primary maternal preoccupation: in other words, the therapist becomes so attuned to his patient's state of mind that much communication is non-verbal, and for a period of time he becomes as absorbed in his patient as a mother in her newborn infant. Bollas writes movingly about this aspect of Winnicottian technique:

> [S]uch patients seek a special ambience with the analyst, where the analyst's interpretations are initially less important for their content and more significant for what is experienced as a maternal presence, an empathic response . . . In such moments, the patient experiences interpretations primarily for their capacity to match his internal mood, feeling or thought, and such moments of rapport lead the patient to 'reexperience' the transformational object-relation. He appreciates the analyst's fundamental non-intrusiveness (particularly the analyst not demanding compliance) not because it leads to freedom of association, but because it feels like the kind of relating that is needed in order to become well.
>
> (Bollas 1979 [1987]: 22–3)

The most extensive clinical example of the use of dependence to regression remains Milner's (1969) *The Hands of the Living God*. During the long analysis of a schizophrenic young woman, a level of psychological fusion was tolerated until the patient began to emerge at her own pace. Milner gave up trying to interpret:

> Instead I felt I had to learn to wait and watch and let her know that I was there, watching, and not let myself be seduced into this working too hard for her, trying to tell her, put into words for her, her unconscious preoccupations; because, I came to suspect, if I let myself be so seduced, which I constantly did, it could only put off the moment, perhaps disastrously, of her finding what she herself had got.
>
> (ibid.: 42)

Eventually, her patient's paintings became her first pre-verbal means of communicating primitive psycho-physical states, beginning with 'faecal symbols as devils or chrysalises' (ibid.: 63) and a 'turd-baby and strangled feelings' (ibid.: 113), and eventually 'ego nuclei, early body memories and archaic body images' (ibid.: 177).[7]

A clinical example from my time in an NHS clinic comes from the therapy of a young woman I call 'Marilyn', whom I saw from age nineteen to age twenty-six. Marilyn was the child of a seventeen-year-old rock singer who drank and used drugs heavily. She was born with congenital eye and heart defects, which required invasive surgery at ages two, five and seven. She had probably experienced little maternal containment and the surgery retroactively exacerbated this deficit by invading her fragile sense of psychic boundedness. Such impingements were compounded by her mother's frequent involvement with men who were violent and abusive. A small crowd of disturbed children assembled in the family home.

Shortly after her initial consultation, Marilyn began to arrive at the clinic every day and request to lie in the recovery room. She curled into a foetal position and for most of the next few weeks lay there most of the day, Monday to Friday. I worked at the clinic four days a week. As it became clear what level of treatment was needed, I saw Marilyn for a fifty-minute session on each of those days.[8]

For nearly a year, she simply lay in silence with me. Then she began to report vivid and disturbing dreams of being attacked and cut open by monsters and ogres, which I simply interpreted as intrusions into her need to be quiet and feel held. More actively interpretive work became possible later when she gradually began to reduce the amount of time she lay in the rest room.

Regression to dependence is also discussed in Chapters 7 and 8.

THE EROTICS OF MOVING ON

> [I]n the course of my work with every one of my patients who has progressed to, or very far towards a thoroughgoing analytic cure, I have experienced romantic and erotic desires to marry, and fantasies of being married to the patient.
>
> (Searles 1959b [1986a]: 284)

Regression to dependence lasts only for a period of analysis. At a later point, when she is psychologically ready, the patient will move on to more differentiated and triangular relating as a sexual adult capable of symbolizing at least some of her experience. The forms this transition can take are theorized by Benjamin (1995), Searles (1965) and Ogden (1987, 1989b), using Winnicott's (1971) concepts of transitional objects, play and 'the third area' or 'intermediate' or 'transitional' space. Neither self nor not-self, a transitional arena permits a gradual disillusionment from infantile omnipotence and a beginning of more individuated relating through play. Winnicott thought this area could be continually revisited in adult life in cultural experiences, which provide an opportunity for contained regression to a state in which boundaries between self and other are not yet absolute and thereby permit enrichment and reinvigoration of self experience. Transitional space and transitional objects both precede and are co-extensive with the testing of the boundaries between self and other through the 'use of an object', discussed a little later in this chapter.

Ogden sets his view of the recognition of separateness, difference and alterity within the mother/infant and analyst/patient dyad, but within a re-conceptualization of the onset and working through of the Oedipus Complex using Winnicott's description of transitional experiences (Ogden 1987 [1989a], 1989b). He thinks Freud's account of the Oedipus Complex would be too great a shock to be tolerable to a young child and liable to result in narcissistic defences and withdrawal. Outlining different paths for girls and boys, he describes how a non-traumatic discovery of triadic relationships might be grounded in a secure dyadic one.

Ogden locates the onset of the Oedipus Complex in the recognition of another in the mother's mind, perhaps a mother's internal object relationship with her own father. For a little girl, this may involve the discovery of a father in the mother, and for a small boy the discovery of a more separate Oedipal mother within the secure context of a pre-Oedipal maternal environment. Lacan (1953) theorized 'paternal function'—*Le Nom* (*Non*)-*du-Père*—(discussed in Chapter 3) as existing primarily within the mind of a mother, with possible supplementation from an actual father or significant other. Ogden's revision of the Oedipus Complex does not involve the relinquishment of either parent, and hence avoids the splitting that some argue to be problematic within more traditional psychoanalytic accounts of gendered development (Butler 1990; Campbell 2000). The discovery of difference in an early maternal relationship allows for gender to be located in a 'dialectic' of diverse masculine and feminine identifications.

Searles (1965, 1979, 1986b) also details the step-by-step discovery of separateness and triangular relationships using both Winnicott and his own fearless scrutiny of his countertransference. He too argues the need for a therapist to be attuned to her disturbed patients' states of mind and need for privacy in order to recuperate what may have been a catastrophic experience of disillusionment (Searles 1962). Separation processes must be gradual: '. . . the first experienced separate object tends to be sensed as a twin of oneself' (Searles 1986b: 13). The erotic transference which heralds the beginnings of Oedipal relating is often matched with an intensely erotic countertransference, however difficult or uncomfortable an analyst may find this (Searles 1959b).

An example of the use of a transitional area to negotiate separation and sexuality within the transference comes from the therapy of an Afro-Caribbean patient I call 'Patrice'.[9] After an intense and delusionally merged transference lasting for several years, this creative young man invented an idea that we were in 'Peru'. I came to understand 'Peru' as a transitional space or culture where he and I could have an unambivalent and playful experience outside and beyond black and white and all they symbolized for both of us and signified in the social dynamics of our relationship.

He started to send me love messages on cards 'from Peru'. I still received hate messages, but these arrived on ordinary British writing paper. He gave me a beautifully decorated Peruvian bowl, and for three sessions after that carried a Peruvian pipe under his T-shirt which looked like an erect penis. In this way his sense of his sexuality, previously associated in his mind with ugliness and rage, came to be modified. In 'Peru', we could enjoy a calm, almost magical transitional space. He said it felt like 'being in a tranquil lily pond with frogs'. And after this experience, he became able to see me more clearly and less delusionally as a separate person with a mind and feelings of my own.

All Independent theorists agree that when a patient moves on from regressed dependence, non-interpretation and quasi-maternal attunement are replaced by more challenging and triangulated levels of interpretation.

AGGRESSION AS PART OF THE LIFE FORCE AND THE USE OF AN OBJECT

> [T]he primary, powerful innate urge to self-realization [is] the basis of aggression.
>
> (Winnicott 1954a: 1363)

Aggression as well as love is essential to moving on and separation/individuation for today's Independents. Winnicott (1950) considered human aggression to be part of the life force and likened it to that which is needed for a chick to break out of an egg. In infant life, it is an aspect of motility and a part of primitive, ruthless love. Ken Tynan instinctively grasped the wonder of benign aggression when he wrote of Katharine Hepburn: 'Her very nerve-ends tingle with glee . . . and her aggressiveness is that of the sun at high noon' (Tynan 1989: 41).

Aggression only becomes pathological when turned against the self and others as a result of trauma or environmental deficit or as a reaction to impingement. A therapist must therefore survive her patient's aggression without retaliation, and, by this process alone, the patient will arrive at 'a feeling of real' and a joyful sense that there is another person out there, who has not been destroyed, to be discovered. This process, which Winnicott (1969) called 'object usage', represents an alternative and supplementary route to the Kleinian depressive position towards alterity, triangulation and symbol-formation. It heralds a breaking out of projective mechanisms and a re-integration or re-fusion of instinctual aggression. Winnicott wrote a vivid description of the object's survival of aggressive assault:

> From now on, the subject says: 'Hullo object!' 'I destroyed you.' 'I love you.' 'You have value for me because of your survival of my destruction of you.' 'While I am loving you I am all the time destroying you in unconscious *fantasy*.'
>
> (ibid. [1974]: 105–6, his emphasis)

Here, Winnicott depicted a profound discovery of external reality and difference, and a crucial stage in separation/individuation processes. The use of an object results in an alive, energized experience for the subject. It is a joy-based theory of development, in contrast to the guilt-laden depressive position (both are necessary, of course). Winnicott's 'use of an object' is arguably the more integrative experience. The subtle dissociation of aggression in depressive processes can lead to what Phillips dubs 'a kitsch seriousness' (Phillips 1998: 3).

The 'use of an object' is a fruitful concept in Independent theory today. It offers internal freedom as well as greater separateness. It enables both the recognition of and identification with difference as a route to growth, and has generated a shift in the way we think about intersubjectivity, which now includes the recognition of maternal subjectivity as important in itself and not just in how it impacts on a baby (Benjamin 1995). As one of the constituents of Ogden's (1994a, 1997) 'analytic third', the 'use of an object' has become part of a revision of the analytic process and what may constitute its curative, or at least mutative, factors.

Benjamin's (1995) theories of the beginnings of more differentiated relating within the early maternal dyad constitute a radical extension of the concept of object usage and a development of the concept of intersubjectivity. Through a mother's capacity to withstand her small child's aggression, a child comes to experience her as a separate person with a mind of her own. If the mother caves in, retaliates or withdraws, she is not properly recognized as a separate other but as part of the child's omnipotence. Benjamin's account of the discovery of difference prioritizes what goes on in a mother's mind (and not just as a schematic prescription for how to be a good enough mother). A mother has to be found to be interestingly different, with a way of looking at things which is not identical to the child's own.

Benjamin, following Stern (1985), argues that 'affective attunement' begins at eight or nine months of age when we discover that '. . . there are other minds out there' (Benjamin 1995: 34). And, if relating is indispensable to emotional and psychic growth, we then have to recognize the role of aggression in pushing growth forward. The intersubjective space between mother and child lays the foundations of the distinction between symbol and symbolized, helping to differentiate between internal and external reality and thereby initiating triangular space. This intersubjective moment between mother and child both has many applications as a clinical concept, and opens the route into a far broader and more flexible account of gender acquisition and sexuality, described a little later in this chapter.

Like Benjamin, Ogden both grounds the discovery of difference in the early maternal relationship, and extends the concept of intersubjectivity to decentre subjectivity and relocate it in a constantly evolving matrix of relationships with others (Ogden 1987, 1989b, 1994a, 1997; Black and Mitchell 1995). He takes from Green's (1975) challenge to the concepts of the blank screen and analytic objectivity, and also his argument for an expansion of the concept of countertransference to incorporate the fact that the analyst is herself an integral part of the analytic process. Her patient's material is not external to her, and an analyst, too, is changed by the interaction with her patient. Green uses the term 'analytic object' to denote a new entity which is born from the analyst/analysand relationship. Ogden coins the term 'intersubjective analytic third' to describe the 'dynamic interplay of subjectivities' generated in the analytic encounter (Ogden 1994c [1994a]: 65).

For Ogden, this 'analytic third' is reborn in every analytic session, thereby presenting a version of psychoanalysis with some psychological equality. 'The intersubjective and the individually subjective each create, negate and preserve the other' (ibid.: 64), and '[t]here is no analyst, no analysand, no analysis, aside from the process through which the analytic third is generated' (Ogden 1995 [1999]: 30). Ogden is not referring here to psychological fusion (although, as we have seen, this may be necessary for a period in the early years of analysis with some patients), but to the ways in which the interplay of two separate minds create an experience different from an individual perspective. Again, in this process, aggression is indispensable: '. . . the analyst must listen to (through) the roar of destruction from its edge, not ever being certain where that edge lies' (Ogden 1994a: 4).

Bollas continually re-emphasizes the centrality of benign aggression in the capacity to use life itself as an object, creatively, generously and, if need be, ruthlessly (Bollas in Molino (ed.) 1997). In his accounts of the 'human idiom' (Bollas 1989) or *Being a Character* (Bollas 1992), forms of object usage are invoked to expand subjectivity and render it more complex and fluid: '. . . the true self is not an integrated phenomenon but only dynamic sets of idiomatic dispositions that come into being through problematic encounters with the object world' (Bollas 1992 [1993]: 30). One radical and challenging instance might be an 'aleatory object', or one that appears by chance, which can be used by those with sufficient internal freedom and security to enjoy it. Like free association, which in Bollas' (1995) terms is a sophisticated accomplishment, aleatory object usage has the '. . . mysterious ability to evoke from within our own unknown depths surprises to us about ourselves and what (and whom) we have been unwittingly harbouring' (Grotstein 2002: 78). Like Lacan's emphasis on the value of surprise, Bollas' schema for transfigurative moments in a fruitful life involves the unexpected at its core.

EGO ORGASM AND THE ECSTATIC TRADITION

> [I]n the analysis of the artist (whether potential or manifest) in any patient, the crucial battle is over the 'language' of love, that is to say, ultimately, over the way in which the orgasm, or the orgastic experiences, are to be symbolized.
>
> (Milner 1950 [1971]: 151)

Winnicott's (1958b) concept of 'ego orgasm', a climax of id-impulse in satisfactory play for children and in aesthetic experience for adults, inspired Milner to theorize the role of 'ecstatic' experience in infant and adult development. Today, this represents a distinctive aspect of contemporary Independent sensibility and approach. Although we are more familiar with the ways in which contemporary Independent analysts have emphasized the aesthetic dimension of analysis (and indeed life), references to ecstatic experience can be found throughout the work of Milner, Khan and Eigen, and sometimes in Bollas' and Ogden's writings. McDougall (1982) uses the term 'ec-static', in reference to Freud's 'libidinal stasis', to describe states of body/mind in which blocked pain is released.

More commonly in Independent writing, 'ecstatic' is used to refer to formative epiphanic or crystallizing moments. Khan, for example, quoted Baudelaire's (1863) account of genius as rediscovered childhood:

> It is to this profound and joyous curiosity that one should attribute the firm and sensually ecstatic gaze of children when confronted with anything new, be it a face or a landscape, light, gilt, colours, soft fabrics, their enchantment with beauty heightened by *la toilette*.
>
> (Khan 1983 [1989]: 26)

Milner considered 'ego orgasm' a seminal aspect of early infant development and adult enrichment through cultural experiences. She developed a visceral theory of creative perception, with the locus of active imagination in the body, and emphasized the value of experiences in which there is no absolute differentiation between self and other. Truth, for Milner, was an affective experience—like Bion, she affirmed the emotional and intuitive basis of knowledge. One potential emergence of 'true self' phenomena became the transient sense of fusion or unity characteristic of orgasmic or ecstatic experience (Milner 1957). Bollas, using quasi-religious and sexual language, also highlights the role of the ecstatic in formative 'true self' engagements and cathexes: '. . . we consecrate the world with our own subjectivity' (Bollas 1992 [1993]: 3), and (of object choice): 'This selection constitutes the *jouissance* of the true self, a bliss released through the finding of specific objects that free idiom to its articulation' (ibid.: 17).

Milner's vision of creative humanity included extremes of plenitude and emptiness sometimes too readily assigned to disturbance or pathology in classical psychoanalysis. As Bollas (1992) asserts, there is a restricted vocabulary for a range of experiences in health in psychoanalysis. For Milner, new insight came about through the rhythmic reciprocity between fusion and differentiation like Bion's account of a necessary fluctuation between paranoid/schizoid and depressive processes in thought and psychic evolution. She centralized the value of illusion in transitional experiences or areas as a '*reculer pour mieux sauter*' (a movement back to enable a better leap forward), a necessary means of breaking down and extending an already established sense of self (Milner 1952).

The formative value of aesthetic and ecstatic experience is also discussed in Chapter 9.

CONTEMPORARY INDEPENDENT THEORISTS

I will now introduce some individual theorists. My comments here are not intended to be exhaustive, but to set the scene for a comparative discussion in Part II.

Three British Independents: Masud Khan, Marion Milner and Christopher Bollas

Khan's three books speak of the ineffability and unknowability of true self experiences (Khan 1974, 1979, 1983). An eloquent exponent of Winnicott, he emphasized the provision of a psychological environment which is mindful and attentive to every shade of feeling, but never intrusive. He deemed many forms of interpretation to be unnecessary and premature attempts to organize an analysand's experience for him: '. . . language can become a usurper of the space of illusion and experience' (Khan 1974 [1996]: 269).

Instead, the analytic object (the entire analytic setting including the mind of the analyst) furnishes the space in which dreams become possible and may need to remain private to the patient. 'True self' experiences may begin to coalesce within a sensitive, nuanced emotional environment: being, experiencing and, only later, knowing (Khan 1969). With equal delicacy, Khan (1963, 1964) described types of analytic provision which enable a patient to begin and go on being herself in a quasi-maternal environment: the auxiliary ego and psychic shield, aspects of a Winnicottian holding environment which can be internalized by the patient as a sense of boundedness as well as an internal resource.

Khan (1963) formulated 'cumulative trauma' as damage caused even by seemingly benign or minor infringements of an analysand's, or small child's, psychic space. Cumulative trauma may result in precocious ego development and defensive establishment of a prematurely separate self in reaction to impingement. Khan's theories of perversion, discussed in Chapter 6, were an extension of his thinking about premature ego development.

A devotee of European Romanticism, Khan, following Blake, established '. . . the sovereignty of intensity, immediacy and imagination' in the analytic process (Khan 1983 [1989]: 24). When the analytic space becomes a holding environment where 'true self' experiences can establish themselves without the premature intrusion of interpretation, it can function as a 'dream space', a place of 'mysteries' or even a habitat for '*lying fallow* . . .', a mode of being that is alerted quietude and receptive wakeful lambent consciousness', that most essential prerequisite to creativity (ibid.: 183, his emphases).

Like Winnicott and Khan, Milner emphasized both the value of illusion as a transitional experience or area and the clinical importance of benign regression to dependence for a period of analysis for very disturbed and/or damaged patients. She was primarily concerned with '. . . the problem of psychic creativity' (Milner 1956: 169), whatever the level of disturbance of her patients. Like Blake (1793) and Castoriadis (1997), she saw perception of external reality as in itself a creative act and impossible without imagination. The 'integrative force' (Milner 1957: 216) of visceral perception, indissoluble from bodily experience, precedes potentially restrictive rational thought: '. . . the inherent rhythmic capacity of the psycho-physical organism can become a source of order that is more stable than reliance on an order imposed either from the outside, or by the planning conscious mind' (ibid.: 224).

Milner argued for paradoxical, not dissociative, awareness, or forms of consciousness which permit incorporation of apparently incompatible extremes. She approved Blake's proverb: 'Without contraries is no progression' (Blake 1790, quoted in Milner 1956: 168). She considered idealization necessary to intense cathexis, and not just a defence against ambivalence. Ecstatic experience, for Milner, incorporated perception, active imagination and extremes of experience reduced and constricted in ratiocinative endeavour.

Bollas centralizes the aesthetic experience or moment as a formative cathexis in 'true self' experiences activated through intense engagement with significant others and a plethora of different forms of 'object usage' (Bollas 1987, 1989, 1992, 1995, 1999, 2000). The complex evolution and enrichment of the self through object usage includes, amongst others, 'mnemic objects' (1992) (which like Proust's *madeleine* evoke earlier projected self-states), 'conservative objects' (1987) (in which a child stores experiences he may not have the means to process), and 'structural objects' (1992) (which through the particular form of their composition shape self-experience). There are also 'endogenously determined' or 'imagined' objects, contrasted with 'actual' objects (ibid.), and 'projective objects', which for Bollas constitute an imaginative rendering of reality necessary to creativity and subjective richness. 'Sensational objects' (ibid.) extend the self in auditory, visual and muscular dimensions. The 'transformational object' (1979 [1987]), or the early maternal environment, may be revisited in many forms throughout life.[10]

Trauma, for Bollas, is constituted by an over-simplification or restriction of the process of object usage: in his view, there is nothing worse than to be trapped in another's idiom without sufficient liberty to articulate one's own. He argues certain forms of marriage or coupledom constitute a retreat from the complexity of individuated subjectivity into the regressive compensations of quasi pre-Oedipal relating (Bollas 1992). In contrast, a fulfilling life involves endless actualization of potential aspects of self through aesthetic engagement with external and internal reality:

> I think that character is an aesthetic. If our way of being refers to our very precise means of forming our world, both internal and inter-subjective, then each of us is a kind of artist with his or her creative sensibility . . .
>
> It is a pleasure to express and articulate the self: there's an erotic dimension to that kind of representation . . . the erotics of the instinct drive is not simply in its final gratification through an object; it's the entire process . . .
>
> (Bollas in Molino (ed.) 1997: 8–9)

> Through free associating the patient unconsciously selects objects of desire and articulates, through these objects, evolving self experiences. We're talking here, of course, of mental objects: of objects that come into mind through which nascent self-states are released into articulation.
>
> (ibid.: 22–3)

These quotations exemplify the pleasure that Bollas derives from writing and speaking. The quality of subjectivity is the *sine qua non* of development throughout life and its enjoyment en route. The complexity of subjectivity is constituted in myriad potential and constantly evolving self states, evoked and brought into being by numinous or affect-laden meetings or matings with self-selected objects. In this way Winnicott's 'true self' becomes in Bollas' capable hands a post-modern concept. Through our 'aesthetic intelligence' we live out our 'destiny drive' through object choice and usage. There is pleasure in the deconstruction of subjectivity through its resituation in encounters with objects and in free association (Bollas 1995). Bollas' version of psychoanalysis can, at best, be oriented towards the discovery and elaboration of future potential selves.

In contrast, character pathology involves inhibition or perversion of these potential processes. The 'anti-narcissist', who destroys another's investment in him, and the 'ghostline personality', who refuses transitional objects in real life and prefers a schizoid fantasy world, present a clinical dilemma in so far as their relating to objects occurs only in the most destructive and deadening forms (Bollas 1989). Similarly, 'normotic illness' describes that restriction of subjectivity now recognizable in people who choose to invest adhesively in material goods or status in place of loving or evocative relationships or creative solitude (Bollas 1987). (All the former are discussed in Chapter 6). However, despite his vivid and specific chronicles of psychic damage, Bollas, like most contemporary Independents, considers the nature of psychopathology less important than the quality of subjectivity and intensity of object cathexis (Bollas in Molino (ed.) 1997).

Although Bollas' debt to Winnicott, and to a lesser extent Bion, is visible throughout his work, after 1995 he draws from some Lacanian theory and from Jean Laplanche. For example, he argues that certain forms of self experience lie beyond representation and could accurately be described as belonging to the Lacanian 'real'. Like Milner's embodied perception, Bollas' 'real' is a bodily experience. In the right milieu, whether maternal or analytic, the unconscious situated in the body is a creative and generative experience in and of itself. Through the breaking up of ordered rational coherence, we gain access to the possible 'dissemination' of our unconscious riches.

'Psychic genera', contrasted with 'trauma', begin life as unconscious 'inherited proto-nucleations' (Bollas 1992: 70). Generative psychic forms are constellated throughout life when lived experience evokes intense psychic interest (ibid.: 88) and are creative, whilst trauma, as 'psychic incubation', condemns us to defensive repetition (ibid.: 67). Through the tolerance of 'generative chaos', as through Bion's return to paranoid/schizoid processes, one may be able to discover a fundamentally new perspective, vision or realization, and the moment may feel revelatory.

Two North American Independents: Thomas Ogden and Jessica Benjamin

Ogden's primary influences are Freud and Winnicott and to a lesser extent, Bion and Lacan (Ogden 1982, 1986, 1989a, 1994a, 1997, 2001, 2005). He refines and extends classical psychoanalytic theory and introduces some new concepts, including the 'autistic-contiguous position' and the 'analytic third' (Ogden 1989a, 1994a, 1997).

The 'autistic-contiguous position' (Ogden1989a), like Kristeva's concept of the 'semiotic' (discussed in Chapters 3 and 9), describes both a cardinal stage of early life and a continuing mode of generating and developing experience in childhood and adult life. Ogden describes it as a pre-symbolic and pre-paranoid/schizoid means of forming connections between sensory impressions or a '. . . primitive psychological organization [which] under normal circumstances contributes the barely perceptible background of sensory boundedness of all subsequent subjective states' (ibid.: 50).

Only in psychopathology (on the autistic spectrum), because of high infantile anxiety as a reaction to maternal deprivation or impingement, do the defences of this position become rigid and out of communication with other phases of development. Under 'good enough' circumstances, the mother's attunement to her baby will be such that the infant's increasing awareness of his separateness will be staged in manageable and non-traumatizing doses, and then the autistic-contiguous position becomes one of several different modes of generating experience in adult life. It may co-exist with paranoid/schizoid, depressive, aggressive and imaginative forms of relatedness, and is likely to be a factor in ecstatic, sensual and aesthetic experience. Ogden argues: 'Sensory contiguity of skin surface, along with the element of rhythmicity, are basic to the most fundamental set of infantile object relations: the infant's experience of being held, nursed, and spoken to by the mother' (ibid.: 52). A baby's ordinary experience of laying his cheek against the mother's breast, the rhythmic regularity of sucking and the 'dialogue' of cooing, like Tustin's (1990) 'rhythm of safety', provide the sensory background for all later development. Gradually, from this unorganized state, shapes as well as sounds come to assume recognizable forms in an infant's subjectivity.

Ogden's 'analytic third' (Ogden 1994a, 1997), as I have said, is part of the new emphasis on psychoanalysis as a venture shared by analyst and patient in the North American relational and interpersonal schools (see for example Bass 2001). Although Bion's description of maternal and analytic reverie and his emphasis on the analyst's openness to the unexpected in every session paved the theoretical way to these developments, Ogden shows us how it actually works. His associative musings are always understood as unconscious countertransferential information, and demonstrate how a therapist's unconscious furnishes a constant counterpoint to her patient's

transferential experiences. There is no longer a sense of a daunting requirement to keep one's mind impossibly empty, as some have interpreted Bion's
(1970) 'without memory and desire'. Nonetheless the discipline Ogden
describes in the lightning speed of recognition of the analyst's association
and return to his patient's material from a new perspective also takes many
years to hone to clinical usefulness.

An example comes from the therapy of a client I shall call 'Anne'. Anne was
born into a comfortably middle-class English family, whose intentions were
benign but whose capacity to deal with their own and their children's feelings
was restricted. Their difficulties had been compounded by her father's incar-
ceration as a prisoner of war in Japan in the Second World War and the cot
death of their first baby two years before Anne, their second child, was born.

Anne became a successful manager but was restricted and inhibited by her
lack of capacity to deal with her own, her husband's and her two sons'
feelings. In a session several years into her therapy, she described a dilemma
related to opening some boxes in her attic which held objects from her past
associated with one of her sons, who had become a heroin addict. I found my
attention apparently wandering to the jug on my desk which, as usual, held
flowers. The jug, as it happened, had belonged to my favourite aunt who had
died of breast cancer when I was nine. I could have dismissed this as irrelevant, but instead I realized that it encapsulated Anne's dilemma: how to hold
onto emotional value whilst dealing with the pain associated with that value.

In a later book, Ogden (2001) suggests we listen to our patients' material
not just as if it were a dream, but also as if it were a poem. In beautifully
written poetic exegeses and accounts of session material, Ogden shows how
the tone, rhythmic structure, alliteration and spaces in the patient's communications provide as rich a source of information as the words themselves. In this way, although he does not declare it as such himself, he
brings us back full circle to the underlying infrastructure of the 'autistic-
contiguous position' in human experience, and shows how it can add a
hitherto little-explored dimension to technique. Like Bollas, Ogden is a
pleasure to read for the sensitivity and grace of his writing and takes core
concepts from Freud and Winnicott to new levels of intricacy and meaning.

Like both Bollas and Ogden, their contemporary, Jessica Benjamin,
draws from richly varied allusive sources. In her three books (Benjamin
1988, 1995, 1998) Benjamin uses sociological theory (particularly Jürgen
Habermas under whom she studied, and Theodor Adorno), infant research
and observation (Trevarthen 1980; Stern 1985), philosophy (Hegel 1807;
Husserl 1935), feminist psychological research (Chodorow 1978; Gilligan

1982) as well as Winnicott and Mahler (1975). Unlike Bollas and Ogden, Benjamin's primary focus is not always clinical, although she is a practising psychoanalyst in New York City and her work has profound clinical implications. She theorizes the cultural determinants of female submissiveness in heterosexual relationships (1988), the discovery of difference and otherness in the early maternal dyad (1995) and the evolution of subjectivity and the ownership of desire within gendered development (1998).

Much of her work centres on an elaboration of Winnicott's (1969) 'use of an object'. For example, she argues it is necessary for women to survive psychological destruction and reclaim their subjectivity in heterosexual relationships to '. . . offer men a new possibility of colliding with the outside and becoming alive in the presence of an equal other' (Benjamin 1988 [1990]: 221). She later argues the capacity to recognize the mother as a subjective other is a critical stage in infant development (Benjamin 1995). The discovery of difference is not left to the father and the Oedipus Complex. She traces the child's recognition of alterity in the early maternal dyad through the mother's survival of the necessarily aggressive component of primitive love, which enables masculine, perhaps paternal, identifications for a small girl, and feminine, perhaps maternal, identifications for a small boy. She stresses the necessity of homosexual as well as heterosexual desire for both genders, and allows for a 'spectrum' of identifications and object love in adult life.

Oedipal processes are never completely left behind, but can be used as a resource to extend the self and open new possibilities of identification and experimentation with diverse ways of relating. Benjamin's thinking complements Ogden's (1987, 1989b) expanded account of Oedipal processes and Lacan's three stages of the Oedipus Complex (discussed in Chapter 3). In Benjamin's view, the multiple identifications and forms of desire of the Oedipal phase and 'postoedipal' configurations permit a far more flexible approach to identity, sexuality and gender: 'The postoedipal form is constituted by sustaining the tension between contrasting elements so that they remain potentially available rather than forbidden and the oscillation between them can be pleasurable rather than dangerous' (Benjamin 1995: 73).

She dismantles any lingering notions that issues of power and authority exist only between and in a world of men, and shows how female submissiveness is psychologically constructed within the deep structure of gender complementarity. She shows us how both parents can be figures of attachment and separation for their children, and how within 'the dance of mutual recognition, the meeting of separate selves . . . desire escapes the borders of the imperial phallus and resides on the shores of endless worlds' (Benjamin 1988 [1990]: 130). Identification with difference becomes possible in a more complex and multiple configuration of shifting movements within triangular relationships, thereby augmenting opportunities for growth and development throughout life and enabling richer and less restricted relationships. Paternal identifications, within traditional Western family structures, can play a particularly positive role in the achievement of autonomous female subjectivity.

Two French Independents: André Green and Joyce McDougall

The French Independents comprise one of the most muscularly eclectic sections of the analytic population and provide a bridge between the British and French schools. Green's massive, complex and inclusive oeuvre is only as yet partially translated into English (Green 1986, 1988 [2001], 1997 [2000], 1999a, 1999c, 2002, 2003, 2005a, 2005c). Green has kept his finger on the pulse of most innovative psychoanalytic developments over more than thirty years, and I will merely touch on some of his central themes here. He declares Winnicott, Lacan and Bion the three primary influences on both his own thinking and on twenty-first-century psychoanalysis (Green 1986, 2005a). Although he attended Lacan's seminars from 1961 to 1967, describes Lacan as 'a tremendous intellectual stimulant' and uses his insights throughout his work, he never 'bought' Lacanian theory wholesale, and disagrees with Lacan's formulation of the linguistic structure of the unconscious (see Chapter 3). He prefers the tenor of the British school:

> The writings of Winnicott (and of his followers, especially Masud Khan and Marion Milner) had an incomparably true ring, clinically: one was struck by the originality of his concepts, their newness and, I would add, their freshness. They gave an airing to psychoanalytic space, stripping classical technique of its rigidity and giving renewed freedom to the analyst-analysand pairing.
>
> (Green 1986 [1997]: 10)

Despite this technical preference, Green deplores the British tendency to disavowal of the centrality of sexuality. The British, he claims, relegate sexuality to genitality and, even then, often proceed to ignore it, sometimes with dire consequences. Instead Green claims all forms of sexuality as the life force and as love of life and others.[11]

> What I think we are doing in analysis is to enable the people who come to us to increase their feeling of freedom . . . to liberate the forces which are present in themselves to enjoy life, not as scared people looking for all sorts of safety, nor as repenting sinners . . . Analysis should improve their capacity to cathect something. We don't have to say what, they will find out . . .
>
> (Green 1995: 25).

'Sexual ecstasy' (ibid.) should be part of this, as should passion (Green 1980), which involves the ownership of our destructive impulses.

Green shares Bollas' and Ogden's preoccupation with forms of aliveness and deadness in the analytic setting, or in his terms cathexis and radical decathexis (Green 1999b). His extended work on the 'negative' (Green 1981, 1998, 1999a, 2000) focuses on the dual aspect of negation introduced by Freud (1925), and Bion's (1959) distinction between 'no-thing' and 'nothing', and links both these conceptualizations with Winnicott's transitional space. The negative can facilitate the unknown or a new thought through tolerance of frustration or a '. . . state that is *between* absolute loss and excessive presence' (Green in Abram (ed.) 2000: 5, his emphasis), or it can result in destructive foreclosure. At worst, the negative is at work in *'psychose blanche'* (blank psychosis) where the blocking of symbolization and splitting of the object result in a core of emptiness combined with a sense of persecution (Green 1975).

'Blankness', in anxiety and mourning, extends to a psychical 'hole' at the centre of the ego as the result of an early experience of a depressed mother. This 'dead mother complex' comprises a fusional identification with a dead 'frame' mother and creates a core of decathexis which can inhibit love and pursuit of life in many forms (Green 1983). Radical decathexis with its inevitable entwinement with destructive instincts is integral to Green's (2001) structural work on narcissism, discussed in Chapter 5.

Joyce McDougall, also a practising psychoanalyst in Paris, declares herself a Freudian although her work incorporates an understanding of Lacanian, post-Kleinian and Winnicottian theory. In her four books (McDougall 1978, 1982, 1989, 1995), she explores forms of psychopathology (narcissistic, perverse and psychosomatic) through which a precarious self is constructed from early deficit (see Chapter 6). Her groundbreaking work on alexithymia, or an inability to symbolize affect, with its concomitant 'operatory thinking' (McDougall 1978, 1989), facilitates clinical work with people who do not seem to have feelings and might traditionally have been considered unsuitable for analysis. These difficult patients may function at a psychosomatic level, or they may, like the 'anti-analysand' (McDougall 1978), foreclose the possibility of making psychic connections.[12] McDougall's predominant clinical focus lies in primitive emotional states in which neither the mother's mind/body nor the baby's psyche/soma are experienced as separate entities, the manifestations of this state of affairs in the transference and its analytic management.

THE SPIRIT AND TENOR OF CONTEMPORARY INDEPENDENT THOUGHT

Winnicott stressed spontaneity as a developmental achievement and as the first emergence of 'true self' manifestations (Winnicott 1960). Today's

Independents never speak or act mindlessly, but a spirit of lightheartedness (in the service of seriousness) permeates the work of Winnicott, Searles, Nina Coltart and Adam Phillips, and sometimes also Ogden and Michael Eigen. Coltart (1986) discusses the importance of laughter in psycho-analysis, and deems '. . . if [psychotherapists are] not enjoying their work . . . then somehow they're on the wrong wavelength' (Coltart in Molino (ed.) 1997: 166). Humour, surprise, and the impact of a startling new perspective can be more skilful (and spontaneous) expressions of a ther-apist's clinical repertoire than a seriously spelt-out transference interpreta-tion (see Chapter 8).

Openness—never in the sense of personal disclosure to the patient—but in maximal deployment of an analyst's self and unconscious processes is central.[13] A willingness on the part of a therapist to be taken into unfam-iliar terrain and areas of herself with which she may not always be comfortable has become a benchmark, leading to an emphasis on particular freedoms and forms of aliveness.

Phillips cites '. . . the comedian and the lover and the mystic' (Phillips in Molino (ed.) 1997: 133) as suitable models for analytic states of mind and interventions. The erotics of instinctual life, as we have seen, are indis-pensable to moving on to greater levels of separation and individuation, whilst also informing the multiple pleasures of self representation and self expression (Bollas in Molino (ed.) 1997). The erotics of object usage take many of these theorists into aesthetic and ecstatic dimensions. In an almost Leavisite fashion, the aesthetic savouring of free association (or the closest we can get to it) and the rendering of the self in interaction with a patient are among the hallmarks of an engaged and creative analysis. Poetry (Ogden), art (Milner) and the poetics of space and form (Bollas) are as great, or greater, sources of inspiration than classical psychoanalytic theory. Indeed, Bollas (2004, 2005) has recently turned to the comic novella as a new vehicle for exploring psychoanalysis.

All these theorists, without exception, give space to the patient—space to be in an unorganized state without demands for analytic compliance, space to be private and silent, space to become and articulate themselves in their own unique idiom. All give priority to the patient's perspective, under-standing and creativity. Patrick Casement (1985, 1990, 2002) shows how a patient's comments, at least unconsciously, denote their 'supervision' of the analyst as feedback on their experience of him.

Unsurprisingly, women also gain a new freedom within this respect for the other's perspective and alterity. Janine Chasseguet-Smirgel (1964, 1986), a French Independent, incorporates an understanding of the cultural determinants of gender inequality. She argues a girl's difficulty in separ-ating from her mother might lead to a tendency to idealize men, and male defences against a phantasy of maternal omnipotence might include deni-gration of women. Her work on the construction of gendered identity and

Benjamin's use of intersubjectivity in the early maternal relationship open the possibility of less rigid and constricted gender roles. At the same time, Benjamin, Bollas and Ogden's versions of object usage and their stress on intersubjectivity in emotional development show how the recognition and valuation of difference in the other's subjectivity are crucial factors in growth.

Some Independent analysts, particularly Eigen and Symington, but also occasionally Bollas, Phillips, Coltart and McDougall, extend the erotics of instinctual life and the privacy of the patient's self into the domain of spirituality. Symington (2001) contends the realm of the spiritual to be indissoluble from sanity, unwittingly echoing Lacan's (1959–60) belief that the converse of psychopathology is ethics, and never 'normality', whatever that may be taken to mean. Eigen, the self-proclaimed *Psychoanalytic Mystic* (1998), writes in a fluid, staccato, contrapuntal style, so that meaning builds and is sparked from a flash of juxtaposition more than from organized 'rational' thought. None of these theorists goes as far as Lacan in his openly proclaimed adherence to certain principles of *Zen* or '*Dhyana*' Buddhism and Hindu '*Dhvani*' in 'oracular' interpretation (Lacan 1953, 1953–4) (see Chapter 8).

Contemporary Independent praxis is marked by its style, its range of cultural influences, its subtlety and delight in clinical work and writing.

NOTES

1. For slightly more detail, see Chapters 1 and 5.
2. Theoretical eclecticism denotes the ability to mix ideas from different paradigms. Pluralism is the conscious application of differing perspectives to the same issue whilst remaining fully aware that the paradigms from which the perspectives originate may not be entirely compatible. This book is intended to be pluralistic rather than eclectic.
3. Husserl (1935) posited that the ego acquires a sense of the other or of the alter ego through a series of experiences which define transcendental intersubjectivity as the reality out of which an individual ego emerges. Habermas (1970) used the expression 'the intersubjectivity of mutual understanding' to describe both an individual capacity and a social domain.
4. The theorists who developed these specific concepts of Winnicott are: 'ego orgasm' (Milner, Bollas); the true self (Khan, Bollas and Ogden); the use of an object (Benjamin, Bollas and Ogden: each mutates this concept in a different arena—Benjamin uses it to break open constructions of gender through Oedipal processes, Ogden uses it in his clinical concept of the 'analytic third', and Bollas describes and distinguishes between a plethora of different forms of object usage); regression to dependence (Milner, Khan, Bollas and McDougall); the third area or intermediate or transitional space (Milner, Khan, Bollas and Ogden). All these concepts are elaborated in more detail later in this chapter.
5. The term, 'ruthless', as intended in Winnicott's 'use of an object', signifies a trust in the object to survive one's aggression, indispensable to both infantile

and erotic expression—and by extension in adult life, the capacity to act decisively and effectively when necessary. Necessary ruthlessness is also a powerful strand of Lacan's post-1964 theorization of 'the subject in the drive' (see Chapter 9). My use of the word 'ruthless' is in no way intended to imply either amorality or any form of habitually unconcerned self-seeking behaviour.

6. By 'disturbances of the self', I refer to those people whose characterological defences are organized in such a way (and there are many possible ways in which this can happen) as to protect them from more overt disturbance. These patients are traditionally categorized as 'borderline' or 'narcissistic', and some-times 'perverse'. For more detail about all these concepts, the reader should turn to Chapters 5 and 6.

7. Milner's work on primitive psycho-physical states prefigured Kristeva's 'semiotic' (see Chapters 3 and 9) and McDougall's theorization of the psychosomatic dimension in analysis (see later in this chapter and Chapter 6).

8. This therapy took place before Thatcherite cuts in public services in Britain prohibited such a level of treatment. I was helped by the understanding and containment of a sophisticated consultant psychiatrist and staff team.

9. The earlier stages of Patrice's therapy are discussed in Chapter 4 as an example of Bion's theories of psychopathology.

10. See also Gabriella Mann: 'Transformational, Conservative and Terminal Objects: The Application of Bollas' Concepts to Practice' and James Grotstein: '"Love is where it finds you": The caprices of the "aleatory object"' in Scalia (ed.) (2002).

11. These views were expressed by André Green in an interview with Jan Abram at the Institute of Contemporary Arts in London on 27th February, 2004.

12. One might compare McDougall's 'anti-analysand' with Bollas' (1987) 'normotic personality' and Bion's (1962) '-K'.

13. Some American relational psychoanalysts do advocate personal disclosure in limited and appropriate ways (Bass 2001), but, with the exception of Margaret Little and Coltart on one occasion, this has never been an aspect of British or French Independent technique.

Chapter 3

Lacanians

[L]a terreur n'est pas française ('. . . fear is not a French emotion').
(Rimbaud 1873 [1962]: 306)

Lacanian theory needs to be approached in the context of French intellectual and cultural traditions. French schoolchildren study philosophy at secondary school. There is more widespread respect for the intellectual and the abstract than in Britain or the USA, and a less rigid separation between academic disciplines. The main theoreticians I discuss in this chapter—Julia Kristeva, Luce Irigaray and Jacques Lacan himself—write in a different style from the British or the Americans. They combine elegance with passion and erudition. They are often witty and flirtatious.

Lacan, in particular, often seemed to be having enormous fun in playing with words: he coined over seven hundred neologisms. He was provocative, iconoclastic and sometimes rude—for example, he described Anna Freud's technique as '*postiche*' (hairpiece) work (Roudinesco 1993 [1997]: 251). Kristeva and Irigaray pay serious attention to the art of writing as writing, and so did Lacan in his *Écrits*. His *Seminars* were delivered as lectures and often included audience participation (Rabaté 2003a). They were transcribed by his son-in-law, Jacques-Alain Miller, and are masterpieces of oratorical style. Lacan did not intend to be accessible, except in his early seminars in which he was a witty raconteur of detective stories, Greek philosophy and psychoanalytic theory alike. His later seminars involved far more compression, ambiguity and play on linguistic mechanisms.

Unlike their Anglo-Saxon counterparts, a logical argument is not always followed through to its conclusion in an obvious way: the multi-layered, richly textured, joking and punning capacities of language are exploited to give a complex associative experience which privileges unconscious mechanisms. To the more staid British, the French can sometimes make amazing associative and intellectual leaps. Kristeva, for example, illustrates a statement about the impact of global capital with clinical material (Kristeva 1993 [1995]: 27–44).

Lacan thought that the unconscious was structured like a language, with metaphor and metonymy assuming the space of condensation and displacement (Lacan 1954–5, 1956–7, 1958a; Dor 1985). The unconscious is formed through the subject's problematic entry into language. Lacan reversed Ferdinand de Saussure's version of structural linguistics: the signifier (the idea/concept in the mind) and signifying chain structure perception and are thereby formative of human experience.[1] There are no pre-existing objects or order which language represents, as in Freud's distinction between the 'thing-idea' and the 'word-idea' (Freud 1915b [2005]: 83). As language organizes experience through its own processes, in so doing unconscious mechanisms reflect those of language. There is no fixed referent between signifier and signified, meanings slip and slide and vary according to their linguistic context, and language is as potentially polyvalent as unconscious symbolism.

Lacan was situated in a cultural milieu which included contact with avant-garde writers, artists, philosophers and anthropologists.[2] He could read in English, German, Latin and Greek, as well as French, and had a thorough knowledge of ancient and modern philosophy, frequently citing Plato, Aristotle, Kant, Kierkegaard and Heidegger. Although he was neither a practising nor a believing Catholic, the influence of his Roman Catholic upbringing and his Jesuit education permeated his work (Schneiderman 1983). The paternal metaphor, '*Le Nom (Non)-du-Père*' (the Name (No) of the Father) (discussed later in this chapter), is the opening phrase of every Roman Catholic religious service.

LANGUAGE AND THE UNCONSCIOUS

Je est un autre ('I is an other')
(Rimbaud 1871 [1962]: 6)

For Lacan, a child is ineluctably born into the desire and the language of an Other, initially incarnated in the mother. This big Other (*le grand Autre*) includes the set of parental expectations and unconscious desires which structure the child's first experiences both pre-verbally and through language: at the beginning of life, a child has no means of differentiating between this Other's language/desire and her own. In addition, the Other (*le grand Autre*) carries and is inseparable from the sets of meanings and principles socially inscribed in language as the symbolic system: in Lacan's terms, the 'Law'. The child's unconscious mind is thereby formed in and through language, even before birth, as Lacan claimed (Burgoyne 1997). In its internal form, the Other comes to represent both the unconscious and a fantasied place of knowledge and certainty.

These observations are supported by modern linguistic theory. Noam Chomsky (1957) argued that the principles and syntactical structure of language are genetically determined by the structure of the human mind. Lacanian theory apparently reversed this perspective in the view that we are spoken by our signifiers, but in effect exploded the dualism between nature and nurture (Shepherdson 2000).

Linguistic context determines meaning. Lacan (1953) argued that the principles later discovered by linguistic theorists were already implicit in Freud's work. His observations on the similarity between linguistic and unconscious mechanisms are borne out by Freud's (1900) 'The Interpretation of Dreams', with its emphasis on the overdetermination of words and verbal wit and punning. For Lacan, the divide between the signifier and signified expressed the problematic relationship between what is said consciously and what is barred from conscious discourse (Gurewich 1999a), and the unconscious can be understood as a complex network of signifiers (Lacan 1957). Lacan's view of the interrelationship between language and the unconscious has multiple implications for psychoanalytic technique, explored in Chapter 8, and was powerfully formative of his own writing and lecturing style.

Like the other precursors of twenty-first-century psychoanalytic theory, Winnicott and Bion, Lacan was an erudite and gnomic writer, but of the three he was the only joker. He punned and played intellectual games to startle the reader out of a too ready understanding of his work. His advice to a young psychoanalyst was: 'Do crossword puzzles' (Lacan 1953 [2001]: 62). His often joking punning style was the medium through which the message became the interrelationship between language and the unconscious. Meaning derives from synchrony or a word's position in relation to its context within a particular linguistic structure, rather than a solidified, historically accrued univalent reference. Both the *Écrits* and the later *Seminars* need to be worked over: one reading alone will not begin to yield their meanings.

For example, in *Seminar XX, 'Encore: On Feminine Sexuality, The Limits of Love and Knowledge'*, '*encore*' (again) also means '*en corps*' (in the body) (Lacan 1972–3 [1998]: 5). It refers to the fact that desire can never be satisfied and therefore always wants more, and could also be a reference to female multiple orgasm and Lacan's view of something '*en plus*' or surplus in feminine *jouissance* which is not reducible to symbolization.[3] '*L'amour*' (love) is also '*la mur*' (wall) and '*amure*' (an old sailors' term for tack) (ibid.: 4)—both of these signify Lacan's ideas about the impossibility of love and sexual relationship, explored later in this chapter. Everyone will imbue these double, or triple, or quadruple entendres with their own penumbrae of meaning. Their polyvalence enriches the experience for the reader and, critically for Lacan, who was concerned to subvert fixed systems of meaning, it enables the reader to make their own sense, or non-sense, of the text.

As well as being playful, witty and deliberately ambiguous, Lacan's mode of speech illustrated his interpretation of the structuralist principles of the signifier's independence of the signified and the retroactive and contextual construction of meaning. Like some of the avant-garde writers he was influenced by (particularly James Joyce), Lacan's style was densely structured and opaque, and its possible interpretations are, at least in theory, endless. It requires an act of creativity from the reader and becomes something personal to the reader. In Bion's terms, it is 'unsaturated'[4] and promotes the possibility of acquiring further meaning(s) as the reader reads on, dreams and reflects on it. Most of all, it resonates with unconscious mechanisms—indeed Lacan '. . . modelled his discourse on the very rhetoric of the unconscious he believed to have discerned in Freud's foundational accounts of dreams, slips of the tongue and jokes' (Nobus 2004: 196).

PSYCHOANALYTIC CONTEXTS

Lacan read widely amongst his psychoanalytic contemporaries. To a limited extent, he was influenced by the writings of Winnicott, Klein and Bion in his earliest theoretical writings. Although he did not always agree with them, he appreciated the radicalism of their ideas (Roudinesco 1993). He used Winnicott's concept of the transitional object in his account of how the subject begins to separate from the Other (Lacan 1960 [2001]: 345). Lacan himself proclaimed his theoretical orientation as a return to Freud: up to 1964, and particularly in 'The function and field of speech and language in psychoanalysis' (the 'Rome Discourse') (Lacan 1953) and 'The agency of the letter in the unconscious or reason since Freud' (Lacan 1957), he focused on a creative and critical re-reading of Freud (Bowie 1993). However, as Foucault (1977) pointed out, a 'return to' does not necessarily entail respectful imitation but a type of reading which is also a rewriting (Rabaté 2003b).

Although Lacan continually referred back to Freud throughout his massive opus, after 1963 he broke ground with many Freudian concepts. The unconscious came to assume a new status in his work and he developed his own cohesive metapsychology, which introduced a new paradigm into psychoanalysis. In this introduction to some foundational Lacanian concepts, it is critical to bear in mind that this is a different paradigm. Even words which may sound familiar from other psychoanalytic theories take on new meanings within this context. What follows is not intended to be a comprehensive account of Lacanian theory but to whet the appetite of those readers not yet familiar with Lacanian theory to read this consummate theoretician, whose contribution to twenty-first-century psychoanalysis cannot be ignored.

Lacan brought sexuality, the drives, the symbolic father and the radical and subversive power of the unconscious back into a psychoanalysis which in his view was becoming attenuated by ego psychology and almost exclusively focused on the mother/infant dyad. He was emphatically against:

> . . . any attempt to strengthen the ego in a type of analysis that took as its criterion of 'success' a successful adaptation to society—a phenomenon of mental abdication that was bound up with the ageing of the psychoanalytic group in the diaspora of the war, and the reduction of a distinguished practice to a label suitable to the 'American way of life'.
>
> (Lacan 1960 [2001]: 339)

There are as many versions of Lacanian theory as there are Lacanian apologists, and, although it is possible to detect national biases, it is also impossible to represent him without distortion and simplification. The task is rendered more complex by the fact that Lacan frequently revised his own theories. He was never interested in writing a '*Que sais-je?*' (or Beginners' Guide) (Lacan 1964a [2004]: 158).[5] His implicit, like Bion's explicit, theory of knowledge was that it is constantly on the move. One aspect of his admiration for Freud came from Freud's working and re-working of his own theories:

> The value of Freud's texts . . . in which he is breaking new ground, is that like a good archaeologist, he leaves the work of the dig in place— so that, even if it is incomplete, we are able to discover what the excavated objects mean. When Mr. Fenichel passes by the same ground . . . he gathers everything up, puts it in his pockets and in glass cases . . . so that nothing can be found again.
>
> (Lacan 1964a [2004]: 182)

Lacan was continually going 'beyond' his own theories: 'beyond' is the word which recurs most frequently in his work. His output was prolific. In addition to his *Écrits*, he gave seminars in lecture form from 1953 until 1979. He effectively produced a book a year, twenty-six in total, but as yet only a small proportion of Lacan's seminars have been officially translated into English.[6]

Lacan in the USA, where in recent years Lacanian theory has had a greater clinical impact than in Britain, is a different animal from the British or South American Lacan. Bruce Fink introduced Lacanian clinical theory to mainstream American psychoanalysis—it took five years for his first book to be published (Fink 1995). Fink's work is closely allied with that of Jacques-Alain Miller, Lacan's editor, and represents a considerable systematization of Lacanian theory. Fink writes with great clarity and contextualizes Lacanian concepts within American culture. He claims, for example, that a different form of transference to the analyst is initially generated in the United States, Americans being prone to demands for immediate

gratification and less likely than the French to have respect for psychoanalysis as an intellectual discipline (Fink 1997). In 1994 a number of
distinguished French and American psychoanalysts met in Paris to debate
core clinical concepts at a conference organized by Judith Feher Gurewich
and some of her colleagues (Gurewich *et al.* 1999b). The subsequent series
of publications, 'The Lacanian Clinical Field', included works by Joël Dor
(1985 [1998], 1997, 2001), Juan-David Nasio (1990 [1997]) and Philippe Van
Haute (2002), and introduced a more linguistically based Lacan to the USA.

In Britain, meanwhile, a debate between Kleinians and Lacanians, spon-
sored by THERIP,[7] took place in 1994–5, and resulted in *The Klein–Lacan
Dialogues* (Burgoyne and Sullivan (eds) 1997). On the whole, in Britain, the
Lacan of Nobus (1998, 2000), Nobus and Quinn (2005), Burgoyne (1997)
and Benvenuto and Kennedy (1986) is more recognizably Freudian. Some
South American versions pay more attention to Lacan's (1964a) revision of
drive theory (Harari 2004). All these at times bear little resemblance to the
French Lacan, who is of course the most sophisticated and complex
creature.

The impact of Lacanian theory is now global, although its clinical influence has yet to catch up with its widespread usage as an instrument of
cultural analysis, particularly in film studies. Lacanian concepts are widely
used as deconstructive tools to lever open the monolithic cultural constructs
of our age—gender and sexuality, or as the French say '*sexuation*', and
more recently, racialization in postcolonial theory (Lane (ed.) 1998;
Campbell 2000). Its clinical impact has been less universal, but is now
beginning to make inroads into Britain and the rest of Europe, the USA,
South America and Australia.[8]

My focus, as always, is on the clinical applications of Lacanian theory. It
is important to remember that Lacan was primarily a clinician. He began
his professional life as a psychiatrist working with the criminally insane at
Sainte-Anne Hospital in Paris, focusing particularly on the impact of
paranoia in some famous murder cases,[9] and until his death in 1981 was
still seeing large numbers of analysands, albeit by this time with controversially unpredictable session lengths.

I will now introduce some foundational Lacanian theory, and later in this
chapter, consider how it has been used by Julia Kristeva and Luce Irigaray.
In this chapter, I will primarily draw from pre-1964 Lacan, and in Chapter 9
I will explore some of the revolutionary developments in *Seminar XI*
(1964a) and after. Throughout the book, I refer to a spectrum of Lacanian
theorists including Joël Dor and Juan-David Nasio (France), Bruce
Fink (USA), Dany Nobus, Bice Benvenuto, Roger Kennedy and Bernard
Burgoyne (Britain), Paul Verhaeghe and Philippe Van Haute (Belgium) and
Roberto Harari (Argentina). I will not introduce these individual theorists
in this chapter as they are primarily concerned with the exposition of
Lacan's work, albeit from different angles and with differing emphases. It is

impossible not to present an over-simplification of Lacanian theory because of its complexity and also its ambiguities, double entendres and paradoxes. So I present, unavoidably, my own version of Lacan.

THE REAL, THE IMAGINARY AND THE SYMBOLIC

Despite his stated purpose of breaking open fixed systems of meaning, powerfully systematic elements can be found in Lacanian theory. These depend not only on an understanding of the role of language in the construction of psyche, but also on Lacan's distinction between the psychological realms of the 'real', the 'imaginary' and the 'symbolic', developed between 1955 and 1964. These three modes of psychic experience are irrevocably interlinked: each depends on the existence of the other, in the way Lacan later represented with his diagram of the 'Borromean knot' (Lacan 1972–3 [1998]: 124).

If one circle of the knot is broken, the others come undone too.[10] These three forms of experience not only depend on each other but generate each other's capacity to function. This will become clearer as I exposit each mode individually.

The real, which must never be confused with 'reality', constitutes that primary unmediated realm of experience which has not been subject to symbolization, or any form of organizing representation. Hence the real can never ultimately be known, and we can only apprehend its existence through symbolic functioning. The real took on different meanings as Lacan's work evolved and became a more central part of his metapsychology and model of psychoanalysis from the 1960s onwards.

In Lacan's early work, the real comprised that residue of experience which had resisted the 'cut', or formation, of symbolization (Lacan 1953–4). At this stage of Lacan's thinking, it was comparable to Bion's concept of *beta* elements, or raw experience which has not begun to be

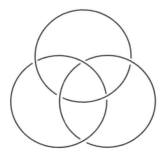

Figure 1 The 'Borromean knot'.

processed through *alpha* function (the initial stages of symbolization which are the prerequisite to verbal thought) (Bion 1962). The real was the arena in which trauma is set, and could be overcome in analysis through partial and progressive symbolization, unless the person had an underlying psychotic structure (Fink 1997).

An example comes from the therapy of a young woman I call 'Ruth'. At age sixteen Ruth had been in a rebelliously enmeshed relationship with her mother, when her mother was killed in a car accident. From being a spirited and troublesome adolescent, she became paralysed by fear and anxiety, and attacked and sabotaged any attempt to further her education. She began therapy at age eighteen. Her opening dream was of a frozen circle of rabbits surmounted by another ring of attacking wolves outside a circus.

This entrenched vicious circle barred her from the carnival of life. Over a very difficult year of intense resistance, we gradually became able to understand her unconscious fear that her aggression had killed her mother, and that in the way familiar from Freud's 'Mourning and melancholia' (1917), she had internalized her ambivalent relationship with her mother as a form of self-hatred and persecution. Only then was Ruth able to begin to mourn her mother's death. In Lacanian terms, only when the traumatic 'real' of this disaster could begin to be symbolized and metabolized, could Ruth begin to move on in her life.

After *Seminar XI*, the real took on a more dynamic role in Lacan's philosophy as the impossible (Lacan 1964a). Henceforth, the real was not just conceived as something which was left over from or resisted symbolic process, but as the potential to encounter something new. Lacan referred to Aristotle's concept of '*tuché*' (an encounter with the real) to denote the possibility of a critical aspect of experience which escapes the '*automaton*' of the signifying chain, although it is inherently elusive—like the unconscious (of which it may be a part), it can only be apprehended as being about to arrive or having just vanished (ibid.). In this theorization, the Lacanian real is much closer to Bion's concept of 'O' or ultimate reality: that stark inchoate area from which experience can be wrought or a fleeting contact with something beyond cognition which can only be reached towards at the highest levels of evolution of mind. For both Lacan and Bion, the real can be internal or external (and by its very nature challenges that distinction). In Lacan's terms, it is extimate: '. . . the intimate exteriority or "extimacy", that is the Thing' (Lacan 1959–60 [1992]: 139). In the 1970s, Lacan's concept of the real changed yet again, and became something which is generated by the signifier: 'The real can only be inscribed on the basis of an impasse of formalization' (Lacan 1972–3 [1998]: 93).

Lacan's concept of the 'imaginary' (image-inary) realm of human experience derived from his formulation of the 'mirror stage' between ages six and eighteen months in human development (Lacan 1949). The unco-ordinated infant, '. . . sunk in his motor incapacity and nursling depen-dence', misrecognizes himself 'in a flutter of jubilant activity' as his specular image and as whole and ideal (ibid. [2001]: 2). As Dor (1985) points out, the mirror stage has three phases, which all take place in the imaginary dimension: in the first, the self and Other are confused; in the second, the child can distinguish image from reality; and in the third, the dialectic between self and image constitutes a structuring factor of identity. The misrecognition (*méconnaissance*) constitutes an identification, the 'Ideal-I', which forms the basis of the ego, an imaginary illusory structure. The imaginary, like a fairground mirror, is always a distorted representation. This theorization underlay Lacan's antagonism to those who saw the strengthening of the ego as an objective of analysis.

The 'mirror stage', however, is a necessary aspect of development: it is a first step in internal psychic separation from the primal Other. However all Lacan's concepts should not be considered as developmental stages so much as structural moments constitutive of subjectivity in complex and mutually interdependent ways. The mirror stage is primordial, narcissistic and a distortion. The imaginary order it institutes is a continuing mode of generating experience throughout life. Its narcissistic basis leads to the erroneous assumption that others are similar to oneself and hence to 'aggressivity' and rivalry, since inequivalence is unbearable within this mode of being (Van Haute 2002).

'Aggressivity' was not necessarily a destructive phenomenon for Lacan. Like Winnicott, he saw it as part of the life force and, like Freud, as an aspect of ordinary ambivalence. Aggressivity '. . . underlies the activity of the philanthropist, the idealist, the pedagogue and even the reformer' (Lacan 1949 [2001]: 8), and aggression is a necessary aspect of the insistence of the drives (Lacan 1964a), only becoming destructive in response to frustration.

Just as, in post-Kleinian theory, the paranoid/schizoid and depressive positions are mutually interdependent, so in the very different paradigm of Lacanian theory the imaginary register constitutes a precondition for linguistic and symbolic functioning, but is also structured and created by the symbolic order. The child enters the symbolic realm, the law and language through the 'master signifier' or the 'paternal metaphor': '*Le Nom (Non)-du-Père*' (the Name (No) of the Father), the gateway to subjectivity (Lacan 1953). Only in the symbolic register is a true birth of the human subject possible.

Lacan took the term 'symbolic' from Claude Lévi-Strauss's 'symbolic function' (Lévi-Strauss 1949). Lévi-Strauss theorized social infrastructures as governed by the regulation of kinship and the exchange of gifts. Communication as exchange of words is an intrinsic and fundamental aspect of social structure and law: '. . . the law of man has been the law of language since the first words of recognition presided over the first gifts' (Lacan 1953 [2001]: 67). The concept of the symbolic evolved in a complex way throughout Lacan's work, and was always linked with his revision of Saussurean linguistics to replace any fixed correspondence between signifier and signified with the signifier's acquisition of meaning through its linguistic context in relation to other signifiers. In effect, as I have said, this means that language plays a part in structuring reality as we know it, and the only way to attempt to express the truth is in the symbolic register, but this truth can only ever be partial and limited.

The entry into language also creates the human subject: 'Man speaks, then, but it is because the symbol has made him man' (ibid.: 72). The concept of the subject evolved throughout Lacan's work. Prior to 1953, the subject connoted little other than a human being, but in 1953 Lacan established a distinction between the subject (symbolic) and the ego (imaginary). Lacanian psychoanalytic treatment addresses itself to the subject and not the ego, and the subject is unconscious and internally riven owing to that which becomes lost when the symbolic order is instituted. The act of saying 'I' involves the 'fading' of the subject, in that the signifier 'I' occludes the unconscious subject who can articulate it (Lacan 1960 [2001]: 347; 1964a). Lacan's vision of the structural formation of the human subject was revolutionary, and built on different foundations from Freudian theory (Gurewich 1999a). Becoming a subject involves a sequence of irreversible losses: the acceptance of lack, difference and separateness instated through the negotiation of the Oedipus Complex, which Lacan conceived of in three stages and which in Lacanian theory is co-terminous with entry into symbolic functioning (see later in this chapter). Lacan thought that one of the tasks of analysis was to shift the mode of relating from imaginary to symbolic.

NEED, DEMAND, DESIRE . . . AND *JOUISSANCE*

Lacan's distinctions between need, demand and desire were an aspect of his differentiation between the psychic realms of the real, imaginary and symbolic and a crucial part of the journey of subjectification. All three terms describe lacks in the subject (Rodriguez 2001), and all three are, of course, mediated through language and the symbolic order. 'Need' refers to something basic and physiological such as a young child's need for food or warmth. It can never be known in a pure form: it must be articulated as a demand (even in the form of a baby's cry) and becomes contaminated with experiences of pleasure and satisfaction.

'*Demande*' in French implies something less strong than the English 'demand': it is closer to 'request' (Fink 1997: 227), usually for something straightforward or concrete, and is linked to that which is impossible in satisfaction. In Lacanian theory, demand belongs to the imaginary register. A small child's demands are frequently repeated until she receives a straightforward 'no'. In analysis, demand might be formulated as a request for relief from certain symptoms or an objective goal such as a relationship.

> A client began his initial consultation with the litany: 'This is no good. What I need is a girlfriend. What I need is a girlfriend *now*. I can't sit here talking to you and then go home and be on my own again tonight. What I need is a girlfriend *now* . . .' etc. etc.

This example illustrates the implicit function of demand for unconditional love: '. . . demand annuls (*aufhebt*) the particularity of everything that can be granted by transmuting it into a proof of love' (Lacan 1958b [2001]: 317).

One of the central and early goals of analysis is to transform the space of demand (imaginary) into the space of desire (symbolic), a very complex Lacanian concept. 'Desire begins to take shape in the margin in which demand becomes separated from need' (Lacan 1960 [2001]: 344). Desire is always unconscious. It emerges from the subject's discovery of lack and separation from the Other, a process I am about to describe (Lacan 1960).

Desire is by its very nature unsatisfied. True ownership of one's desire, and separation from the desire of the Other within oneself, is indissoluble from the traversing of fantasy and the beginnings of subjectification: 'Desire merely subjects what analysis makes subjective' (Lacan 1958a [2001]: 287). When set free from neurotic fixation through 'dialectization' in analysis, desire can shift its objects, and is essentially, as Lacan continually re-emphasized, a question. Green put it thus: '. . . desire is the movement by which the subject is de-centred' (Green 1988 [2001]: xix). This will become clearer as I embark on an account of the Lacanian 'precipitation of subjectivity' (Lacan 1945).

Jouissance, on the other hand, refers to the child's original experience of the (m)Other as omnipotent. It is a legal term referring to the right to enjoy the use of something (Gurewich 2003). Desire is necessary to protect the child from maternal *jouissance*. This term came to acquire considerable further meanings as Lacan's work developed, including orgasm (Lacan 1958c). It is further discussed later in this chapter and in Chapter 9.

THE CREATIVE SPARK OF THE METAPHOR . . .
FLASHES BETWEEN TWO SIGNIFIERS

(Lacan 1957 [2001]: 173)

At the beginning of life, as I have said, a baby is psychologically born into the desire and language of an Other. This Other usually coincides with a (m)Other, whose unconscious desire for her child is determined by her own and her family history, but also by the social and historical sets of meanings she was born into. For example, religious and ideological systems are part of 'the discourse of the Other' ('*discours de l'Autre*'), as are the stories that parents and grandparents tell about generations of their family (Van Haute 2002). The discourse of the Other is therefore a complex fabric of contradictory stories, commands and prohibitions. We are dependent on this discourse as a system of signifiers, or what Lacan termed 'O . . . the locus of the signifier's treasure' (Lacan 1960 [2001]: 336), without which we cannot exist as subjects, but the subject never coincides with the Other except in psychosis (see Chapter 6). It should be remembered that although the Other may be co-terminous with a mother at the beginning of life, the meanings and implications of discovery of lack and separation from the Other are far broader than a quasi-naturalistic account of separation from the mother, as for example in object relations theory, and cannot be elucidated in those terms.

For the human subject to enter the symbolic order, she must be able to relate to the Other in a way that is different from the imaginary function of the ego. The gap between demand and need introduces a rupture into the relationship between a child and her mother, and this rupture opens the potential for desire to develop—in the following way. Lacan thought the traditional psychoanalytic ascription of the child's first experience of herself as omnipotent was an 'idiotic cliché' (ibid.: 344). Instead, the child experiences the Other as omnipotent in fantasy, and can begin to break from this through a transitional object, as an 'emblem', a 'representative of representation', whilst retaining her primary attachment (ibid.: 345).

This partial substitution of one object for another constitutes the beginning of 'metaphorization', or the institution of symbolic functioning. The lack disappears into the unconscious, where it continues to function as the little other or '*objet petit a*'.[11] *Objet a* constitutes the mainspring or cause of human desire as its fantasy object and also as its agent provocateur. The forms *objet a* can take offer compensatory mechanisms against the lack found in and of the Other. These fantasy structures form the epicentre of the unconscious. Therefore, the origin of desire remains hidden from sight and its dynamism lies at the heart of the transference in psychoanalysis. *Objet a* is further discussed a little later in this chapter.

THE NAME OF THE FATHER, *OBJET a* AND
THE TRAVERSING OF FANTASY

After 1960 Lacan, like Bion, turned increasingly to diagrammatic and mathematical formulations to represent the structural moments constitutive of subjectivity. In his 'graph of desire', Lacan (1960) put together the primary signifying structures and movements through which a person becomes able to separate from the desire of the Other and to begin to represent herself symbolically. As we have seen, the mirror stage (Lacan 1949) constitutes the structural preconditions for the development of verbal thought, supplemented by the transitional object as 'representative of representation' (Lacan 1960 [2001]: 345). The final primary structural moment is achieved through the paternal metaphor: '*Le Nom (Non)-du-Père*' (the Name (No) of the Father) (Lacan 1953–77), and its institution depends in turn on the negotiation of Lacan's version of the castration complex.

Lacan's use of the word 'phallus' always connotes a fantasy or a signifier as opposed to the anatomical penis. It is a complex concept and used in six different forms in Lacanian theory (Evans 1996). Here, I will focus on the imaginary and symbolic uses of the word 'phallus': it is important to remember that these constitute two entirely different entities. As early as the mirror stage, Lacan claimed the imaginary 'phallus' signified a crack in the illusion of wholeness in the specular or mirror image because it could 'be detached' in the double sense of the French '*se détacher*'—either 'to come off' or 'to stand out' (Lacan 1960; Van Haute 2002: 182). Lacan claimed the child tries to become the 'imaginary' phallus for the mother or the object of the mother's desire.[12] To seal the break between child and (m)Other in unconscious phantasy, the child must abandon this futile enterprise through the 'Name (No) of the Father' (Lacan 1960).

Because of the child's fantasy of the omnipotence of the Other, a law is needed to protect the child from being delivered over to the Other's *jouissance* (ibid.). This law, *Le Nom (Non)-du-Père* (the Name (No) of the Father) or paternal function, operates as the first signifier of 'thirdness'. The mother's absences indicate that her desire is not limited to her child. As an element in the mother's discourse, the 'paternal metaphor' signifies the mother's capacity to bear in mind some form of other (her husband, her partner, her work, her belief in what her developing child may need) which interrupts her total absorption in her child. This symbolic father is not necessarily incarnated in an actual father. For Lacan, fatherhood was quintessentially symbolic as it is culturally instituted through the father's conferring of his name.

Through the paternal metaphor the child gives up any belief that he can satisfy the mother's desire, and hence is freed to find his own desire. As the representative of the Law and symbolic discourse, the paternal metaphor forms the structural possibility for abandoning fulfilment. Symbolic (as opposed to imaginary) castration in Lacanian theory constitutes the process whereby the phallus is transformed into the signifier of lack and the impossibility of fulfilment of desire. In the symbolic realm, the phallus functions as pure signifier and relates to the anatomical penis only in so far as something can be missing. This acceptance of lack constitutes the truth of desire.

Objet a (which, as I have said, operates as the motivational epicentre of unconscious dynamism) is the term Lacan used to signify a fantasy which supplements the discovery of lack. *Objet a* underpins symbolization: it both functions as the fantasy object of and causes desire in neurotics (Lacan 1964a [2004]: ix). In the various forms of neurosis (hysteria, obsessionality and phobia), different subject positions are assumed in fantasy in relation to *objet a*. Hence, Lacan's dictum '*l'inconscient est le discours de l'Autre*' means 'the unconscious is a discourse *about* the Other' (Lacan 1960 [2001]: 345). (The ways in which a fantasied relationship to *objet a* are constituted in neurosis are discussed in Chapter 6.)

From 1960 to 1964, Lacan introduced a new dynamic notion '*la traverse du fantasme*' (the traversing of fantasy), meaning a shift in subject position in relation to '*objet a*' as a goal of analysis. (The implications of this in terms of the transference are explored in Chapter 7.) As an example, Lacan considered that the fundamental fantasy of the hysteric involves being the sole object of desire for the Other, a position she maintains through unconscious manoeuvring in relationships and in analysis.

My patient, Ruth, for example, would probably have been diagnosed as a hysteric in Lacanian terms. As soon as one problem was resolved, another appeared. She often tried to conduct her session in question and answer form, apparently assuming I was a fount of information about her! Both these unconscious strategies could be understood as attempts to keep herself as the object of my desire in the sense that she proffered me the opportunity to occupy a position of great knowledge and authority in relation to her. The far deeper issue, and the one temporarily obscured by her mother's death, was therefore this remaining subjection to the other. In Lacanian terms, she had not yet subjectified the cause of her desire.

In analysis, the Other's (usually the parents') desire which brought one into the world must be taken responsibility for, subjectified and made one's own. Analysis must involve '. . . this repositioning of the ego as subject in this *a* that I was for the desire of the Other, and no disentangling is possible of the enigma of my desire without this re-passing through the *a*-object'

(Lacan 1964–5 (23): 9). Thus, instead of 'It happened to me' or 'They did this to me', the subject is able to say 'I did this' or 'I chose to respond in this way' (Fink 1997). Meaning is only created after the event. All memory is retroactively constructed or reconstructed (*nachträglich*). The traversing of fantasy can also be thought of as increasing symbolization of the Other's desire, reducing alienation and beginning to take responsibility for oneself and one's own desire. As Stephen Mitchell said, the aim of Lacanian analysis is to make possible a fuller embracing of one's destiny as one's own (Black and Mitchell 1995).

In the traversing of fantasy, the subject takes the cause of their existence (the Other's desire: *objet a*) as their own and becomes open to their own desire, thereby embarking on a potentially endless subjective journey. The liberation of desire through its 'dialectization' means it is potentially continually in motion. Fink translates this as '"*Wanderlust*": lust that wanders, or the taking pleasure in wandering/wondering' (Fink 1997: 231). Desire does not seek satisfaction but rather its own continuance and furtherance.

For example my patient, 'Ruth', once she became more independent from the 'other' inside herself and from myself, decided that she wanted to discontinue her relationship with a kind, supportive man whom she loved but was not passionately in love with. She felt the relationship was too 'limited', a state of affairs she was happy to take responsibility for. She thought this was the only form of relationship she could have managed in her previous, rather debilitated state. She felt that eventually she would like a more complex and challenging relationship with a man, but for the time being she wanted to be by herself so that she could explore the new possibilities life seemed to be offering her.

FURTHER IMPLICATIONS FOR ANALYSIS

The Lacanian subject, then, being the subject of the unconscious and internally riven, is never the subject who speaks, except in the unconscious manifestations of dreams, slips of the tongue, jokes and symptoms. Psychoanalysis always addresses itself to the unconscious subject, and never to the ego or the speaking subject. The analyst must therefore hunt for the slips and gaps in the analysand's discourse.

In the 1960s, Lacan tried to pinpoint the evanescent beginnings of the subject's life in what is not said to the French use of '*ne*' in phrases like '*avant que je ne me réveille*' (before I do/do not wake up) (Lacan 1964a [2004]: 56) or '*avant qu'il ne soit avéré qu'ils n'y comprennent rien*' (before it becomes obvious that they have missed the point) (Lacan 1960 [2001]: 330). Here, uncertainty or ambiguity is introduced into discourse, and evidence of a conflict between an intended statement and unconscious feelings. A very rough equivalent in English might be something like: 'Not that I didn't admire her'. This internal contradiction, for Lacan, signified the first flickering appearance of the human subject, an extremely elusive being. He even claimed: '. . . take out that *ne* and my enunciation loses its attack. *Je* eliding me into the impersonal' (Lacan 1960 [2001]: 330).

This subject 'surges forth' like a spark between two signifiers in slips of the tongue, bungled actions, linguistic tropes and parapraxes. Lacan's metaphor suggests the firing of a synapse or other forms of energic ignition such as fire or passion. Therefore, although analysis still involves the progressive symbolization of areas of fixation or blockage in the familiar classical way, it is only through these '*kinks in the symbolic order*' that the beginnings of the subject of the unconscious can come to life (Fink 1995: 30, his emphases). This dual aspect of the subject (its internal split) resonates with the double meaning of Lacan's phrase 'the precipitation of subjectivity' (the same in French as English) (Lacan 1945 [1999]: 205). Here, precipitation refers both to a process of sedimentation as in the depositing of solids within fluid (the symbolizing aspect),[13] and to precipitation in the sense of haste or even falling headlong (where the subject 'surges forth' in the gap between two signifiers) (Fink 1995). This latter aspect of subjectification (precipitation as haste or a spark flashing) in the '*inter* (*intra*)-*dit*' (between what is said/what is forbidden) (Lacan 1960 [2001]: 331) constitutes a significant and radical opening of the subject:[14] '. . . the *one* that is introduced by the experience of the unconscious is the *one* of the split, of the stroke, of rupture . . . It is always a question of the subject *qua* indeterminate' (Lacan 1964a [2004]: 26, his emphases).

The 'surging forth' of the subject in the gap between two signifiers like metaphor's creative illumination brings about a new configuration of thoughts and a new signifying chain. Lacan thought that this is how people change. Therefore, Lacanian analysts never fill in the meaning for the analysand—their interventions are instead intended to confuse the ego to create more space for the unconscious to emerge. The implications of all this for psychoanalytic technique are explored in detail in Chapter 8.

In his later work Lacan often repeated such phrases as: 'I write that, but I don't write after it "the end", "amen" or "so be it"' (Lacan 1972–3 [1998]: 4). Something crucial becomes lost in symbolic representation. As from *Seminar XI* in 1964, Lacan shifted his emphasis from desirousness to the *jouissance* of the drive as the ultimate goal of analysis, thereby radicalizing his dethronement of the ego and his privileging of the deep unconscious as the route to aliveness and development still further. The 'dialectization of 'desire' was still necessary, but there was another route beyond even that. These later developments in Lacanian theory are explored in Chapter 9.

THE THREE STAGES OF THE OEDIPUS COMPLEX, AND *SEXUATION*

Lacan (1949) considered the beginning of the Oedipus Complex to be co-extensive with the mirror stage when, in however rudimentary and illusory a form, the small child begins to experience himself as somewhat separate, although in fantasy still the sole object of the mother's desire or the imaginary 'phallus'. Next, a third element is introduced, the symbolic father or paternal function, in the form of prohibition, frustration and privation and a representative of the Law (Dor 1985). At this second stage, the child recognizes his lack, and the way is henceforth open to the third stage: symbolization. Only through the primary metaphor, the 'Name (No) of the Father', 'the structural crossroads of subjectivity' (ibid. [1998]: 81), can the subject's journey begin.

Lacan (1972–3) suggests that, in analysis, separation and the traversing of fantasy can take one beyond Freud's 'rock of castration', signifying a more radical internal freedom. However, there are different paths for men and women. Lacanian constructions (and deconstructions) of gender are exceedingly complex. What follows is a great simplification and must be read as my own gloss on the subject.[15]

Lacan used the term *sexuation*—the same in English as in French—to imply the psychological constitution of gender through language via social and familial agency. The 'cut' of the signifier inscribes the body '. . . which has the effect of projecting in their entirety the ideal or typical manifestations of the behaviour of each sex, including the act of copulation itself, into the comedy' (Lacan 1958b [2001]: 321). He repeated gnomic utterances such as: 'Love is impotent . . . because it is not aware that it is but the desire to be One, which leads us to the impossibility of establishing the relationship between "them-two" (*la relation d'eux*). The relationship between them-two what?—them-too sexes' (Lacan 1972–3 [1998]: 6)[16], or '*La femme n'existe pas*' (The woman does not exist) (ibid.: 7). Nobus translates the first of these sorts of aphorisms as signifying the impossibility of a 'perfect match' (Nobus 2000: 139), whilst Rose (1986) stresses how our unconscious construction divides subjects both to and from each other. Nasio (1992) interprets the impossibility of sexual relationship in Lacanian terms as referring to the absence of any signifier to represent *jouissance*. It may also refer to Lacan's conception of the psychological construction of women as commonly hysterical and men obsessional (Lacan 1955–6, 1958–9, 1960) (Lacanian diagnostic categories are discussed in Chapters 6 and 7). As these two neurotic structures of subjectivity represent completely different psychological positions in relation to *objet a*, complementary emotional contact is impossible. They are unable to relate because the ways in which psychological 'men' and 'women' '*jouissent*' (or enjoy/experience *jouissance*) are incompatible. Phallic *jouissance* (which is associated with castration and lack) is available to both genders, whilst feminine *jouissance*, which has an ineffable, inarticulable element, is in the real and is mainly the preserve of women and mystics (Verhaeghe 2001).

The woman does not exist because 'man' (or '*l'homme*') is used as a generic term for human beings, and 'woman' (or '*la femme*' with the '*la*' barred) is excluded from this category. 'Woman' is produced by and through male discourse (and, by implication, men's projections) as a lack, an other. As the object onto which lack is projected and through which it is disavowed, woman is a 'symptom' for man. Woman also comes to stand in for what has been lost, or *jouissance* (Rose 1986). A number of feminist psychoanalytic writers in France, Britain and the USA have found versions of Lacanian theory to be powerful intellectual instruments in the questioning and reconceptualization of gendered identity. Indeed, by the time Lacan delivered *Seminar XX* (1972–3), he was respected by many feminists and considered to have made a very significant contribution to their work (Schneiderman 1983).

Freud's (1905) problematization of sexuality and gendered identity also produced a generation of feminist theoreticians and militants. Bertha Pappenheim (Anna O.), who translated Mary Wollstonecraft's *Vindication of the rights of women*, became the first president of the International Council of Women and investigated prostitution in Eastern Europe, Russia and the Middle East. Lacan (1964a) insisted on referring to Bertha Pappenheim by her real name and called her 'the Queen of social workers' (Lacan 1955–6 [1993]: 103). Some of the first feminist psychoanalysts included Joan Riviere who, in 'Womanliness as a Masquerade' (1929) argued that all 'feminine' women dissimulate in some degree in order to disguise aggression. Lacan thought all sexual identifications were a masquerade and referred to Riviere with approval as a groundbreaking theorist. Lou Andréas-Salomé advocated sexual emancipation for women. Hélène Deutsch, who had been a communist revolutionary, became a lucid psychoanalytic exponent of female masochism. Emma Goldman, the anarchist and advocate of 'free love', came from London to Vienna to attend Freud's lectures (Appignanesi and Forrester 1992).

Lacan broke with 'biology' or 'nature' in a more radical way than Freud. *Sexuation* is structured with the entry into language and the symbolic order: the body is overwritten with signifiers. Sexual identity becomes a fraud—an idea taken up in recent feminist theory in concepts such as 'performance' (Butler 1990) or even 'carnival' (Stallybrass and White 1986). In *Seminar XX*, Lacan attributed to 'woman' a particular 'more than *jouissance*' which transcends symbolization and patriarchal discourse, which is '*en plus*' and may be seen to have a mystical dimension (Lacan 1972–3 [1998]: 76–7). This 'en plus', along with Lacan's theorization of the birth of the human subject as breach in the real,[17] have been expanded in Kristeva's (1974) use of the 'semiotic' and by Irigaray's (1985) call for the creation of a female imaginary and in her lyrical renditions of female sexuality.

LACANIAN FEMINISM

Many feminist psychoanalysts and theoreticians today work with a version of a Lacanian paradigm, although they may have contributed their particular gloss or original concepts within it. They include Julia Kristeva, Luce Irigaray, Hélène Cixious, Toril Moi, Catherine Millot, Juliet Mitchell and Jacqueline Rose. Whilst the two most original, Kristeva and Irigaray, use Lacanian concepts in the service of very different metapsychologies, they are both preoccupied with questions of how subjectivity can be generated, and for Irigaray the potential of a multiplicity of feminine discourses, in preference to a static monolithic entity. In this way, they both contribute to Lacanian accounts of subjectification, and especially in Irigaray's case, subjectification within gendered identity. In the following brief account of some of Kristeva and Irigaray's work, I shall focus on the clinical applications of their theories. I shall not engage with the many feminist debates about their work: both have been criticized (for different reasons) for alleged 'essentialism', or the pre-symbolic situation of identity, and for an over-privileging of the realm of the maternal.[18]

Kristeva is a linguist, a novelist and a cultural theorist as well as a psychoanalyst. She is a clinical writer of great significance although her reputation as a cultural theorist sometimes eclipses this fact, and unlike Lacan and Irigaray, she sometimes illustrates her theses with clinical material. I will return to the subject of Kristeva as clinician in Chapters 6 and 9. She could almost be classified as a contemporary Independent in terms of the eclecticism of her theoretical bases and her model of containment and attention to affect—the latter derived from Green (1999c). However, since much of her thinking falls into a modified Lacanian paradigm, I include her here.

She focuses on the creative possibilities inherent in what remains of early maternal experience for both sexes in later life and those aspects of subjectivity only partially bound into the norms of psychic and social life. Her concept of the 'semiotic',[19] an area of pre-symbolic, pre-Oedipal experience, is comparable with Ogden's (1989a) 'autistic-contiguous position' but more drive-related, and can be seen as an amalgam of Lacan's registers of the imaginary and the real. The semiotic is a form of sensual bodily affect, experienced in body/mind integrity, non-verbal and composed of '. . . sound and melody, rhythm, colours, odours and so forth' (Kristeva

1993 [1995]: 104). The semiotic emanates from the pre-imaginary, undifferentiated space of the mother/baby dyad, which Kristeva names the '*chora*',
after Plato's mediating space of eternal form: '. . . the *chora* precedes and
underlies figuration and thus specularization, and is analogous only to
vocal or kinetic rhythm' (Kristeva 1974 in Moi (ed.) 1986: 94). The '*chora*'
as maternal space and source of creativity could supplement Winnicott and
Bollas' depiction of the maternal environment (see Chapter 2) and Bion's
concept of maternal 'reverie' (see Chapter 4).

The semiotic, like primary process, furnishes the necessary preconditions
to linguistic functioning and indeed impels it forward. The symbolic is
formed through the repression and sublimation of the semiotic but is
unable to exist, has no raw materials or energetic force without the semiotic. Kristeva uses this concept clinically to access areas of pre-symbolic
mind/body 'unity', like McDougall's (1989) theorization of the psychosomatic dimension in ordinary development discussed in Chapter 6.
Kristeva says:

> It could be hypothesized that this imaginary level of semiotic *meaning*
> (as opposed to linguistic *signification*) is closer to the drive represen-
> tatives particular to the lower layers of the brain. Thus, it can act as a
> relay between these layers and the cortex that controls linguistic
> production, thereby constituting supplementary brain circuits able to
> remedy any psychobiological deficiencies. Consequently, when we are
> faced with a child who fails to make active use of symbolic communi-
> cation, and who is unlikely to retain much of what he takes in from the
> outside world, the imaginary is a way of gaining access to more archaic
> affective representations, if not to linguistic signification itself. It can
> also be a way of accessing the drama that underlies these repre-
> sentations, a drama that never ceases to overwhelm, torment or amuse
> the child.
>
> (Kristeva 1993 [1995]: 104, her emphases)

Kristeva illustrates her theory of the semiotic in the grace, rhythms,
alliterations and poetry of her writing. It offers a way into the 'feminine' for
men since we have all partaken in this level of experience. She makes huge
claims for both the semiotic and psychoanalysis: the semiotic as an
instrument of cultural disruption and psychoanalysis as a remedy for late
capitalist alienation:

> [T]he current onslaught of psychological illness, which takes the form
> of 'soap operas' that inevitably cater to the other side of the society of
> performance and stress, seem to call out to psychoanalysis. 'Tell us the
> meaning of our inner turmoil, show us a way out of it.' . . . As a result,

psychoanalysis wagers to modify the prison of the soul that the West has made into a means of survival and protection, although this prison has recently been revealing our failings. This wager is therapeutic as well as ethical, and incidentally, political.

(Kristeva 1993 [1995]: 29)

Kristeva has been criticized by some feminists (e.g. Campbell 2000) for her concept of 'abjection' which describes how the pre-Oedipal mother becomes an object of horror, distaste and fear when children of both sexes separate from her (Kristeva 1980b). Never fully repressed, she remains '. . . a magnet of fascination and repulsion', '. . . a locus of horror and adoration' for both sexes (Kristeva 1993 [1995]: 118–9), as may be seen from the depiction of female monsters (Amazons, Sirens, the Medusa) and witches in the myths of many cultures. The recognition and symbolization of this powerful imaginary area of early experience is arguably less demeaning to women than its unwitting enactment. Kristeva specifies the social and historical context of signification and subjectivity, which Lacan implicitly universalizes.

Irigaray, who is a philosopher, a political activist and a linguist as well as a psychoanalyst, has written relatively little that is directly clinical in content, partly because of the different status of psychoanalysis in France as a public discourse in dialogue with many other intellectual disciplines. Nonetheless, the clinical significance of her work may be applied to men as well as women. She is concerned to develop accounts of female subjectivity in its own right as opposed to the representation of women as object or other, and derelict in their exclusion from masculine discourse and language (Irigaray 1974). Lacan himself pointed out that *la femme n'existe pas*' (the woman does not exist) (Lacan 1972–3 [1998]: 7), but Irigaray was the first psychoanalytic theorist of any persuasion to take up this challenge, followed later in a different paradigm by Benjamin (see Chapter 2).

Irigaray's primary preoccupation lies in how women can represent their own experience. In her critique of psychoanalytic theory, she refers to the impossibility of speaking from an ungendered position (Irigaray 1985). She claims that Lacan's symbolic subjectivity is founded in a male imaginary in which the phallus is defensively overvalued (Irigaray 1974). In consequence, woman is construed as a 'commodity', an object of exchange. Irigaray, like Blake (1790–3), Bachelard (1958, 1971) and Castoriadis (1997), construes the imagination as a site of radical activity. For her, a female imaginary would not be based in the binary oppositions and definitive categories of masculine discourse, but would instead incorporate apparent paradoxes and multivalences (Irigaray 1985). A female imaginary would be mobile and fluid, and '. . . a *disruptive excess* is possible on the feminine side' (Irigaray 1977 [1985]: 78, her emphases). As Whitford (1991b) points out, Irigaray posits that what has been excluded from masculine symbolic discourse as its residue or waste, 'woman', might in fact be symbolized differently, but this would inevitably involve a different means of apprehending experience.

Whilst Irigaray's relationship to the writings of both Freud and Lacan is respectful[20]—she describes Freud as an 'honest scientist' for example, and cites Lacan frequently—she is scathing about the heuristic status of psychoanalytic discourse. This, she claims, is a prime example of a claim to be universal, whilst all the time writing from the perspective of men and considering women only as either lacking or subjectivityless: as mothers, as objects. Hence, frigidity and masochism are construed as women's problems, whilst, she argues, they are caused by a discourse which excludes and objectifies them (Irigaray 1977) and, at least implicitly, sanctions male aggression. She reconstructs hysteria as a culturally induced symptom with revolutionary potential (Irigaray 1974) (see Chapter 6).

Irigaray argues that sexual *difference* should be acknowledged. Female subjective discourses, in her view, would open the way to a creative and fertile dialogue with men: '. . . the production of a new age of thought, art, poetry, and language: the creation of a new poetics . . .' (Irigaray 1984, in Whitford (ed.) 1991a: 10). This 'amorous exchange' she deems to be '. . . the symbolic representation of fertile creative intercourse between men and women both recognizing each other as the other of the other' (Minsky 1996: 198). Irigaray thinks this would go some way to counter the deadening and destructive impact of a monosexual culture.

Whilst Irigaray's project has been described as utopian in its generalization and is sometimes erroneously simplified as the creation of a female language, she is merely concerned that women may become able to speak from their own subjectivity, whatever forms that may take. In this way, she augments our understanding of the construction of the analytic relationship. She argues that transference operates on both sides of the analytic relationship (Irigaray 1985). The analyst's transference to the patient—and this includes the sexuate dimension, constructed in language and culture—is as or more important than the patient's transference to the analyst because the analyst's preconceptions and attitude determine the containment and facilitation of open speech for the patient and whether the patient can be heard:

> Within sexual difference, this peace and this harmony would signify acceptance and accomplishment of one's own sex, without will to outdo the strange or the stranger who insists in the other. This dimension of sexual difference constitutes a horizon for the potential deployment of analysis as opening or enigma, rather than as peremptory imposition of the authority of a word, a language, or a text . . . For this to be a possible alternative, the analyst must always keep in mind the dimension of his or her own transference, must always remain close to and

yet distant from the one to whom he or she listens, in a transferential relationship, reversible and open, linking up all possible positions in space and time.

(ibid. [2002]: 245–6)

Irigaray's work is important because she opens the possibility of a new dimension in psychoanalysis: consideration of the impact of alienation, marginalization and exclusion from language on female patients. Through becoming aware of our own projections onto this 'other', we may become more able to facilitate her construction of her own subjectivity through speech.

There is a visionary dimension to Irigaray's work: she is, after all, concerned to change society, and has remained a political activist. She argues passionately that a female imaginary (yet to be created) could serve as the basis for a multisexual expansion of language which opens out the logical and binary confines of masculine discourse. This dimension of her work bears comparison with Kristeva's 'semiotic' but it is more radical in that she appeals to something which does not as yet exist. For Irigaray, the imagination is the site of possible futures and possible new forms of relationship, individual, social and analytic.

Kristeva and Irigaray use Lacanian theory to step beyond its confines. Lacan's expositors would not necessarily agree with their views. Nonetheless, in keeping with my contention that the ability to generate difference is a sign of the vigour of a psychoanalytic paradigm, these two theorists must stand amongst the most original of a Lacanian persuasion today.[21]

NOTES

1. For more detail on Lacan's reconstruction of Saussurean linguistics, see Nobus (2003).
2. Writers in Lacan's cultural milieu included Georges Bataille, Raymond Queneau, Jean-Paul Sartre, Simone de Beauvoir, André Malraux and André Breton; artists included Pablo Picasso, Salvador Dali and Alberto Giacometti; philosophers included Alexandre Kojève (expositor of Hegel), Maurice Merleau-Ponty, Roman Jakobson and Martin Heidegger; the anthropologist Claude Lévi-Strauss was also an influence (Schneiderman 1983; Roudinesco 1993; Nobus 2000).
3. In Lacanian theory, *jouissance* has multiple meanings and connotations—Dylan Evans (1996) lists seven—but always implies some form of satisfaction and excess, either of pain or pleasure, and marks the limits of the pleasure principle. *Jouissance* is further discussed later in this chapter and in Chapter 9.
4. Bion's (1962) term 'unsaturated' refers to a mental capacity, a 'pre-conception', which is open to acquiring further meaning (see Chapter 4).
5. *Que sais-je?* was the name given to a popular series of cheap introductory books published in France.
6. Cormac Gallagher has translated most of Lacan's seminars into English in a private publication unavailable for resale.

7. THERIP: The Higher Education Network for Research and Information in Psychoanalysis.
8. Accounts of the spread of Lacanian clinical psychoanalysis vary. Some claim there are now greater numbers of Lacanian than IPA analysts, and that the majority of South American analysts are Lacanian (Vivien Burgoyne: personal communication).
9. Lacan worked with Marguerite Pantaine ('Aimée'), who tried but failed to stab the actress Huguette Duflos. He also wrote about, but did not work with, the Papin sisters—two servants who viciously murdered their female employer and her daughter, gouging their eyes out and hacking their bodies to pieces (Lacan 1932; Roudinesco 1993). The Papin sisters provided the inspiration for Jean Genet's (1962) *The Maids*. For Lacan's theory of paranoia, see Chapter 6.
10. This version of the knot is not tied in psychosis (see Chapter 6).
11. Lacan insisted that *objet a* should not be translated into English in order to emphasize its status as an algebraic sign (Sheridan 1977 [2001]: xiv). I retain the French here in order to avoid confusion with the object relational or Kleinian use of the word 'object'. *Objet petit a* connotes a lack rather than an introjection.
12. This idea underlies Lacanian theorizations of perversion (see Chapter 6).
13. This aspect of the precipitation of subjectivity can be compared to Bion's theorization of the transformation of raw experience through *alpha* function (see Chapter 4).
14. The other aspect of the precipitation of subjectivity could be compared with Gaston Bachelard's (1958) idea of poetry's creation of the new.
15. For fuller accounts of Lacanian constructions of gender, see Mitchell and Rose (1982), Rose (1986), Grosz (1990) and Shepherdson (2000).
16. '*La relation d'eux*' means both the relationship of two people (*deux*) and the relationship of or between them (*d'eux*) (Fink 1998: 6).
17. 'The real, I will say, is the mystery of the speaking body, the mystery of the unconscious' (Lacan 1972–3 [1998]: 131).
18. For an excellent account of these debates, see Rose (1986).
19. Kristeva's work belongs in the semiotic tradition begun by Roland Barthes (1955), in which analysis of language developed into a critique of the stabilizing illusion of the sign.
20. Amazingly respectful considering Lacan excluded Irigaray from teaching when he took over the psychoanalysis department at the University of Vincennes in 1974 (Schneiderman 1983: 42–3).
21. Within cultural theory, the work of Slavoj Žižek develops Lacanian theory into new arenas.

Chapter 4

Post-Kleinians

The Kleinian group in London evolved a cohesive identity after the tripartite division of the British Psychoanalytic Society in 1944.[1] These 'contemporary Kleinians of London' (Schafer 1997b) focused historically on the understanding and treatment of severe disturbance, chiefly borderline and psychotic states, and more recently on analyses with people who are difficult to reach or psychologically stuck as a result of complex defensive psychic organizations. The Kleinian group in London are relatively inward-looking, and their analytic, supervisory, tutorial and personal interrelationships sometimes result in shared authorship of innovative concepts.

The depth of their studies of the psychoses and severe forms of narcissistic disturbance has resulted in widespread percolation of their ideas. Contemporary Jungians (Fordham 1995) and Independents, in particular, borrow heavily and occasionally steal from the Kleinian group. Despite their influence, post-Kleinian clinical technique remains idiosyncratic and restricted to the Kleinian group. Its hallmarks are greater emphasis than any other contemporary school on the transference interpretation as the principal mutative instrument, and more systematic application of their theory than contemporary Independents in the understanding of clinical phenomena. Even so, their work has revolutionized the treatment of the severely disturbed in many parts of the world—in South America, particularly Argentina (Racker 1968; Langer 1989, 2000) and Chile (Grinberg 1990), and also in Europe, especially in Britain, Scandinavia and Italy.[2]

Melanie Klein's radical and challenging theoretical innovations have been well documented and discussed (Klein (1921–45) 1975a, (1946–63) 1975b; H. Segal 1973, 1979, 1981; Meltzer 1978; J. Segal 1985; Spillius (ed.) 1988a, 1988b; Hinshelwood 1989, 1994; Schafer 1997b; Sayers 2000). Most contemporary Kleinians still adhere to the theoretical building blocks she inaugurated: the paranoid/schizoid and depressive positions, internal objects and part-objects, constitutionally high levels of destructive aggression and envy, infantile sadism, and intrusive projective identification (Klein 1975a, 1975b). In Kleinian theory, the term 'object' is used to describe people in internal and external reality, and 'part-object' to denote a more primitive state of affairs in which one aspect of a person only is experienced, for example breast or penis. Several eminent contemporary Kleinians have made substantial theoretical extensions and refinements within this fundamental paradigm. Betty Joseph, for instance, amplifies the clinical usage of the transference by extending it to include the 'total situation' of unconscious intrapsychic constellations of internal objects and part-objects, phantasies, impulses and defenses, living and changing from moment to moment in the consulting room and through 'parallel process' in supervision (Joseph 1985). Hanna Segal elaborates and expands a range of Kleinian concepts, notably in symbol formation where she adds the dimension of 'symbolic equation' in the psychotic, using an example of a young man who cannot play his violin in public because he equates it, literally, with masturbation (Segal 1957). Both Segal and David Bell have made groundbreaking use of Kleinian theory in social and political arenas: Segal about the nuclear arms race and its attendant psychotic anxieties and Bell with the underlying mindset of the Thatcherite 'reforms' in the National Health Service in Britain (Segal 1987; Bell 1997).

Here, I will not focus on the many developments of the original Kleinian theoretical building blocks, which provide fertile ground for clinical discovery and social and organizational application, but instead prioritize those post-Kleinians who made paradigmatic shifts in theory. Perhaps the most radical of these, Wilfred Bion, moved the Kleinian frame of reference into another register and constructed an entirely new theory of mind, which has had extensive impact on contemporary psychoanalytic theory. Donald Meltzer expounded and, in some instances, made fresh use of Bion's theory, as well as furnishing his own original and noteworthy contributions: in particular the concepts of the 'claustrum', 'aesthetic reciprocity' and 'aesthetic conflict' (Meltzer 1992, 1988) (see later in this chapter and Chapters 6 and 9).

Herbert Rosenfeld remained within a Freudian and Kleinian metapsychological framework but with his formulation of a 'gang' or 'mafia' organization of destructive impulses in severe disturbance made a conceptual leap of such virtuosity as to transform the psychoanalytic treatment of borderline, narcissistic and psychotic patients. J. Henri Rey (1979) fleshed out a theoretical area adumbrated by Klein (1955) and Riviere (1952), and thereby added a new dimension, that of the temporal/spatial, to Kleinian theory. Lastly, John Steiner and Ron Britton, two recent innovators, refine some key areas of theory and open new dimensions for exploration. Steiner's (1993) *Psychic Retreats*, or forms of gridlock 'pathological organization', expands Klein's theorization of narcissism as an internal refuge within an idealized internal object and Rosenfeld and Meltzer's work on destructive narcissistic organizations (Rosenfeld 1971; Meltzer 1973) (see later in this chapter and Chapter 5). Britton's (1989) groundbreaking re-conceptualization of the internal unconscious phantasy of the primal scene as the psychological template of how mental links may be forged or evaded is an extension and application of the work of both Klein and Bion (Klein 1945; Bion 1970), and is explored at the end of this chapter.

W. R. BION

W. R. Bion (1897–1979) was one of the most profoundly radical psycho-analytic thinkers. As Ogden (2004) points out, his analytic work comprised two periods with markedly different conceptions of psychoanalysis. I focus on Bion's earlier work in this chapter, and explore his later work in Chapter 9.

Groups

Bion (1961) transformed the practice of group psychotherapy in his work with traumatized soldiers at Northfield Hospital after the Second World War. He conceived of three powerful unconscious sets in group mentality, which he called 'basic assumptions', as evasions of the pains of uncertainty and lack that Bion deemed necessary to thought.

For example, a group might idealize a person in or outside itself, or a belief, and behave as if this imagined entity held magical solutions: this Bion dubbed the dependent group or 'BaD'. If a group, or a large part of it, became paranoid about phantasied enemies in or outside itself and prone to thoughtless action, Bion deemed this a fight/flight or 'BaF' mentality. If a group became enthralled by an internal or external couple and phantasized their offspring, either literal or symbolic, as the holders of omnipotent powers, this was termed a pairing or 'BaP' mindset. Bion thought these unconscious constellations were operative in society: the church held BaD, the army BaF and the aristocracy BaP. He contrasted these unconscious evasions of uncertainty or the unknown with what he called 'the work group', whose members are capable of thought and contact with external reality. These ideas paved the way for a galaxy of group relations and organizational consultants, who added further possible 'basic assumptions' (for example, Pierre Turquet's basic assumption 'oneness' (BaO)) and applied Bion's insights in industrial, commercial and public service settings (Turquet 1974; Bain 1982; Miller 1993; Obholzer and Roberts 1994).

Bion's theory of thinking

After his pioneering work on groups, Bion (1962) addressed himself to the study of thought, and disorders of thought, and to what he termed the 'evolution' of mind. His theory of thinking (1962a, 1962b) introduced a process-based concept of self. There remained little trace of a structural model of mind in his work. For Bion, the mind is either in continuous evolution through the workings of 'truth' (the authentic rendition of emotional experience) or thought, or deteriorating through the operation of what Bion termed 'lies'—the evasion of frustration and reality through psychologically omnipotent or omniscient mechanisms. Klein (1928) posited the desire to learn (epistemophilic instinct) as a central drive in development. For Bion, this became the primary motivational force. Emotional growth became a more powerful energizing principle than sexual libido (Symington and Symington 1996).

To briefly compare Bion and Freud's ideas, for Freud (1900) a dream was a hidden desire presented in disguised form; for Bion a dream was the first stage in the synthesis and representation of unorganized aspects of experience. For Freud (1911a) the function of thought was to decrease tension; for Bion its purpose was the management of tension—bearing pain and frustration were necessary prerequisites to developing a capacity for thought. Bion reformed Freud's conceptualizations of primary and secondary processes and replaced them with his theory of thinking: the processing of '*beta* elements' through '*alpha* function', the 'contact barrier' and the increasingly abstract stages of thought represented in his diagrammatic Grid (Bion 1962a [1984]: 22, 54).

Bion drew widely from other intellectual disciplines: from mathematics (the 'selected fact' comes from Poincaré (ibid.: 72)); from philosophy (especially Plato, Kant and Wittgenstein); and from divinity (the Gnostics, Julian of Norwich and St. Augustine). His theory of thinking can ultimately stand on its own as an epistemological system. Bion's work contradicted much of the spirit of Kleinian theory. He emphasized the importance of personal meaning as a goal. Thought involves emotion at its core. Like the eighteenth-century philosopher, Giambattista Vico, Bion thought: 'Men at first feel without perceiving, then they perceive with a troubled and agitated spirit, finally they reflect with a clear mind' (Vico 1744 [1984]: 218). He retained, assimilated and made fresh use of many core Kleinian concepts, but, as the Symingtons point out, he used them in the service of 'a new metapsychology' (Symington and Symington 1996: 11).

Beta elements and alpha function

Bion's theory of thinking rests on the distinction between what he termed '*beta* elements' and '*alpha* function' (Bion 1962a). *Beta* elements represent particles of raw experience which must be evacuated from the mind if they cannot be processed into thought. The evacuation proceeds through projective identification, hallucination, somatization, mindless activity or 'acting out', acting on impulse, chatter or group or herd behaviour (Meltzer 1986). All of these Bion deemed to be psychotic or 'soma-psychotic' phenomena, and therefore anti-thought and damaging to the mind. *Alpha*

	Definitory Hypo-theses	ψ	Notation	Attention	Inquiry	Action	
	1	**2**	**3**	**4**	**5**	**6**	**. . . n.**
A β-elements	A1	A2				A6	
B α-elements	B1	B2	B3	B4	B5	B6	. . . Bn
C Dream Thoughts Dreams, Myths	C1	C2	C3	C4	C5	C6	. . . Cn
D Pre-conception	D1	D2	D3	D4	D5	D6	. . . Dn
E Conception	E1	E2	E3	E4	E5	E6	. . . En
F Concept	F1	F2	F3	F4	F5	F6	. . . Fn
G Scientific Deductive System		G2					
H Algebraic Calculus							

Figure 2 The Grid.

function represents the process by which these elementary particles of experience may be transformed into thought. This takes place first through forming a visual, auditory or other form of sensual image which can be dreamt and then processed into more sophisticated forms of thought. He represented this in the left-hand column of the Grid (see Figure 2), which is a very condensed form of Bion's theory of thinking.

The Grid

Each of the two axes of the Grid provides a perspective on the development of thought. The vertical axis, from top to bottom, represents degrees of evolution and abstraction of thoughts. The horizontal, from left to right, demonstrates the application or uses of the different distinctions or levels of thought, as represented in the vertical axis. The points of intersection between the axes enable the drawing of very fine distinctions between types of thoughts, both inside and outside the psychoanalytic consulting room (Bion 1963, 1977; Grinberg *et al.* 1993). Bion intended the Grid to be used after sessions, not in them, as a means of discerning how the analytic couple are interacting in level and gradation of stages of thought.

All the rows of the vertical axis, except beta elements, represent stages of thought which are unsaturated and open to acquiring further meaning, although rows G and H do not have a psychoanalytic application. Category one of the horizontal axis denotes the necessary tolerance of frustration required of the analyst if she is not to misuse her knowledge of theory and jump to premature conclusions or let her intuition be occluded by preconceptions (represented by the Greek *Pi* in the second category). An example might be a patient who feels her analyst misunderstands her. Her analyst might jump to the conclusion that her patient is being paranoid, or she might wait for images, dreams and thoughts to emerge before realizing something different from her original formulation is taking place. Then she will be in a better position to attend to what she has noticed and think about it.

The contact barrier, the selected fact, Ps↔D, container/contained (♀♂), multiple vertices

I will now briefly explore some other core concepts in Bion's theory of mind: the 'contact barrier', the 'selected fact', Ps↔D, 'container/contained (♀♂)' and 'multiple vertices' (Bion 1962a, 1970). The streams of thought proceeding from the continuous exercise of *alpha* function create the contact barrier. Like a stained glass window or a piece of gauze, the contact barrier performs a protective and divisive function but can sometimes be seen through. It separates conscious from unconscious mind, and safeguards relations with external reality. It also renders the mind less permeable to the influx of projective identifications from psychotic processes in others, for example in a highly charged group situation or with a disturbed patient determined to locate hatred and hostility in their therapist. Bion thought that, due to the operation of *alpha* function, the contact barrier and all the different stages of thought outlined in the Grid, the evolution of mind is potentially infinite, a revolutionary concept at the time and now. As long as one is capable of thought and truth, or the honest, authentic and faithful processing of one's experience, the mind can continue to evolve far beyond the givens of early environmental influence.

In Bion's thinking, the 'selected fact' and 'Ps↔D' were closely interconnected (Bion 1962a). Bion posited a continual—almost moment-by-moment—fluctuation between the paranoid schizoid and the depressive positions. This movement is necessary because it is only through a temporary and partial regression to the relative chaos and fragmentation of paranoid/schizoid processes that the emergence of a new idea is possible.

This fleeting regressive moment does not necessarily involve a great sense of persecution (ibid.: 92), although a sense of pressure might be felt. It might feel, for example, as if the mind is darting about in a chaotic fashion, or intolerably blank and empty and unable to think. There may be a sensation of something pushing from behind, before the relief of a new thought springs out of this inchoate state.

This new idea, or 'selected fact', as Bion termed it, represents an emotion or notion which gives coherence to what is dispersed and introduces order into disorder. It could be described as an intuition or divination—an 'oh' which makes the beginning of a thought possible, and simultaneously incites a movement into the depressive position. In Bion's use of the term, the depressive position therefore loses much of the moral loading it acquired from Klein, and the paranoid/schizoid position loses its unhelpful reputation. In health, Bion suggests, *both* are necessary to the emergence and development of new ideas and thought and, without free movement between the two, change and development are impossible.

The concept 'container/contained' (ibid.) represents an internal relationship—mother/infant, analyst/analysand, coital couple, or, I have argued, teacher/student (White 2002)—which makes thought possible. At the beginning of life, Bion thought, a receptive mother through her 'reverie' contains her baby's projection of intolerable feelings (hunger, discomfort, pain and anxiety) until the baby has internalized a capacity to bear feelings himself (Bion 1962a, 1962b, 1967). Later in life this internal capacity can become a growing, strengthening and increasingly flexible and serviceable 'container/contained', developed through the evolution of thought and mind and by contact and interaction with other thoughtful minds. It can provide the basis for continual learning from experience (Bion 1962a).

The term 'vertex' implies a perspective or point of view. In health and thought (interchangeable in Bion's earlier work), he postulated the possibility of 'binocular vision' or 'multiple vertices': the capacity to hold in mind differing perspectives on the same issue or possibility. This is a powerful method of reality testing (Bion 1965). When multiple vertices from different people converge to reveal a consensus, then a picture or paradigm of external reality emerges, which Bion dubs 'common sense' (Bion 1962a). This underlines his idea that thought proceeds from both internal and external relationships.

At this stage in Bion's thinking, the letter 'K' represented the all-important attitude. K means 'getting to know' rather than holding or having a piece of knowledge (Bion 1962a [1984]: 47). It describes a journey of emotional and intellectual discovery. Later, Bion came to think of K as less important than what he describes as F or faith and 'O' or ultimate reality, either primary and unmediated or that which may be reached towards at the highest levels of evolution of mind (Bion 1965, 1970). These last concepts of Bion's are explored in detail in Chapter 9.

Bion's views on psychopathology

Bion's ideas on psychological disturbance are, put simply, his concepts of psychological growth and the evolution of mind in reverse. As we have seen, Bion thought that in health we have the capacity to tolerate frustration and bear feelings for long enough to allow an experience to be transformed by *alpha* function into a sensual image which can be dreamt, then processed into thought. In illness, the experience, feeling or sensation cannot be borne and has to be expelled through evacuation of *beta* elements. The expulsion of raw undigested experience takes place through projective identification in numerous forms, including acting out and physical illness, but here I will focus on the extreme and hostile projective identification of aspects of a disturbed person's feelings and, ultimately, Bion thought, of parts of the mind (Bion 1967).

Excessive projective identification, with its inevitable concomitant splitting, results in paranoia, as hostility is experienced as external. It both proceeds from and eventuates in very high anxiety: because splitting and fragmentation are so great, catastrophic anxiety about disintegration ensues. This results, Bion and other Kleinians thought, in greater disturbance and possibly psychosis (ibid.).

At the beginning of life, Bion thought, maternal 'reverie' contains a baby's sense of persecution caused by feelings he cannot yet bear. If maternal processing of infantile anxiety does not take place because the mother cannot bear the feelings herself—if she is depressed, disturbed, too anxious or unreceptive for some other reason—or, Bion and other Kleinians thought, if the baby's constitutional levels of intolerance to frustration, hatred, hostility and envy are too high, then projective identification becomes more extreme and destructive. In this latter case, the person relies increasingly on paranoid/schizoid processes instead of moving freely between de-integrated and depressive states. The degree of splitting becomes more severe and a vicious spiral is set up in which a person becomes increasingly persecuted by hostile and angry feelings they have projected out. In this paranoid state, there is no place of calm or safety and hostility is projected with increasing force, a process which can eventually result in a complete loss of contact with external reality (ibid.).

Bion (1957) introduced the, then revolutionary, ideas that, first, we all have psychotic aspects to our personality, and second, even the most disturbed schizophrenic person has a sane part which can be reached by a skilled therapist. One can infer from this that the question of healing then becomes a matter of shifting the balance of the split, gradually and over time—an extremely serviceable clinical insight. Increasing quantities of a disturbed person's experience can be borne by a therapist until they are available to be transformed into thought by both parties.

Bion thought that the ultimate result of extreme levels of splitting and projective identification is the expulsion of fragments of the personality which enter into and are engulfed by their objects, transforming them into 'bizarre objects', or 'dream furniture' (Bion 1967: 39–40). As a result, the psychotic person lives in a waking nightmare and is unable to dream. This explains severely disturbed phenomena such as thinking the television is talking about one or the sensation of being completely surrounded by hostile and persecutory forces.

Bion (1957, 1959) demonstrated how psychotic aspects of the personality are not merely intolerant of frustration, but sadistically attack attempts to bring things together in the mind. These ideas were based on Klein's description of an infant's phantasied sadistic and envious attacks on the breast and the parental couple in the early stages of the Oedipus Complex, and were further developed by Britton (see later in this chapter). Attacking the links that make thought possible results in undermining contact with external reality and ultimately also the capacity for verbal thought. 'L', 'H' and 'K' (love and hate, or ordinary ambivalence, and getting to know), which Bion deemed the motive forces of emotional links and psychological development, become '- L', '- H' and '- K': envious and spoiling destructive attacks on meaning, feeling and vitality. As there is no possibility of containing feelings, 'nameless dread' or unbearable disintegrative anxiety predominates (Bion 1962a, 1963, 1965). *Alpha* function and the stages of thought outlined in the Grid are replaced by the expulsion of *beta* elements through projective identification, resulting in extreme splitting and paranoia, and potentially in bizarre objects, dream furniture and hallucination. Container/contained in both its maternal and Oedipal versions then becomes a destructive attack on linking in any form, including those links which are necessary to the basis of thought. As there is no possibility of the development of a contact barrier to protect the distinction between internal and external reality, they become confused.

Omnipotent and omniscient mechanisms replace any capacity to bear uncertainty and frustration. For Bion, therefore, like Lacan (1955–6), one hallmark of the psychotic personality becomes certainty, which Bion linked with intrusive curiosity, arrogance and stupidity (Bion 1967). A capacity to hold in mind different perspectives on the same experience or situation, or multiple vertices, which Bion deemed the most powerful method for reality testing, becomes instead being stuck in one perspective only and an incapacity to see another point of view.

Some of Bion's views on psychological disturbance were exemplified in the therapy of a young man I call 'Patrice', whom I saw for eleven years, first in an NHS setting and later privately (see also Chapter 2). When he first presented,

Patrice was in a state of near-breakdown with considerable delusional ideation. He believed that an enemy alien planet had shot a black egg into his insides, from which emanated all his troubles. In the transference, at times I was an intergalactic enemy from outer space, who had to be managed with military tactics of interrogation and disorientation (culled, he later told me, from a German war manual) and various threats against my person.

In this way, he gave me an experience of how unpredictable and attacking his entire environment felt, like Bion's (1967) 'bizarre objects'. The extremity of the splitting (outer space), the level of destructive hostility and paranoia and the near-complete confusion between internal and external reality were very apparent. For about two years I merely bore him, a far more difficult enterprise than it sounds, and tried to make some sense in myself of what was going on—Bion's (1962a, 1967) 'maternal reverie'. There was no point in trying to interpret anything to him at this point, because he could only have experienced interpretation as destructive assault or malignant misunderstanding (Britton 1998) (see later in this chapter and Chapter 6). Instead, I tried to remain empathically in tune with his experience.

Patrice was terrified of losing touch with reality completely, and he felt himself to be several different people and to have no control over his transitions between one and another (the level of psychic fragmentation caused by extreme splitting and projective identification). When he first came to see me he wore a white 'disguise'. He thought that I dyed my hair between sessions so that it was sometimes black, sometimes brown and sometimes blonde (I am blonde—Patrice's bizarre perceptions show the extent to which his objects have been fragmented as well as his mind).

Alongside this intensely negative transference, there was also a fierce attachment. Patrice would send me love messages on bits of paper. One day, he brought with him his teddy bear, who was called George, he said, and who was the only other person who really listened to him. 'Would I have listened to him if I had met him on a bus?' Intense love and murderous hate could only be experienced separately, on different days.

After about two years, there began to be evidence of a greater level of integration in his personality. From being an intergalactic enemy from outer space, I became merely a Conservative government agent sent to spy on him, a projection that at one level was almost equally delusional, but was actually closer to home and in the reality we both shared. His rage and murderous hostility could finally be contained in safety and he proceeded through many interesting twists and turns of the transference to become more integrated. As he became able to think about what had happened to him, we both became aware of how his experiences of racism on a daily basis had fed and reinforced the hostility that we finally came to understand he was carrying for his entire family.

My work with this patient shows how, through my bearing and containing experiences which were literally unthinkable, the psychotic part of his personality was very slowly and gradually brought into a mind that could think about and articulate his experiences (Bion 1957).

I have focused on Bion's theoretical innovations in some detail as they form the basis of many subsequent clinical developments.

DONALD MELTZER

Bion's work generated much learned exposition (Grinberg *et al.* 1993; Bléandonu 1994; Lopez-Corvo 2003; Symington and Symington 1996). Meltzer was one of his most erudite apologists and also a major post-Kleinian theorist in his own right. Throughout a long series of books (Meltzer 1967, 1973, 1978, 1984, 1986, 1988, 1992, 1994), he expounded and clarified Bion's concepts as well as introducing several of his own original ideas. He articulated an idiosyncratic but nonetheless post-Kleinian clinical approach and theoretical system, and wrote in a charming and exuberant style:

> A particular analysis begins with a relatively ill person coming to a relatively well one for help. But if the effort to organize and set in motion a 'psycho-analytical process' succeeds, the two people are caught up in an intimacy, a frankness, a revelation of thought and feeling whose intensity, I assert, is unparalleled. It compounds the depth of concentration of the breast-feeding mother and babe, the passion of the coital couple, the artist's urgency to give plastic form to experience, the impulse towards verbalization of the philosopher, and the craving for precision of the mathematician—potentially.
>
> (Meltzer 1973: viii)

Meltzer (1967) detailed the step-by-step internal processes he deemed necessary to maturation and development in child analysis. Starting with the sorting of the zonal and geographical confusions,[3] the transference gradually gathers and deepens,[4] self and object become more differentiated, and eventually the threshold of the depressive position is reached, followed by a weaning process and integration and introjection of whole objects and a benign parental couple—necessary, in Kleinian terms, for true reparative capacity and depressive concern. Here, Meltzer introduced the term, 'toilet breast', to denote the way a child may use splitting to preserve the goodness of her everyday life and objects:

> [T]he most primitive form of relief of psychic pain is accomplished by the evacuation into the external object of parts of the self in distress and the persecutory debris of attacked internal objects, receiving back through the introjective aspect the restored objects and relieved parts of the self.
>
> (ibid.: 21)

Meltzer's depiction of the internal world of objects, part-objects and their concomitant interrelationships and internal (and sometimes external) dramas was one of the most vivid and graphically described in the literature. He introduced a concept of perverse infantile sexuality as the cornerstone of destructive narcissism and '. . . every aspect of psychopathology' (Meltzer 1973: 90).[5] Klein and Rosenfeld focused on hostile aggression, let loose by instinctual defusion, as fuelling intrusive projective identification and phantasies of omnipotent control in narcissistic organizations. Meltzer (1973) highlighted perverse (and manically triumphant) aspects of the personality as dominant in defensive systems which militate against libidinal openness and vulnerability.

Extending the geographical dimension in which the internal world is a living space and generative theatre of meaning, he claimed that a cynical, spoiling aspect of self, composed of destructive infantile omnipotence fused with 'bad' objects or part-objects, gains sway over the rest of the psyche and triumphs over depressive anxieties (ibid.). Its omnipotent delusions of grandeur are achieved through projective identification inside desired aspects of the mother's body in unconscious phantasy. This 'carrier of the mark of Cain' creates chaos and reverses moral values in a confusional process which may eventually lead to breakdown (ibid.: 96–7). In contrast, introjective identification with valued others '. . . contains an aspirational element, tinged with anxiety and self-doubt' (ibid.: 52–3).

Meltzer emphasized adolescence as a critical stage (ibid.). The rigid splitting of the latency period, based on infantile defence structures, must be unsettled in adolescence for adult development to proceed authentically and not be based in imitation or compliance. The wild extremes of adolescent experimentation with identifications and 'flight to the group' or gang phenomena are necessary aspects of contained breakdown:

> [T]he group life presents a modulating environment *vis-à-vis* the adult world and distinct from the child-world, well equipped to bring this seething flux gradually into a more crystallized state—if the more psychotic type of confusion of identity due to massive projective identification does not play too great a role.
>
> (ibid.: 53)

Meltzer (1992) later described an unconscious phantasy scenario resulting from the evasion of separation anxiety through this same massive projective identification. He argued that one aspect of projective identification within internal objects and part-objects, as an intrusive psychotic defence, is into phantasied compartments of the maternal body: head/breast, genitalia and the maternal rectum (claustrum).[6]

Separation anxiety and depressive pain are avoided through an unconscious delusional inhabitation of the inside of the mother. This usually, according to Meltzer, begins in 'head/breast', a magical idealized haven, in which no harm can touch the inhabitant nor loss of phantasied omnipotent and omniscient powers:

> Here we find the big, indolent baby boys and doll's-house little girls, for whom the supreme value is comfort. They are voluptuous without eroticism, curious without interest, obedient from inertia and polite without consideration. What they enjoy seems to them what the whole world is striving for, an eternal holiday with companionship but without relationship, in a pretty world without disturbing aesthetic impact . . . etc. etc.
>
> (ibid.: 86)

However, in Meltzer's view, life in 'head-breast' cannot be sustained for ever. If the intruder (in phantasy) continually backs away from the threshold of the depressive position, there will be an inevitable descent into the other compartments of the phantasied maternal body: 'genitalia' and 'claustrum'. Whilst a measure of protective idealization may be maintained in 'genitalia' with phantasies of irresistibility through masturbatory activity and sexual conquests, life in the claustrum becomes a claustrophobic persecutory nightmare and is characterized by internal and external sado-masochistic relationships.

Meltzer's logic here was that this degree of splitting and projective identification, and their concomitant manic triumph, severely damage both the would-be escapist/intruder and his internal objects. Life in the claustrum resembles Bion's descriptions of the terrifying psychotic results of continuing reliance on projective identification. Here, the struggle is for survival only. Through the confusional states engendered by this level of projective identification, there is a 'perilously slippery chute' from head to rectum, and eventually into delusion formation and psychosis (ibid.: 91).

In contrast, Meltzer (1988) set out the startling thesis that the depressive position precedes the paranoid/schizoid position in infant development. He argued that mother and baby behold each other with depressive awe and wonder, which he termed 'aesthetic reciprocity'. The balance of L, H and K in this state is difficult and precarious to maintain: this 'aesthetic conflict' relates to the difficulty in loving someone so intensely that one could not bear to lose them, whilst retaining a sense of mutual separateness. Therefore when the pains of this state become unbearable, there may be a lapse into paranoid/schizoid phantasies of omnipotent control.

These theorizations inspired some child psychotherapists to write about how children may manage to survive the worst extremes of abuse and deprivation with some capacity to cathect good experiences still intact (Reid 1990; Williams 2000). The crucial factor seems to be a capacity to mourn traumatic loss without destroying the object in unconscious phantasy. The profound implication for psychoanalytic technique lies in looking for a state to be regained, as opposed to being achieved for the first time (see Chapter 9).

A clinical example comes from the patient I call 'Ewan' (see also Chapter 3). He spent his entire initial consultation repeating in endless maddening fashion: 'This is no good. What I need is a girlfriend. What I need is a girlfriend *now*. I can't come here and talk to you and then go home and be on my own again tonight. What I need is a girlfriend. What I need is a girlfriend *now*' . . . etc. etc. In a flash of intuition whose source is still unknown to me—but may be related to Meltzer's idea that aesthetic conflict (which may result in a lapse into omnipotent control) proceeds from the difficulty in maintaining aesthetic reciprocity (love and desire whilst remaining separate)—I said: 'You're the kind of person who can't enjoy the view while he's driving along because he's too busy *honking at traffic*.' Ewan did a double-take, gave me a big grin and replied: 'How did you know that?'

For three years of three times weekly psychotherapy, week in, week out, with no respite Ewan would evacuate his feelings of hatred, envy (of happy people, including apparently myself) and contempt into me through endless maddening bullying repetition of unthought statements about his loneliness, his unhappiness, his boredom at work, his not being able to bear seeing happy people around him etc. etc. until I was at my wits' end. I truly understood what it meant to be a toilet breast.

Now, Ewan did come from a very difficult background. He was one of triplets in a poor and struggling family in a Glaswegian tenement. His father, who sounded very depressed, was killed in an industrial accident when Ewan was six. This may have been a parasuicide as he was found to be using equipment in an unsafe fashion. Ewan perceived his mother as preferring his siblings to himself and giving them all her attention. He reacted to this perceived state of affairs with tantrums and violence from a very young age. He could remember sticking a fork into his brother and smashing his fist through a window when he thought his brothers had been given more sweets than he had. His earliest memory was of his mother pretending to call the police to come and take him away.

Despite the real difficulties in his background, I quickly realized that empathic understanding only resulted in escalating outbursts in which he would rubbish everything I said to him, often with the retort: 'Answers, Jean. I want answers. This is no good. I want answers *now*.' Ewan's intolerance of frustration and evacuation of his feelings drove potential girlfriends away, resulting in a vicious circle which intensified his loneliness and envy. He also had a powerful streak of vengefulness. When I first saw him, he used to call his mother to let her know when he was about to 'bungy jump' (remember how his father died). This behaviour ceased very early in his therapy, but his bullying of me did not. Little by little, I withstood his assaults, and interpreted the way he got rid of his feelings in the way that Bion and Meltzer describe so ably.

Fortunately, Ewan was intelligent, possessed drive and ambition, and could take a tough interpretation on the chin. Over a long period of time, and with great upheavals and reversals, he slowly began to stop harassing me. Interestingly, at this stage in his therapy, he started to have vicious dreams about women. As Bion theorized, once intolerable feelings can be borne for longer, dream images herald the beginning of a capacity to process feeling into thought. These dreams also illustrate a perverse aspect of Ewan, deployed to evade the pains of loss of omnipotent control.

He became able to talk to his mother, who sounded like a genuinely kindly and well-intentioned person. She told him he had been 'a beautiful baby' up to age nine months, when his tantrums started. Meltzer's thesis that the paranoid/schizoid position follows the depressive position because of the pain and difficulty inherent in 'aesthetic reciprocity' may also be borne out by this case.

Eventually, and to my initial amazement, Ewan became able to tolerate short periods of peaceful silence in his therapy—at first followed by just a hint of complaint such as 'Is there any point in coming to see a therapist when they don't say anything to you?' but later quite companionably. He became able to form relationships with women. And at last, he fell in love.

It is not coincidental that I have illustrated post-Kleinian theory with some of the most difficult patients I have seen. In my experience, a knowledge of Kleinian theory, admixed with post-Winnicottian insights about containment, transitional space and the role of external reality, and a more flexible approach to technique, is essential in the treatment of very disturbed people.

HERBERT ROSENFELD AND J. HENRI REY

Rosenfeld and Rey were two theorists of severe psychological disturbance. Both worked with borderline and psychotic patients throughout their careers. Whilst both remained within a broadly traditional Kleinian framework, their theoretical advances have been taken up by a range of psychoanalysts and sometimes within psychiatry.

Rosenfeld (1971) outlined for the first time the psychological mechanisms which underpin the sabotaging of good experiences and the terrifying backlashes after psychological progress encountered in severely narcissistic, borderline and psychotic patients. Rosenfeld posited an internal gang formation composed of idealized fragments of destructive infantile omnipotence, sadism and envy, which pose as helpers but actually attack and undermine the libidinal cathexis of valued people and experiences. This nasty internal phalanx is also ranged against emotional openness, vulnerability and dependence, and the patient's libidinal self. The clinical usages of this phenomenon are discussed at length in Chapter 5 with a clinical example.

Rosenfeld was one of the first analysts to work with schizophrenic patients, and the first Kleinian to publish an account of the analysis of a schizophrenic patient (Rosenfeld 1965; Sayers 2000). Like most other Kleinians, he focused primarily on the psychotic mechanism of extreme and destructively hostile projective identification, which can result in such a massive evacuation as to constitute a loss of sense of self and a resultant inertia and apathy. He described the consequent confusional states and the disturbed person's fear of becoming claustrophobically imprisoned in others. In one case history, he illustrated his psychotic patient's destructive and deadly grandiosity with a dream in which a man who is nine feet tall dominates the patient (Rosenfeld 1971; Hinshelwood 1994).

In Kleinian style, Rosenfeld portrayed the unconscious phantasies dominating his patients' internal lives as a vivid theatre of meaning, and paid little attention to the role of external reality in the aetiology of serious disturbance. He was one of the first Kleinians to describe the moral reversal or perversion of values which can eventuate from the dominance of destructive and deadly mechanisms in psychotic states. He pioneered the investigation of pathological unconscious organizations which serve as temporary bulwarks against further disintegration and overt disturbance, but which also render the person out of emotional contact with others and unable to develop psychologically (Rosenfeld 1987).

Transferential and countertransferential impasses result from the externalization of such organizations in the analytic relationship and may create therapeutic deadlock if they go unrecognized. Rosenfeld's work influenced Steiner's (1993) detailed accounts of the labyrinthine forms such organizations may assume and the anxieties against which they form defences (see later in this chapter).

Rey's (1979) theoretical innovation—the spatio-temporal dimension in borderline and psychotic disturbance—was based on concepts first outlined by Klein (1946), Riviere (1952) and Rosenfeld (1965). Hostile intrusive projective identification results in a sense of being imprisoned or encapsulated by one's objects, internal and external. This produces a tendency for fusion or merger in relationships, and can cause claustrophobic symptoms. Rey's lifetime work with the severely disturbed patients at the Maudsley Hospital in London, or the 'brick mother', afforded him the opportunity to observe these phenomena closely.

Drawing from Piaget as well as Kleinian theory, he differentiated between physical and psychological birth and separation. The infant, he thought, resides in a psychic 'marsupial space', like a newborn kangaroo in its pouch. True psychological birth requires a further process of separation, loss and mourning. He argued that the borderline patient exists on the boundaries of gender and psychosis/neurosis, and resides uncomfortably, in unconscious phantasy, inside his objects. Claustrophobic panic ensues and an urgent need for escape, but once outside, the borderline person becomes afraid he will lose the object on which he so depends and becomes terrified of being alone and exposed in empty space, or agoraphobic (Rey 1979). Rey formulated this as the 'claustro-agoraphobic dilemma', a clinical phenomenon which may require the treatment setting to make allowances for the borderline patient to come and go for a period of time, whilst being continually borne in mind, or to maintain a manageable distance from the therapist. It may be unwise in some cases to see a severely borderline patient at too high a frequency. My patient, Patrice, for example, came only twice weekly. He would also have felt too terrifyingly overwhelmed in greater frequency. A supervisee, whose borderline patient missed huge numbers of sessions, would sometimes countertransferentially experience his patient as enormous and right in his face, whereas in fact she was small and they were sitting a few feet apart.

JOHN STEINER AND RON BRITTON

Steiner and Britton are from the most recent generation of post-Kleinians. Steiner (1985) develops Vellacott's (1971) study of the Oedipus myth, which revealed both a story of an innocent man caught in the web of fate and a psychological drama in which the entire cast—Jocasta, Creon, Teiresias and the chorus, as well as Oedipus—and the audience could see the truth but chose to ignore their better judgement on a remote chance that it could be otherwise. Steiner extrapolates from this second, complementary version of the tragedy to explore the mechanism of 'turning a blind eye' seen in clinical practice with neurotic and perverse patients as an evasion of Oedipal realities and depressive pain.

Psychic Retreats (1993) is Steiner's contribution to the Kleinian literature on narcissism, in which narcissistic withdrawal is not to some idealized version of self (Freud 1914) but to an idealized internal object (Klein 1946, 1952a, 1952b). Steiner conceives of a 'psychic retreat' as a complex defensive pathological organization (of destructive impulses), designed to protect the person from unbearable depressive and/or paranoid schizoid anxieties but which simultaneously pre-empts further psychic development. Steiner thinks these 'organizations' might be operative at all levels of disturbance— neurotic and 'normal', as well as narcissistic, schizoid and borderline. The distinction is one of degree. Whilst a neurotic patient may use a retreat temporarily when under siege from anxieties she finds unbearable and return to a state of greater contact with internal and external reality quite easily, a borderline or schizoid patient may take up permanent psychic residence in a retreat. Steiner postulates a 'borderline position' (not to be confused with borderline personality) as a state we may all withdraw to under duress. The 'retreat' may be idealized as a haven, an island or a house, or it may be experienced as persecutory and malign in the form of a Mafia-like gang (Rosenfeld 1971), a totalitarian government (Meltzer 1986) or a business organization.

Steiner combines Rosenfeld's (1971) theorization of destructive narcissism and Rey's (1979) conceptualization of the spatial element in internal withdrawal. He argues that we need to discover and interpret not just *how* the organization is operative but *why*—what exactly are the anxieties defended against and what are the circumstances which precipitate them. In one of his clinical examples, 'Mrs. A.' (Steiner 1993: 14–24), he shows how the patient would retreat to an idealized but barren haven (reading novels in bed) at times when she heard his comments as persecutory but also when there had been some 'real' emotional contact. Steiner incorporates Meltzer's (1973) work on the role of perverse infantile sexuality in narcissistic organizations to argue that there is no 'innocent' libidinal self trapped by the malign elements in the personality (Rosenfeld 1971), but a perverse collusion of all parts of the personality often choosing sado-masochistic gratification over vulnerability. Because of their labyrinthine nature and provision of some precarious stability, these organizations pose a challenge in analysis and require specific technical interventions if they are not to result in therapeutic impasse. Some implications for technique are explored in Chapter 8.

A clinical illustration comes from a patient I call 'Kevin', whose first few years in therapy were characterized by entrenched defences against emotional contact and terrifying backlashes after times of understanding and progress (see Chapter 5). At a later stage, Kevin became able to enjoy and sustain relationships with women and a far less isolated personal and professional life. However he still had a tendency to withdraw to an internal retreat when he felt threatened by further challenges in therapy and in his life.

At one such stage, he dreamt he was in a beautiful, but old and crumbling, French chateau. He was lying in the middle of a four-poster bed with his girlfriend, Denise, on one side and a 'celebrity' he was attracted to, but had no respect for, on the other. On the ceiling, a contented cherubic baby observed this scene from a slowly trundling conveyor belt. Kevin associated the house with the holiday home of his affluent uncle, Cieran, with whom he was living temporarily, and the conveyor belt on the ceiling with Superman and an experience of a 'roller-coaster' as a child.

This dream clearly represented his temporary psychological position in a half-way formation between fantasy and reality. He lay between his real girlfriend, whom he loved and wanted to stay with, and a fantasy 'relationship' of the type which had dominated his emotional life for many years. There was a pervasive atmosphere of stuckness and lack of movement. The support of his uncle allowed him a vicariously comfortable life but also prevented his moving into a more independent and committed set-up with his girlfriend. The child on the ceiling showed how the infantile gratifications resulting from the partial retreat contributed to a reluctance to emerge from it and the illusion of a superior vantage point from which to view mundane struggles. Kevin said the slow trundling of the conveyor belt represented exactly how he felt—stuck in an uninspiring but well-paid job and unable to move beyond the immediate gratifications of material comfort—yet trapped in a situation which was going nowhere.

Significantly, this dream occurred at a point at which Kevin was becoming more conscious of his reluctance to take the risks involved in moving his life on. The dream also signified a temporary retreat into a partially narcissistic state as a reaction to therapeutic understanding of his preference for fantasy relationships. Steiner's insights enabled us to disentangle the complex interweaving of fantasy and reality involved in his withdrawal.

Phillips' (2000) comments on Steiner's work highlight an important caveat. Whilst this is a major advance in uncovering deeply defensive psychological manoeuvres, there is also omnipotence inherent in thinking we know what level of emotional contact is 'real' or good for our patients. We may all need to withdraw from time to time.

Britton's (1989, 1998) extraordinary insight that some people find the thought of their parents' sexual relationship too painful to bear in mind and refuse an internal phantasy of the 'primal scene' is an application of Freud (1924b) and Klein's (1928, 1945) work on the Oedipus Complex, and Bion's (1970) recognition of 'container/contained' as not merely an internalized form of maternal receptivity but also a triangulated situation in which two people (objects) may share a third to the advantage of all three.[7] Britton deems such an internal evasion may be consequent on a failure of early maternal containment or a reluctance to give up the gratifications of pre-Oedipal relating by not allowing one's parents to come together in one's mind. Such evasions result in concomitant difficulties in bringing ideas together.

Britton observes from clinical experience how the underlying phantasy of the primal scene may form a template on which thought is based. For example, a person who is 'vague' might allow her parents to co-exist in her mind but not allow penetrative active mental intercourse (Britton 1989). A range of 'Oedipal illusions' may also be deployed, such as '. . . horrific, sado-masochistic or murderous intercourse, or as depressive images of a ruined couple in a ruined world' (ibid.: 94).

> For example my patient, Kevin, suffered terrifying and crippling anxiety around my holiday breaks. Whilst this anxiety was initially related to my capacity to survive his rage during breaks (see Kevin's dream in Chapter 7), it became apparent at a later stage that it was also related to what I might be doing and with whom behind his back. Kevin's capacity to think was detonated at these times and he spent his sessions in mute paralysis.

This accords with Britton's insight that a person whose unconscious phantasy of his parents' intercourse is violent and destructive might be able to allow his thoughts to come together sometimes, but only with great anxiety and trepidation. A borderline patient, 'Angela', whose therapy I supervised (see Chapter 6), became exceedingly anxious when her parents, who had divorced when she was two, spent any time together. At these moments, her tendency to volatility increased dramatically and thought and insight were temporarily suspended.

In very serious disturbance, a notion of parental intercourse cannot be sustained in any form. The result, according to Britton, is an absence of a triangular perspective on which insight is based (Britton 1998: 41–58). In such cases, a client may experience any interpretation or *other* point of view as malignant misunderstanding, and a modification of technique may be required, such as Steiner's 'analyst-centred' interpretations (Steiner 1993) (see Chapter 8).

Britton softens the Kleinian approach to the aetiology of disturbance. He considers the role of external reality in his patients' suffering, and argues certain forms of libidinal narcissism to be a necessary protection where there has been a failure of early containment (Britton 2003). These must be differentiated from more rigid narcissistic defences against dependence, openness and vulnerability in people whose parenting has not been disrupted or difficult.

Building from Klein's thesis that '. . . creativeness becomes the deepest cause for envy' (Klein 1957 [1975b]: 202) and Bion's (1959) theory of an enviously attacking self-destructive superego, Britton also explores how this cruel internal construct may exist in people less disturbed than in Bion's original formulation who may have received disturbed or envious parenting (Britton 2003). In such cases actual experience has contributed to the formation of the self-destructive agency. In analysis it may be modified into an ego alien introject which does not occupy the same commanding position as a superego from which to destroy creativity, success and progress in analysis.

Without the groundbreaking post-Kleinian concepts described in this chapter, deep psychoanalytic work with very disturbed patients would be far less possible.

NOTES

1. After Bion's emigration to Los Angeles in 1968, a group of post-Kleinian psychoanalysts with a specifically Bionian orientation assembled in California. They included James Grotstein, Robert Caper and Alfred Mason. Kleinian influence in Latin America, especially Chile, Argentina and Mexico, has always been very significant.
2. Meltzer's (1986) *Studies in Extended Metapsychology* was written with a number of analysts and child psychotherapists, several of whom are Italian (M. Albergamo, E. Cohen, A. Greco, M. Harris, S. Maiello, G. Milana, D. Petrelli, A. S. Scolmati and F. Scotti). P. Bion Talamo, F. Borgogno and S. A. Merciai (eds) (2000) *W.R. Bion: Between past and future* was the result of an International Centennial Conference on Bion's work held in Turin in 1997.
3. In Meltzer's work, zonal confusions refer to the various erogenous zones and products such as nipple/penis; mouth/vagina/anus; urine/semen/saliva. At this early stage, horizontal splitting is necessary to keep the 'toilet functions' separate from the feeding functions. Geographical confusion refers to the confusion between self and other (mother and baby) discussed a little later in this section.
4. Meltzer, like Lacan, thought different levels of transference gradually establish themselves in psychoanalysis, and it takes time to reach the core complexes.
5. For further analysis of destructive narcissistic organizations, see the sections on Rosenfeld and Steiner later in this chapter, and Chapters 5 and 6.

6. Projective identification inside internal objects and part-objects derives from Klein's (1946) concept of narcissism as a phantasied retreat into an idealized internal object. Meltzer amplifies this to a far greater extent. See also Steiner's (1993) *Psychic Retreats* later in this chapter.

7. 'Although I shall speak of the Oedipal situation as if it were the content of thoughts it will be apparent that thoughts and thinking may be regarded as part of the content of the Oedipal situation' (Bion 1963 [1984]: 44).

Part II

Contemporary clinical practice

Chapter 5

A modern view of narcissism

The concept of narcissism highlights a divide between the Lacanian school on the one hand and contemporary Independents and post-Kleinians on the other. Lacan (1949, 1953, 1954–5) thought the ego was a narcissistic formation and although critical in developmental terms, an impediment to access to the unconscious and the opening of the space of desire in neurotics. Lacanians therefore do not work with a clinical concept of narcissism except in the sense in which 'imaginary' processes in all of us may interfere with the work of analysis (see Chapter 3 and later in this chapter).

The concept of narcissism has functioned as a metapsychological watershed since Freud (1914) deemed it the divide between the psychoneuroses and the psychoses. Contemporary post-Kleinians still adhere to this view, using a different conceptual framework. Lacanians posit perversion as a structural position between neurosis and psychosis (discussed in Chapter 6), but Lacan afforded narcissism a unique role as the first structuring moment of subjectivity with the 'mirror stage' (Lacan 1949). Contemporary Independents have contributed some striking new clinical formulations.

The term narcissism is used in at least three different senses—in its popular usage; as a metapsychological concept used to describe deep structures of mind and pathology; and as a clinically diagnostic term. The popular usage conjures up someone rather vain, in love with themselves, self-absorbed, indifferent to the needs of others, and potentially exploitative. These ideas have some bearing on the clinical applications of the term, but are in some instances misleading.

Both the metapsychological and the clinically specific usages, in Kleinian and Independent theory, relate to the withdrawal of libido from others towards some form of self-idealization as a consequence of trauma, deprivation or disturbed parenting. A narcissistic person has been let down, usually badly, and as Green (1988) points out, often by both parents. Put simply, a child may not have had sufficient good experiences to internalize as resources. A narcissistic structure is therefore a defence against psychic annihilation. The ways in which the self-idealization functions and how it is conceptualized vary according to degree of severity of disturbance and depending on which theoretical perspective is being used: these dramatically affect treatment approach.

The metapsychological usage describes diverse underlying psychic structures across a broad spectrum of disturbance, with differing levels of splitting and fragmentation. Anyone who relies primarily on an underlying narcissistic structure is potentially vulnerable to breakdown. This empty split form of self relies on five major defence mechanisms to remain intact: splitting, projective identification, idealization, omnipotence and denial. Disowned aspects of the self are split off and projected into others, so that they do not threaten the precarious stability of the self-idealization. This latter is maintained by infantile omnipotence, or over-valuation of the self's powers and qualities, regardless of the intrusions of reality. Because splitting mechanisms predominate, further fragmentation under threat or stress is always a possibility. In terms of psychic structure, therefore, this is a very different picture from someone with securely established internal resources (or objects), who can make use of the neurotic defences of repression and sublimation without damage to the integrity of the ego.

The spectrum of narcissistic disturbance, as theorized by contemporary Independents, Freudians and post-Kleinians, ranges from 'narcissistic personality' (Kernberg 1975, 1986a, 1986b) to the borderline states, and incorporates psychiatric personality disorders or forms of character pathology, including addictions. Some post-Kleinians think narcissistic structures also underlie the perversions (Meltzer 1973; Waddell and Williams 1991) (see Chapter 6). Narcissistic personality (the third usage) is a specific diagnostic term, at the apparently best-functioning end of the metapsychological spectrum. 'Narcissistic personality' was conceptualized by Kernberg (1975, 1986a), as a regressive fusion of ideal self, ideal object and ego ideal, discussed later in this chapter.[1] This specifically clinical usage of the term must be distinguished from its broader metapsychological applications.

Pathological or structural narcissism is, of course, very different from the traces of narcissism remaining in all our characters, which may be an important resource in child-rearing or a spur to heroic deeds or great achievements. Grunberger (1989) argues life would lack spice and interest if we had no narcissism at all. In contrast, narcissism as a form of disturbance is now widely recognized as extremely difficult to treat, and potentially a dangerous and destructive phenomenon. Many psychoanalysts now think that its malign aspects need to be tackled in the transference, as idealization diminishes or ceases to play a useful or containing role.

The myth of Narcissus and Echo, as recounted by Ovid, contains some germs of the clinical usages (Mollon 1993; Holmes 2001). Narcissus came from a traumatic background: his mother, Liriope, was raped by the river god, Cephisus. He generated envy in others (projective identification) and yet remained unreachable and unobtainable (protective withdrawal). He treated Echo and his other admirers sadistically and Echo became masochistically enslaved (underlying hatred of libidinal attachment and denigration of others). Hamilton sees Echo and Narcissus as mutually trapped in a '. . . mirroring or doting symbiosis which resists change' (Hamilton 1982 [1993]: 137). Just as Echo echoes and mirrors Narcissus' words, so Narcissus is captivated by his reflected image at the pool. There is no separateness or individuality, liveliness, development or real interchange but instead a pervasive sense of alienation, stuckness and deadliness.

More recent versions of this myth include Oscar Wilde's (1891) *The Picture of Dorian Gray* and Will Self's (2002) *Dorian*. Wilde's haunting and savage tale describes a young, beautiful socialite who descends ever more deeply into hypocrisy, dissolution and crime, whilst the only face which bears the marks of his true character is a painting stored in his attic. Wilde's Dorian has no capacity to care for others and is prepared to go to ever-increasing lengths to prop up his narcissistic self-image. Self places his Dorian within contemporary gay culture and British New Labour. This twenty-first-century Dorian uses drugs and promiscuous sexual activity as a substitute for human relationships. His mother, with whom he has no contact, lives in a hotel in Los Angeles. This Dorian has no emotional home. What begins as an attempt to prop up an empty, loveless self ends up as a perverse orgy of murder and murderous sexual activity.

Lasch (1979) and Kovel (1988a) argue that the social requirements of late capitalism produce narcissistic personalities: an ability to sever emotional links and move on without undue pain may now be more useful than sustaining close ties in intimate relationships, family and social kinship, and the economically driven level of material consumption is dependent on a high investment in image and acquisition. Kovel shows how white racism operates through projective identification of disowned aspects of the idealized white self into black people, who are then forced to carry the aggression, hostility, rage, greed, sexual voraciousness and impurity the white 'civilized' person prefers to dissociate (Kovel 1970; White 1989).

Freud (1914) noted the role of illusion, a prominent feature of Narcissus myths, as a factor in disturbance of relation to external reality, and the clinical significance of grandiosity, omnipotent or magical thinking and idealization of self and object. He observed disturbance of recognition of time, the denial of necessity for development, and the narcissistic person's inability to allow for the separate existence of others or to experience concern for them as other and different.

Melanie Klein and Anna Freud (1942–4) debated the existence of primary narcissism as expounded by Freud. Klein argued that babies relate to others from the beginning of life, and in consequence, narcissism is a secondary phenomenon: a regression to a phantasied merger with an idealized internal object. Subsequent research on early life bears out Klein's contention about infant development (Stern 1985; Holmes 2001). However, the distinction between primary and secondary narcissism may become semantic once it comes to the impact of entrenched narcissistic functioning on later pathology.

Narcissistic disturbance varies along a libidinal/destructive continuum, depending on whether idealizing or other-hating aspects are uppermost in the clinical picture. Libidinal or 'thin-skinned' narcissists rely predominantly on idealization and are hypersensitive, vulnerable and prone to depression (of an empty, futile variety) and withdrawal (Rosenfeld 1987). Destructive or 'thick-skinned' narcissists are more hostile and more likely to bully their way through life, exploiting others (ibid.), although Bateman (1998) argues the two function as different sides of the same person. Britton adds the 'as if' personality, in which a void space constitutes inner reality, to Rosenfeld's two categories (Britton 2003). Libidinal and destructive aspects may need to be tackled at different stages in the course of therapy.

A narcissistic transference can be difficult and sometimes damaging for the psychotherapist to negotiate. The level of idealization may be seductively tempting to stay with although it can have clinical uses (discussed a little later in this chapter). Underlying the idealization is extreme unconscious hostility, mobilized against the terror of mutuality. The therapist is usually subject to unconscious denigration and diminishment, and forced to carry those aspects of self the narcissistic person cannot tolerate. Hostility and denigration may be exacerbated by extreme defensiveness against dependence. Although the narcissistic person may seek symbiotic merger to repair early damage, they are simultaneously terrified that traumatic experiences will be repeated and that they could be left intolerably defenceless.

COMPARATIVE PSYCHOANALYTIC APPROACHES

In this chapter, I depart from the contemporary Independent/Lacanian/ post-Kleinian demarcation used in every other chapter in Part II, as the distinctive approaches to the treatment of narcissism do not fall so neatly into these divisions. The different approaches, though, do illustrate the global impact of some American Freudian and self psychologists (Kernberg and Kohut) on contemporary psychoanalytic practice, especially on the Independents.

Narcissism as developmental arrest

Heinz Kohut's (1971, 1977) thesis on both the origins and the treatment of narcissistic disturbance was related to how phases of idealization of self and other are essential in ordinary development. He thought that, in psychotherapy, these primitive idealizations can be held for a developmentally appropriate length of time and disillusioned at a tolerable pace, thereby transmuting them into an emergent ego ideal and eventually a modification of the superego. He believed that early deprivation or trauma can result in fixation and dissociation of primitive idealizations, a consequent freezing of the personality at this stage and pre-emption of further psychological development. They remain split off, are re-enacted in everyday life and relationships, and cannot be integrated into the rest of the personality. Sufficient trauma, in Kohut's view, is constituted by abandonment, impingement, tantalization, or other forms of disturbed parenting.

Kohut (1971) held that, in analysis, dissociated primitive idealizations become reactivated in the transference. They may form either a 'mirror transference', an externalized version of an idealized grandiose self, or an idealizing transference, in which an idealized selfobject is revived and experienced in relation to the analyst (at this stage Freudians and Independents believe self and object are not yet fully differentiated). Kohut argued that these archaic transferences must be held by the analyst without premature interpretation. She must tolerate and support (without actively encouraging) a high level of mutual idealization, which has a powerful clinical function. Because the dissociated part of the personality is contained analytically, the self is held or bound with a consequent improvement in functioning.

However, with analytic breaks or failures in empathy, the patient may be subject to regressive swings dominated by fears of fragmentation. At these times, there may be a tendency to resort to increasingly primitive and disturbed mechanisms to bind the self. For example, a client might withdraw socially and/or analytically, or they might be drawn to extremist religious beliefs or cults, engage in perverse autoerotic solutions or act out. If these regressive swings are empathically interpreted, and if the reactivated primitive idealizing transference can be held in analysis for the requisite time with a tolerable pace of disillusionment, then structural change can take place.

Kohut was criticized by the classical analytic community for his innovations in technique (Siegel 1996). In fact there are great similarities between his methods and a Winnicottian 'holding environment' (discussed in Chapters 2 and 8) and many analysts of all persuasions have disputed the appropriateness of triangulated interpretation in certain forms of disturbance or at certain stages of regression (Lacan 1955–6; Britton 1998; Steiner 1993). However, Kohut's theories are problematic in that they rest solely on a libidinal view of narcissism, or the need to love and over-value oneself in compensation for a deficit of ordinary idealizing experiences early in life. Kohut neglected the destructive and self- and other-hating aspects of narcissism. The negative transference is not to be analyzed, nor is denigration of and hostility towards the object with their concomitant defences. The redirection of the underlying destructiveness and hostility, even in denied or dissociated forms, could create major difficulties for the patient.

Kohut's version of narcissism constitutes a partial theory of development—it enables a movement towards a modified form of narcissism, but not towards object or other-relatedness. As Symington (1993) commented, because all negatives are located externally to the self and the patient is left dependent for reassurance on external sources of approval and affirmation, it is a paranoid theory. With some clients, though, Kohut's ideas can prove effective for a period of analysis—as in the following example.

'Mikhaela' was an Eastern European orphan who had lived in an orphanage in grim conditions until she was two. She had dreams about people banging their heads against walls, or sitting and rocking, or totally withdrawn with their heads in their hands, which may have referred to her time in the orphanage. She was adopted into a British family with one older brother. Her adoptive father had an affair with someone in the same village whom he married when Mikhaela was four. Mikhaela's mother became emotionally absent. Although Mikhaela had a materially comfortable and maternally kind upbringing, she seemed to have received little individual attention. She found a role for herself as the family 'helper'; she cleaned, ironed etc., and made herself unobtrusive. At age nineteen, she married a much older man, whom she later admitted she did not love.

At the beginning of her therapy, Mikhaela was very withdrawn and found it difficult to express herself or to recognize what her feelings were. After a few months she started to blossom and became more outgoing—probably because of a level of attention and individual understanding she had not previously received. I became an idealized selfobject, an unexpected source of support with the lonely burden of carrying herself. She declared, 'Being in analysis is the best thing that's ever happened to me', which felt true to her at the time. She needed her idealization for an extended period of time, as she needed maternal attunement and an undisturbed period of containment in which she could begin to get to know herself and her emotional life, and learn how to articulate it.

Near the beginning of her therapy, she had many dreams of climbing mountains and slipping down again, or driving a car and the brakes failing. These dreams, as Kohut suggested, indicated the precarious nature of the idealization, which needed to become more firmly established in a secure and real relationship, before her personality could have the space and the necessary conditions to begin to cohere. About six months into her therapy, she had a dream in which she was marooned in her childhood bedroom, aged about four, on her bed. The room was flooded, her toes were dangling in the water, and she was beset by tiddler fish getting under her toes and a large shark fish which she was swatting off with her only weapon, a teddy bear. This dream showed her emotional isolation very clearly, and her final fixation at the age of her father's departure. Her only weapon, a material comforter, defended her against the persecutors or destructive forces in her personality which threatened her equilibrium.

After this phase of her therapy she moved on, and no longer needed the same level of self or object idealization. She began to explore the 'nasty hating' side of herself, and became painfully aware of the limitations her difficulty with deep emotional engagement had put on her life. She became enraged with me for my lack of availability outside session times. Her dreams became livelier and revealed deep conflict and internal struggle about depending on and opening herself to another person and her understandably profound fear of abandonment. I cannot explore the later developments here. I hope to have illustrated that she would never have reached a point at which she felt safe enough to experience such conflict with me, if she had not experienced the integrative effect of a period of idealization.

Whilst Kohut (1977) held that regressive drive fixation (for example at an oral or anal stage) was less important than the secure establishment of a child's sense of self within the empathic responses of her parents, the next theorist, Otto Kernberg, bases his theory of narcissism in defensive fixation at an oral stage.

Narcissism as defensive construct: Narcissistic personality

Kernberg's (1975, 1986a, 1986b, 2004) very different view of narcissism is also clinically influential across the world. He propounds a theory of narcissistic personality as a specific differential diagnosis, with a particular underlying construction of self incorporating both libidinal and destructive elements. He thinks that in the absence of good-enough early care, and a background which often includes 'chronically cold parental figures with covert but intense aggression' (Kernberg 1986a: 220), a self is cobbled together out of deficit. As I have said, a regressive fusion of ideal self, ideal object and actual self forms the nucleus of this fragile collage (Kernberg 1975: 231), a defensive construction covering extremely primitive oral rage. He calls this 'narcissistic personality', in contra-distinction to borderline states and other forms of 'personality disorder' such as 'anti-social personality', which might also be based in deep narcissistic structures but require a different therapeutic approach.

In optimal conditions, a narcissistic personality can appear reasonably stable and well-functioning. They can often be highly achieving, but dependent on admiration and adulation from others. Other people are used and sometimes exploited without concern, often idealized while they remain a source of adulation and dropped when no longer useful in this respect. Disowned and unwanted aspects of self are always projected out into denigrated others. Interpersonal relationships are problematic, unless of the merged, symbiotic variety. Narcissistic personalities can be subject to psychotic decompensation—anyone with an underlying narcissistic structure of self is potentially vulnerable to breakdown—and they have few resources to deal with the ordinary hardships and vicissitudes of life. They tend to age badly as they have few internal resources when the external ones diminish in later life. They may become hard and embittered. They become easily bored, and often lead a restless life with much dropping of what has been started and moving on. The narcissistic personality is '. . . a hungry, enraged, empty self, full of impotent anger at being frustrated, and fearful of a world which seems as hateful and revengeful as the patient himself' (Kernberg 1986a: 219), and experiences great resistance to change.

Kernberg claims it is necessary to interpret both libidinal and destructive elements in the transference—the idealizations and the hostile denigration of the analyst. As patients, these people experience enormous fear of dependence and repetition of the trauma which produced the original defensive structuring of self, and the rage which underlies it. They manifest extreme defences against taking in anything good, because of high levels of envy and because receiving from an analyst would entail some recognition of the separateness and value of the other. Kernberg continually emphasizes how wearing this is for the therapist. He warns against countertransferential developments such as unconscious retaliation, and advises psychotherapists to exercise caution lest they internalize what these patients project. He argues they need high-frequency, intensive treatment over many years, and even so, the therapeutic gains may be very limited. He proffers an extremely guarded prognosis, which may be slightly better in those cases where some capacity for guilt and sublimation is already evident.

Kernberg's theory must be applied with great care as it applies to one form of narcissism only: 'narcissistic personality'. Informed differential diagnosis is required to distinguish this structure from the more volatile borderline states, from perverse or addictive syndromes which may cover more fragmented narcissistic structures, or from forms of narcissism dominated by libidinal, as opposed to destructive, aspects. Kernberg neglects the potential benefits of holding a transferential idealization without interpretation for a period of time. His theorization does, though, provide invaluable clinical insights with cases of genuine narcissistic personality, as in the following example.

'Sharon', as I shall call her, failed to arrive at her first consultation because she had become so lost in north London that she had absolutely no idea of where she was. Such was the extent of her terror. She eventually arrived at her second consultation, blaming her twenty-minute lateness on traffic—which was to prove a continuing feature of her therapy.

She had been suffering from depression and anxiety so severe that for periods of a week or two she had been unable to leave her bedroom. Initially, she described her childhood in an idealized fashion—comfortably lower middle-class, wonderful parents, suburban idyll. Simultaneously I experienced powerful countertransferential feelings of profound, overwhelming, almost unbearable, loneliness and emptiness. At the same time, throughout the two years I saw her, I always felt like a poor relation or maybe the cleaning woman—a sort of scruffy nobody of no significance whom she might, if I was lucky, condescend to drop in on—late of course—for a 'chat'. This sort of experience could have led to the countertransferential build-up against which Kernberg warns the therapist and which can lead to unconscious retaliation.

It took more than a year to disentangle and begin to understand her history properly. She was the older child of two, the only daughter. Her brother, eighteen months younger, was the apple of her mother's eye. Her attitude to her brother was, and remained, venomous. Her father, though, seems to have idolized Sharon, and when her parents divorced, Sharon at age six went to live with her father. He subsequently had several depressive breakdowns, with in-patient treatment and ECT. He would confess his suicidal intentions to Sharon, who was terrified, hid in her bedroom and cried herself to sleep, night after lonely night. In the daytime she lived a solitary but magical existence with her dolls.

Aged seventeen, she became a model and rapidly obtained international success. When she came to see me, her looks were fading but she was developing a lucrative business as a lifestyle guru. She was capable of firing an employee who offended her without a second thought and seemed oblivious to the human consequences of her ruthlessness.

It proved very difficult for her to take her therapy seriously enough to get to it, although she contracted to come three times a week. Nevertheless, with a struggle and over time, a terribly bleak internal world began to reveal itself. She rarely remembered dreams. In her first, she went on a picnic with a gang of menacing 'yobs' in a park. This dream, like Sharon herself, was cheerful on the outside with something sinister within. As we continued to work, her depression lifted and her internal world began to show signs of insubstantial life. In one dream, she dreamt about me as a cartoon character, a

Minnie Mouse tripping round her bed collecting dreams. Kernberg emphasizes the marionette-like quality of the populace of the internal world of the narcissistic personality. Now, I think I should have interpreted her denigration of myself and her therapy more vigorously. Nonetheless, despite herself, an attachment was growing, and a grudging recognition of the fact that her therapy had made a very significant difference. At this point, she took fright and flight, in one of the sudden dramatic reversals and droppings the narcissistic personality is prone to. She set up an outpost of her company in another country and packed herself off at no notice.

One year later, she telephoned me in a state of near-breakdown. She came back for a few sessions, and decided to resume her therapy, which up to this time had been paid for by an insurance company. The insurance company announced she had reached the limit of what they would fund. This was used as a flimsy pretext for yet another sudden reversal of plans. Sharon did not suffer from shortage of funds. The reality—the beginning of her recognition of her need for another person, so deep she had contemplated changing her business plans to see me—was unutterably terrifying. Her narcissistic defences, hostile and ganglike in nature, had precipitated an abrupt and ruthless foreclosure of the possibility of change for this very sad woman.

Destructive narcissism

Herbert Rosenfeld (1965, 1971, 1987) concentrated on the most severe and fragmented forms of narcissistic structures which post-Kleinians consider to underlie addictions, perversions and borderline states. Although entirely Kleinian, Rosenfeld's theories proved influential and are used by clinicians of most persuasions when dealing with very serious disturbance. He posited that, in destructive narcissism, self-idealization plays a critical role but in the form of idealization of omnipotent destructive parts of the self directed against any positive libidinal relationship and any libidinal part of the self which experiences the need for an object and the desire to depend on it (Rosenfeld 1971). These idealized infantile sadistic omnipotent fragments are organized into a gang or mafia formation, which exerts a powerfully destructive hold over the rest of the personality (ibid.). Its presence constitutes the greatest resistance to treatment and likelihood of negative therapeutic reaction known to psychoanalysis.

Rosenfeld argued the sane, dependent part of the patient's personality is held in thrall by destructive omnipotence, organized in such a way as to militate against any form of need of or receiving from another. This hugely controlling pseudo-protective gang swings into backlash if the apparent stability of the organization is threatened by good external experiences, by understanding or uncovering in analysis, and/or by greater recognition or strengthening of the patient's libidinal self, all of which would expose its essentially hostile nature. The gang formation, as idealized fragments of envious spite and hostility, is solely aggressive and destructive in intent, both internally and externally (ibid.).

Rosenfeld depicted this form of internal narcissistic organization as the product of instinctual defusion, or the pathological separation of the loving and hating aspects of the personality, rendering the hateful side potentially deadly to self and others. He thought the operation of the death instinct was at work in the self-destructiveness of this form of narcissistic organization. In analysis, its internal work is manifest through obliteration of good experiences or understanding, forgetting, blanking, acting out or even psychotic episodes in reaction to progress. It thereby constitutes intense, virulent and prolonged resistance. With greater analytic progress, the gang formation may eventually be unmasked, and may appear as a gang or similar constellation in the patient's dreams.

Rosenfeld's theory provides an extremely useful form of understanding when working with very disturbed people, especially in relation to the bizarre and vicious forms of attack and self-attack which often follow insight, understanding, greater dependence and progress. But it has serious drawbacks and limitations. Rosenfeld offered no recognition of the role of external reality in the aetiology of serious disturbance: interpretations based on his understanding, without any empathy for traumas the patient may have undergone, can be experienced as persecutory and so prompt further resistance or negative therapeutic reaction. As he did not recognize a potentially benign role for idealization, there is little emphasis on timing. Interpretation of destructive elements alone from the beginning of therapy can prove counter-productive: it can increase paranoia, resistance and possibly flight, although there may be cases where it is necessary to combine this approach with an understanding of the circumstances that produced this intransigent constellation.

Rosenfeld's theories proved valuable with the Irish patient I call 'Kevin', whom I saw for seven years four times weekly psychoanalytic psychotherapy some years ago. He was eighteen when I first saw him and suffered such severe panic attacks that he would sometimes literally lose an afternoon, and have no recollection of where he had been or what he had been doing. His anxiety and internal persecution were so intense that thinking or being in touch with any kind of human feeling was very difficult. We quickly discovered that he was not 'held' by twice or thrice weekly therapy, whilst four times weekly provided a sufficient bulwark against his disturbance to enable analytic work to be done.

Kevin was the only child of a woman who suffered from schizophrenia. His father died when he was two. He lived alone with his mother until he was sixteen. His mother became increasingly disturbed, often needing in-patient psychiatric treatment. Kevin learnt how to keep his distance, and not provoke her disturbance or become too disturbed himself by her rage and withdrawals.

After travelling to England where he had relatives, he broke down, became incapacitated by anxiety, and left two periods of psychotherapy after about six months each. When I first started seeing him, his internal world was terrifyingly bleak and empty. He dreamt about deserted landscapes and highways at night, with dustbins littered with parts of corpses. After he had settled into me four times weekly and it became clear that this therapy was going to 'take', violent and vicious conflict began to manifest itself in his internal world. For example, he dreamt that he was in a war zone with his friend, Sid, whom he associated with Sid Vicious, an internal identification with the destructive side of his personality. Kevin and Sid were in a procession of refugees, maimed, mutilated and hobbling along, trying to escape from the war zone. He had to scale a high wall to try to get out. Two Arab men helped him climb up but when he reached the top, they threw paraffin over him, set him alight, and shoved him back down into the war zone. He then joined forces on a war plane going on a bombing mission into Iraq (this dream took place during the first war on Iraq). Nonetheless, it illustrates clearly Rosenfeld's theory that idealized omnipotent destructive fragments of the infantile self may pose as helpers to further resistance to treatment. It also demonstrates the vicious circle Kevin was locked into internally—he responded to the failed escape by joining forces with the destructive elements in his personality, thereby increasing persecution and paranoia.

As his treatment progressed and his libidinal self grew stronger, Kevin became increasingly able to stand up to the thugs and gangs in his internal world. About two years into his therapy was a dream much closer to home, in itself a sign of integration and movement. He dreamt he was attacked by a gang of stereotypical thugs, with eyepatches, shaven heads and scarred faces, in a deserted street in Hackney, east London. He was beaten into abject submission and rolled into the gutter. Then, in the dream he thought 'I don't have to put up with this', and rose up and succeeded in fighting the thugs off. Eventually, whole healthy people began to appear intermittently in his dreams. On his twenty-first birthday, he dreamt I was pregnant, and I invited him into my home where my husband was looking after a little boy of Kevin's age when his father died. I cooked them a delicious dinner. Although the level of idealization was apparent, this dream heralded a shift towards the restoration of good internal resources which could nurture and sustain him.

Kevin continued to struggle with the destructive elements in his personality, but over the years he became increasingly able to sustain feelings of attachment, regard and love. He enjoyed his first proper relationships with women, held down a job and was promoted to a responsible position, and became capable of genuine human emotion. He knew he needed to remain in four times weekly therapy until his internal resources were securely established, even though he did not like the expense or the restrictions psychotherapy imposed on his life.

Some post-Kleinian theorists developed Rosenfeld's concept of an internal gang or mafia-like constellation at the core of destructive narcissism. Meltzer (1973) incorporated destructive narcissism into a model of perversion in which a cynical spoiling aspect of self gains dominance over libidinal, dependent tendencies (see Chapters 4 and 6). Steiner (1993) elaborated Rosenfeld's theory into a range of 'pathological organizations' which may protect from more overt disintegration and breakdown, but by the same token pre-empt development into more depressive areas (see Chapter 4). Britton (2003) distinguished between forms of libidinal narcissism as a necessary safeguard where there has been a failure of parental containment, and more rigid forms of narcissistic organization where parenting has not been obviously disturbed but there is '. . . an excess of object-hostility in the infant' (ibid.: 164).

Comparative Lacanian approaches

Although Lacanians do not work with a clinical concept of narcissism, in the form of the 'mirror stage' it plays an important ontological role as the basis of ego formation (Lacan 1949, 1953–4) (see Chapter 3). For Lacan, narcissism derived from the realm of generating experience he described as the 'imaginary' (Lacan 1949, 1953–4) and is present in all of us as the ego is an imaginary function serving (imaginary) mastery (Libbrecht 2001). Aggressivity is always a correlative of narcissistic identification—hence its predominance in paranoid disorders (Lacan 1948 [2001]: 18). Analysts may adopt an imaginary position in relation to their clients, and transference/countertransference difficulties and mistaken diagnoses can ensue (Lacan 1953–4; Nobus 2000: 147).

For Lacan, the ego is an instrument of '*méconnaissance*' (misrecognition): the sense of integrity it assumes is illusory. He considered it a problem and a barrier in analysis, and did not deem its strengthening to be a goal. He criticized the 'ego psychologists' repeatedly for conducting analyses on the basis of a requirement that analysands form an imaginary identification with their analyst.

We are all internally riven in Lacanian theory. There is no distinction between a narcissistic ego and an object-related one since the ego is always based on imaginary identifications. This perspective lends an interesting dimension to other discussions of narcissism, which traditionally assume a contrast between narcissistic modes of (non)relating and the ability to form object relations, eventually leading to a mature genital relationship which Lacan considered a fiction (Lacan 1954–5). He thought that we all need to recognize lack and symbolic castration in order to begin the journey of 'subjectification' and ownership of our desire. This view may seem to stand in inverse relation to the Kleinian insistence on the need for internal dependence on securely established 'good' objects and a benign parental couple.

Severe narcissistic disturbance, as defined by Kleinian and Independent theorists, would probably be classified as psychotic within Lacanian differential diagnosis. As the symbolic father cannot be recognized, paternal function is apprehended on the imaginary plane and is not inscribed in any triangular dialectic (Lacan 1955–6 [1993]: 204). Therefore a truly Other point of view cannot be borne and the analyst's positioning in the transference has to be that of an imaginary other. This poses a clinical dilemma. Within most other contemporary perspectives, narcissistic structures can slowly, and with long, painstaking and difficult work, be transformed into better internal resources and a capacity to recognize difference. For Lacanians, a psychotic structure can only be maintained, more strongly buttressed and enabled to function without breakdown (as discussed in Chapter 6).

Relatively recently, Jacques-Alain Miller (1996) argued that the concepts of perversion and narcissism are linked in some women who have difficulty distinguishing themselves from the Other.[2] I think there could be parallels for both sexes, and an exchange of views between the different approaches, such as the debate about borderlinity (Gurewich *et al.* 1999), could prove fruitful. A perspective in which theories of perversion and narcissism were not reductively synthesized but harnessed to supplement each other could furnish fresh insight into both these forms of disturbance. For Lacanians, the analytic task in perversion is to manoeuvre the transference so that the analyst can become the cause and object of the perverse analysand's desire, as opposed to the pervert's remaining, in fantasy, the imaginary phallus. This formulation, discussed in Chapters 6 and 7, has some bearing on therapy with patients classified as narcissistic by other psychoanalytic schools, in that a long-term goal is for the analyst to be perceived as a separate, differentiated person who is needed and related to.

Two pluralist approaches: Joyce McDougall and André Green

Although neither are Lacanians, both McDougall (1978) and Green (1988) incorporate some Lacanian insights into their work on narcissism, whilst also drawing from Independent and post-Kleinian theory.

McDougall succeeds in weaving between Lacanian concepts of perversion and theories of narcissistic organization influenced by some post-Kleinians, Kohut and Winnicott. She sees some narcissistic organizations as a response to object loss and a defence against overwhelming and unbearable need, such that a person might feel threatened by being swamped by close interaction. Others may be in search of a perfect illusion of fusion as a confirmation of their existence and a defence against an acute terror of separation (McDougall 1978).

Green (1988) argues that primary narcissism must be understood as a structure and '. . . the Desire of One under the trace of the Other' (Etchegoyen 1999: xii). Like Rosenfeld (1971), Green sees the death instinct at work in negative narcissism '. . . in which excitation tends towards zero' (Green 1988 [2001]: 26). This form of radical decathexis is related to Green's concept of 'blank psychosis', where a delusional neo-reality of 'zero object' is inscribed through the destructive work of the negative: 'The ultimate aim of narcissism is the obliteration of the trace of the Other in one's desire, therefore the abolition of the primary difference, the difference between One and the Other' (ibid.: 149) (see also Chapter 2). Green's narcissism is an empty bleak place: 'Narcissistic wholeness is not a sign of health but a mirage of death' (ibid.: 149). His 'moral narcissist' is closely related to the intellectual narcissist: in both, infantile megalomania is tied to the ego ideal. A moral narcissist is in retreat from the shame of being nothing more than he is. He makes himself into a sacrificial object and uses '. . . morality as a crutch in order to free [himself] from the vicissitudes involved in the tie to the object' (ibid.: 145).

Narcissism as existential choice

Until Symington's *Narcissism – a new theory* (1993), Kohut, Kernberg and Rosenfeld's theories represented the chief polarities around which debates about narcissism waged. Symington's work can most easily be criticized as too sanguine, as making the relinquishing of a narcissistic option sound too simple, but it did, nonetheless, add a new dimension to understanding narcissistic phenomena. Some of his concepts are radical and require a revision of the field; others are a restating in helpfully bold and precise form of some insights of other theorists, including Freud and Rosenfeld.

In brief, Symington posits narcissism as an existential choice. A narcissistic option will, of course, be precipitated by an external trauma, or more likely cumulative trauma (Khan 1964), but unless a child's spirit is completely broken, Symington upholds that she has, at a deep unconscious level, a choice. As turning away from the other is a choice, it can be reversed. Symington contends life offers everyone several opportunities to reverse the choice of the apparent safety of a narcissistic cocoon and opt for what he conceptualizes as 'the lifegiver'. These opportunities could include an exceptional relationship or set of circumstances which provide both security and an opportunity for regressive transformation, hitting 'rock bottom', and of course psychoanalysis or psychotherapy. However, Symington fails to investigate the lengthy, painstaking level of emotional containment and the analysis of complex, circuitous defences needed with a narcissistic patient.

The lifegiver, a complicated concept, is a psychic object which only comes into being at the moment at which it is chosen. It is neither self nor other but also both:

> It is a psychic object located in relation to a breast, a penis, a vagina, the self, the analyst, or the therapist. While it is not any one of these primary objects of fertilization or nurture in itself, it has no existence apart from them.
>
> (Symington 1993: 35)

Opting for the lifegiver is an existential opening to life at a very deep level, implying trust in the unknown and a leap of faith. With this concept, Symington unites an ability to relate to another in an open, trusting way, and access to an internal source of autonomous creativity and spontaneous action. As Grotstein (1993) observes, we make an unconscious choice either towards the lifegiver (its authenticity or spontaneity) or towards its disavowal through the use of magical pretence in order to evade psychic reality and to avoid external reality.

Symington sees narcissism as a radical turning away from both relatedness to others and from the deepest sources of life and autonomous thought and action in the self. He thinks there are many parallels between narcissism and autism, particularly in the way described by Frances Tustin (1972, 1981, 1990). Tustin thought autism arose from premature violation of the symbiotic bond between mother and child, and patients in whom there is an autistic area noticeably take 'the easy way out'—they do not fight or struggle. Both constitute an opting out of interdependency, and for a manipulative, parasitic relationship in which the object may be seduced and controlled to permit the autistic or narcissistic subject to remain omnipotent and protectively encapsulated. Symington sees this as an unconscious choice between aliveness and deadening, between openness and foreclosure. He posits a level of perverse excitement generated by killing and self-killing.

There is no narcissism without self-hatred (Symington 1993).

Symington claims narcissism is the source of all pathology. At one level, there is nothing new in this startling formulation. Freud said this, more or less, when he asserted that narcissism was the divide between the neuroses and the psychoses. Symington illustrates his contention with the example of 'the cauliflower man', a patient he was in the habit of letting run over time. One day he stopped him in mid-flow. There was no apparent reaction but the next day 'the cauliflower man' arrived fifteen minutes late because he had been buying a cauliflower at the request of his wife. Symington shows how this patient cut himself off in an instant from any emotional response to his session being ended summarily:

> Frustrated and hurt, his response was to cut off inwardly—a much more serious cutting off. When he cut himself off inwardly he killed something in himself . . . a psychic killing generates excitement and gives motivational energy, but the autonomous source feels hopeless.
>
> (ibid.: 117)

The cauliflower man then relied on the 'discordant source', false feelings were substituted for true feelings, and he projected the killer into his wife. The discordant source, according to Symington, paralyzes the autonomous source; it detaches feelings from their true locus and attaches them to the exact reverse; it falsifies judgement; it splits intellect from feeling and enslaves reason to the discordant source—a process called rationalization; it expels a psychic constellation from inside the mind into an outer figure, thereby impoverishing the mind; it implodes an outer object into the inner constellation. The cauliflower man's feelings were cut off from his intellect, his knowledge of his own action was eradicated, he propelled a part of his functioning into his wife, and he seriously reduced the power of his own creative autonomous action. When a situation such as this is intensified by a certain magnitude, Symington claims, schizophrenia could be the result.

So is narcissism the basis of all pathology? Post-Kleinians concur and contemporary Independents afford narcissism a special position within psychopathology. Lacanians privilege the role of narcissism in developmental terms and see it clinically as a problem for all of us. Interestingly, all psychoanalytic models of development and growth, including the Lacanian one, describe or imply movements away from narcissism.

NOTES

1. See also Fairbairn's (1952) theorization of narcissistic factors in schizoid personalities.
2. For a discussion of Lacanian theories of perversion, see Chapter 6.

Structures of psychopathology

As we saw in Chapter 5, many psychoanalysts today consider narcissism the divide between neurosis and deep structures of psychopathology, potentially vulnerable to breakdown. Lacanians, however, conceive of perversion as a structure between neurosis and psychosis (explored in detail later in this chapter). Levels of psychopathology are often thought abou᷑ in terms of degrees of internal separation from the primary other (or Othᶜr). A capacity to symbolize experience and to 'triangulate', or look at thinɡs from a perspective other than one's own, is established in inverse proportion to the severity of disturbance.

Differential diagnosis is a vexed and controversial area within psychoanalysis. Unlike psychiatric nosology, it is not always a primary clinical tool—although most contemporary psychoanalysts work with a cautious hypothesis of their client's psychopathology. Bollas (in Molino (ed.) 1997) suggests we remember that many profound differences between people cannot be accounted for by psychoanalytic psychodiagnostics. Depth and intensity of object-usage, for example, can cut across forms of psychopathology, although generally narrower and with fewer evocative, generative experiences in illness (ibid.: 28). Nonetheless, diagnostic guidelines are necessary to avoid dangerous pitfalls such as treating a narcissistic patient as if she were neurotic: she might need an extended period of idealization, for example. Equally tricky would be approaching a perverse client as if he were borderline. A perverse struggle with symbolization may sometimes seem similar to the borderline tendency to switch to another state of mind when emotionally threatened, and both perverse and borderline patients tend to feel taken over by their therapist at times, but these phenomena stem from different underlying causes, and require different levels of interpretation and management (explored later in this chapter).

To avoid dehumanizing the patient, many clinicians find a rolling diagnosis or a discrimination between different states of mind and being preferable to a fixed hypothesis. Areas of complexity and overlap always exist. An element of improbable surprise, often the hallmark of a lively psychoanalytic therapy, can explode a diagnostic presupposition.

For example, my patient, 'Ewan' (described in Chapter 4), relied so heavily on projective and evacuative mechanisms that he could easily have been (mis)taken for borderline or narcissistic. However, his ability to take a tough interpretation on the chin without emotional reaction, and his capacity to make use of such interpretations so that they radically altered his state of being even though they sometimes needed to be repeated many times, suggested instead a deficit in maternal containment.

Contemporary psychoanalytic models of an ability to change and move on describe fluid processes, open to the recognition and use of difference, and the acceptance of lack, limitation and desire which will never be fully gratified (see Chapter 9). Contemporary theorizations of psychopathology are rooted in concepts of blockages or restrictions to growth and/or in developmental processes in reverse—for example Bion's views on psychopathology constitute the opposite of the evolution of mind (see Chapter 4). Although entrenched defences and forms of character pathology are necessary for psychic survival when there has been privation or abuse in childhood, they inhibit a fully engaged life and may render a client vulnerable to breakdown or illness. Underlying structural psychopathology makes the process of therapy difficult and arduous for both parties: the painstaking work of containing and sorting the anxieties defended against, or holding and managing the regression essential to the facilitation of new forms of growth, demand skill, knowledge, patience, endurance and intuition. In this chapter, I will discuss the diagnostic possibilities of psychosis, psychosomatosis, borderlinity, perversion and neurosis. A limitation of this book is the omission of the autistic spectrum.

Lacanians work with a clearly defined system of psychopathology. Following Freud but involving new linguistically based accounts of aetiology, Lacan (1953–4, 1955–6) theorized the three primary structural categories as psychosis, perversion and neurosis. Neurosis was further subdivided into hysteria, obsessionality and phobia. Post-Kleinians believe there are psychotic areas in everyone's personality and that intransigent narcissistic structures of various forms underlie severe psychopathology (Bion 1957; Rosenfeld 1971; Steiner 1993). On the whole, contemporary Independents use less systematic accounts of psychopathology but distinguish between different treatment approaches for patients with disturbances of the self (or character pathology) and neurotic patients. Bollas (1987, 1989), Ogden (1989a) and McDougall (1978, 1989) introduced new distinctions in psychopathology, and Khan (1979) refined the diagnosis and treatment of perversion.[1] Independents emphasize areas of health and creativity within psychopathology. Bollas, for example, differentiates between the very disturbed Sylvia Plath's profound relationship to her cultural objects and other borderline personalities who may have 'dead souls' (Bollas in Molino (ed.) 1997: 24–5).

I will now consider the various concepts of psychopathology from a comparative contemporary perspective.

PSYCHOSIS

Lacanians conceive of psychosis as a failure to recognize lack and separate from the Other. The Name of the Father is foreclosed and no negotiation of symbolic castration or symbolic Oedipal process is possible. Hence, the psychotic patient does not enter the Law and language in the same way as the neurotic patient. Consequently (and terrifyingly), he is not internally divided, has no unconscious as such and his relationship to language is always disturbed. Intense paranoia is usually an attempt to bring the Other into existence as a separate entity (Lacan 1955–6).

Lacan's theorizations of psychosis changed over the course of his long career. He began work as a psychiatrist with the criminally insane. His doctoral thesis focused on a novelist, 'Aimée', who had tried to stab a well-known actress (Lacan 1932). Lacan interpreted this as a paranoid attack on an ego ideal, resulting in a psychosis of self-punishment and of the super-ego. More than twenty years later, he revised Freud's theory of psychosis in the Schreber case (Lacan 1955–6). Freud (1911b) interpreted Schreber's delusions as the product of the denial of his homosexual feelings. Lacan prioritized the mechanism of foreclosure (*Verwerfung*) and saw it as a refusal of the primary (paternal) metaphor, resulting in a failure to enter the symbolic realm through language and a return of the foreclosed elements in the 'real' as hallucination.[2]

Twenty years after that, Lacan reconsidered the implications of a psychotic structure, using James Joyce as his model (Lacan 1975–6).[3] He thought Joyce's writing constituted in a topological sense a 'symptom' ('*sinthome*'—saint man; '*synthomme*'—synthetic/self-creating man), a fourth potential ring of the Borromean knot but one which constantly threatens to come undone and thereby undo the entire structure (Thurston 1996).[4] In psychosis, in place of the paternal metaphor, a delusional metaphor is constructed in the imaginary realm. This 'suppletion'[5] can bind the subject if it is not challenged by an Other, opposing point of view. Suppletion can take the form of creativity or psychosomatic illness, which buttress the delusional metaphor. Joyce's 'epiphanies' (sudden spiritual manifestations), for example, transformed unmetabolized experience into delusional certainty (Joyce 1916, 1929, 1939; Grigg 1998).

After an early age an underlying psychotic structure cannot be changed, even though the person may never break down (Fink 1997). Therefore, in analysis the primary task becomes the strengthening of the delusional metaphor in order to improve the ability of the psychotic person to function. Lacan (1975–6) thought many psychotic people were capable of making important scientific or artistic contributions. However, symbolic function is 'imaginarized' in psychosis (Fink 1997): instead of being assimilated as a radically different order which restructures imaginary functioning, it is imitated from other people. The metaphorical use of language is not available to psychotic people due to this failure of the primary signifier, the paternal metaphor (Lacan 1955–6). In analysis, if the Name-of-the-Father is '. . . called into symbolic opposition to the subject' (Lacan 1957–8b [2001]: 240), the psychotic person will break down. There is no space for a symbolic Other within the delusional metaphor, as paternal function '. . . isn't inscribed in any triangular dialectic' (Lacan 1955–6 [1993]: 204). These insights support Britton's (1998) thesis that triangulation or the introduction of another point of view in work with borderline patients may be experienced as malignant misunderstanding and can trigger paranoia or even a psychotic break. They also accord with the importance of narrative emphasized by Schafer (1981) and Spence (1982), and with some psychiatric research which found that schizophrenic patients who have elaborated their delusional systems to interpret their psychotic symptoms function better than those for whom this is not the case (Roberts 1992).

Russell Grigg emphasizes Lacan's description of Schreber's symptoms as 'transsexual' (Grigg 1998: 55). Schreber, in a state between sleeping and waking, had 'the notion that it must really be a rather nice thing to be a woman undergoing intercourse' (Freud 1911b [2002]: 6). The foreclosure of the Name-of-the-Father results in an absence of 'phallic meaning', the symbolic phallus being the signifier of the possibility of lack on which sexuation is founded. Lacan thought transsexualism in psychosis was linked with a demand for the missing endorsement from the father: it is a symptom rather than a determinant (Lacan 1957–8b [2001]: 210). In *Horsexe* (1983) Catherine Millot argues that it is vital for clinicians to discern whether there is an underlying psychotic structure in people who request transsexual surgery, lest the surgery itself precipitate a psychotic break.

Bion also correlated psychotic structure with failure to negotiate Oedipal triangulation, and its Kleinian concomitant, the depressive position. Despite their obverse paradigmatic contexts, there is a clear correlation here with Lacanian theory. But whilst Lacan emphasized the linguistic, Bion focused on the destructive aspects of this impasse: they both stressed the damage to symbolic function and verbal capacity. Bion thought an excessively cruel superego renders the entry into depressive processes too difficult for some people (Bion 1967, 1992), an idea Riviere (1936) described as a betrayal of the superego through happiness. Bion linked this form of superego with Oedipus' arrogant quest after the truth at any price: the combination of

stupidity, arrogance and curiosity were hallmarks of the psychotic personality (Bion 1967). Bion, like Klein and most other Kleinian theorists,
characterized psychotic processes as excessive and ever-increasing splitting
and projective identification, fuelled by high levels of envy and destructive
aggression. His core concept, 'attacks on linking' (Bion 1959) (discussed in
Chapter 4), described the tendency of the psychotic part of the personality to
aim at the destruction of all unifying functions, internal and external, hence
preventing verbal thought through *alpha* function. These processes can
ultimately result in 'bizarre objects' and 'dream furniture', or a nightmarish
engulfment ensuing from evacuation of fragmented aspects of the self (Bion
1967). Lacan's account of the way what has been foreclosed from the
symbolic returns in the real as hallucination is a description of the same
phenomena from a linguistic and structural perspective (Lacan 1955–6,
1957–8b).

Many other Kleinian theorists published accounts of work with psychotic
patients (for example Segal 1950; Rosenfeld 1965; Rey 1994; O'Shaunessy
1992). Rey (1979) described claustro-agoraphobic mechanisms in psychotic
and borderline patients for whom intimate relationships, whether erotic or
psychotherapeutic, spell merger and intense paranoia resulting from lack of
separation/individuation and consequent confusion of their savage, persecutory internal worlds with another person. Meltzer's (1992) 'claustrum'
depicted the end result of projective identification inside phantasied compartments of the internal mother and is another version of a nightmarish
persecutory internal world. (Rey and Meltzer's work in this area is discussed in Chapter 4.)

In tune with the Kleinian emphasis on constitutionally high levels of
destructive aggression, and Freudian accounts of the defusion of the life
and death instincts in severe psychopathology, North American 'Moderns'
emphasize the role of unbound destructiveness in illness (Spotnitz 1976,
1985; Meadow 2003). Meadow cites a case of a schizophrenic patient whose
symptoms improved dramatically when he became an avid bowler. They
stress the importance of not merely seeking discharge for destructiveness
but outlets through which hostile impulses can be fused with libidinal
drives, claiming that otherwise illness, sadism and war may be the result.

Recent Independent theorists work with less systematic theories of
extreme disturbance and offer fewer accounts of work with psychotic
patients, with the very major exceptions of Milner (1969) and Searles
(1965). Independents focus more frequently on forms of 'character
pathology', or entrenched defences against disturbance, than on psychosis
per se. Winnicott (1960) thought a 'false self' covered states of fragmentation, and when held in a sufficiently adaptive psychoanalytic environment, recovery might occur spontaneously through the gradual coalescence
of maturational processes (Winnicott 1954b). An adaptive psychological
environment involves complex and lengthy psychoanalytic work—either

high-frequency (four or five times weekly) psychoanalysis or an informed and specifically adapted institutional setting (White *et al.* 2001).

Potentially a dangerous idea in the wrong hands, Winnicott's observation runs the risk of making the treatment of psychotic illness sound too sanguine: like Symington's (1993) opting for 'the lifegiver' (see Chapter 5), we are left with a notion that something may or may not happen fortuitously. Although the Independent emphasis on the possibility of redressing early environmental failure in analysis and the unpredictability of much of what happens is necessary, the arduous nature of work with psychotic disturbance is addressed in the rigour of post-Kleinian and Lacanian theory.

In Milner's detailed account of her work with a schizophrenic patient referred to her by Winnicott, she described the step-by-step process of going '. . . to pieces in order to come together in a new way' (Milner 1969: 59). Over sixteen years of five times weekly work, Milner showed how a patient, who had '. . . lost her soul' (ibid.: xix) and maintained that neither she nor her analyst existed, came to revisit a fusional dependence she had first experienced with her psychotic mother, but this time without being driven mad. Her patient re-experienced the '. . . ground of her being' (ibid.: 410), represented in her drawings of a coiled serpent and coiled shell, from which she gradually emerged in pictorial form as a baby seal. Eventually, she came to feel fully alive for the first time (see also Chapter 2).

Searles (1965) published some of the most extensive, humane, honest and funny accounts of work with psychotic clients. I will restrict myself to two of his central theses here (further discussion of Searles' ideas on the treatment of psychosis can be found in Chapter 7). Prefiguring R.D. Laing (Laing 1961; Laing and Esterson 1964), he contends that some people are driven mad as the 'carriers' of psychotic disturbance for a parent or an entire family (Searles 1959a), and demonstrates how these dynamics can be revisited in psychotherapy (Searles 1958). The schizophrenic person may experience a therapist's unconscious processes as an aspect of himself and express them in hallucinations, vituperative outbursts and/or acting out. If the analyst is not scrupulous in monitoring her countertransference, she will increase her patient's disturbance by unwittingly forcing him to carry her dissociated feelings.

Both these factors applied in the therapy of the patient described in Chapters 2 and 4 as 'Patrice'. His family were not obviously disturbed. His parents were hard-working, decent people. They regarded themselves, as Patrice later graphically described it, as 'psychologically squeaky clean'. All their issues and conflicts about their 'blackness' and immigrant status were unconsciously located in Patrice, the oldest of their five children, the most sensitive and rebellious, and the blackest member of his family.

These dynamics were recapitulated in Patrice's therapy when I discovered, to my horror, that my fear of him was not just related to his violent threats against my person but to the fact that he was black. When I finally recognized my own participation in a psychosocial mechanism in which violence, rage and disturbance may become projected into black people, the level of Patrice's disturbance and threats subsided significantly (White 1989).

Adam Limentani (1979) emphasized possible transsexual aspects of psychotic illness in (unacknowledged) accordance with the Lacanian view that psychotic illness involves a very early disturbance of symbol formation as a possible consequence of intrusive or absent (inappropriate) paternal influence and an identificatory fusion with a phallic mother, which can result in a confused sense of gender. A note of caution is needed here. Butler (1990) demonstrates how the laws of gender we take for granted as natural are part of a social construct in which existing norms of gender are imposed at some psychological cost. Some Independent theorists (Ogden 1987, 1989b; Benjamin 1995, 1998) show how a fluid and complex acquisition of a sense of gender can enable less constricted lives and relationships. Whilst a transsexual dimension may be part of severe disturbance, this recognition must be set within a sophisticated understanding of gender acquisition and enactment.

PSYCHOSOMATIC ILLNESS OR 'PSYCHOSOMATOSIS'

Lacan (1975–6) noted that psychosomatic illness might constitute one form of 'suppletion' of a psychotic structure and, using a different conceptual framework, so did Bion (1961) and Meltzer (1986). In his work on groups, Bion postulated the existence of 'proto-mental phenomena' or deeply unconscious matrices in which the physical and psychological are not yet differentiated (Bion 1961: 101). Meltzer developed this 'proto-mental apparatus' to include 'soma-psychotic phenomena' (Meltzer 1986: 38–49). Extending Rosenfeld's (1971) concept of deeply pathological internal organizations, Meltzer posited a proto-mental 'establishment', connected to the immunological system, through which physical illness might develop as a response to the threat of change or disruption of the organization (Meltzer 1986: 39). In Bion's terms, one route for the evacuation of *beta* elements could be through the body.

Referring to Lacan, Bion, Klein, Mahler, Winnicott, Kohut and Ogden, McDougall (1989) expounds a comprehensive theory of psychosomatic disturbance as a pre-symbolic form of mind/body expression. 'Psycho-somatosis' should not be confused with post-symbolic conversion hysteria (discussed later under 'neurosis'). McDougall draws from the Paris psycho-somaticians, Marty, de M'uzan and David (1963a, 1963b), who formulated an economic theory of psychosomatic transformation and a psychosomatic personality structure. The newly termed 'psychosomatosis' involves lack of symbolic representation of instinctual conflict or affect, or 'alexithymia' (Nemiah 1978), and impoverished use of language and 'operatory', or pragmatic and concrete, thinking.

> McDougall gives an example from a patient who had injured a mother and child in a car accident. When asked 'Were you upset when you ran over the woman with the baby?', she replied 'Oh, I was insured against third party accident.'
>
> (McDougall 1978 [1990]: 360)

The psychosomatic mode of functioning is archaic. Pre-symbolic and pre-verbal, it harks from a primitive stage of development in which neither mother and baby nor mind and body are experienced as separate. The 'desomatization' of psyche depends on the introjection of a benign and soothing maternal environment which can contain and process primitive affect. When this is disturbed for some reason, the person may function in a psychosomatic fashion in adult life, and this may include, at times of stress, a lowering of immunological barriers.

> A clinical example comes from a patient I call 'Tracy', married for twenty years to a man who was a friend but not her lover for over a decade. She had previously contemplated leaving her husband for a man she was deeply in love with, but she had suffered a mild stroke. Although this was successfully treated, she abandoned her plans to go, and remained in an unsatisfactory and fictive relationship.
>
> Tracy was extremely deprived. From a working class background, she had been the youngest of eight children of a loveless and violent marriage. Several of her siblings were more obviously disturbed. After a period of intensive therapy in which she regressed to dependence and was able to work through confused and claustrophobic aspects of her internal world, Tracy became more able to bear and articulate her own feelings. Eventually, she fell in love again, and this time she and her partner decided to emigrate to Lanzarote and

set up a bar. Although Tracy's entire family were aghast and punitive, they eventually forgave her and became able to move on in life themselves. She suffered no further strokes and seemed to be extremely happy.

The 'Moderns' conceive of psychosomatic manifestations as the result of the inhibition of destructive impulses, a product of a struggle with conflicting drive tendencies. They claim that health can be built through actions which integrate both sets of impulses, a difficult and precarious achievement. Meadow states in forthright fashion: 'It is easier to die than live' (Meadow 2003: 65).

BORDERLINITY

'Borderline Personality Disorder' is a particularly controversial diagnostic category. Some have argued that within psychiatry, at least, clinicians tend to define the clients they find most difficult to work with as borderline (e.g. Ramon *et al.* 2001). Within psychoanalysis, borderline states have been extensively theorized as a specific and volatile syndrome suffered by those, often from severely abusive backgrounds, whose struggle to survive has necessitated the dissociation of traumatic experiences with their corresponding self states.

Borderline states in psychoanalysis are usually conceptualized structurally as fragmented forms of narcissism and standing between psychosis and neurosis (Kernberg 1975). Dissociated self states may consist in '. . . archipelagos . . . delineated by void space' (Green 1977a [1997]: 78). Whilst people who are borderline may be vulnerable to psychotic breakdown, the degree of internal fragmentation may be covered by a 'false self' personality organization (Winnicott 1960). Winnicott saw this as a '. . . *freezing of the failure situation*' (Rayner 1991: 192, his emphases). Recent Independent theorists have theorized entrenched character pathology as a defence against further fragmentation (Bollas 1989), whilst some contemporary Freudians argue for an 'as if' personality which creates a new self-representation to avoid dissonance and panic (Sandler and Sandler 1998).

For Lacanians, those described as borderline in other psychoanalytic theories would probably fall into the category of the psychotic. This lacuna, like the lack of a clinical concept of narcissism, reveals a limitation of Lacanian theory, as clinical accounts elsewhere show how it is possible to effect profound structural change through slow, painstaking and informed work with borderline patients (Kernberg 1975; Searles 1986b; White *et al.* 2001). Post-Kleinian and contemporary Independent thinking on borderline disturbance encompasses a temperament or trauma, nature or nurture debate, in their respective treatment approaches as well as their theories of aetiology.

Both these schools agree that within borderline disturbance there is insufficient ego or thoughtful process to contain and symbolize intolerable levels of anxiety or affect, with a consequent shifting of self-states (A. Ryle 1995), or sudden and sometimes dramatic changes in affect with little or no conscious connection to the previous state of mind. For example, someone in whom a dangerously angry outburst has been triggered by an event or remark reminding them of previous abuse may be oblivious to the fact that earlier the same day they were feeling elated or optimistic. Feelings of fragmentation or difficulty in retaining a coherent sense of self may result in resorting to drugs, perverse or obsessional behaviours and/or self-abuse to bind a sense of self and as protection from excessive panic. The borderline client can therefore be impulsive, unpredictable and prone to acting out, but despite all this, they are commonly experienced as creative, interesting, warm, direct and rewarding to work with (Searles 1986b; White *et al.* 2001).

Contemporary Independents, following Winnicott, conceive of borderline disturbance as the product of traumatic abuse, intolerable deprivation, tantalization, intrusiveness or a premature requirement that the baby adapt to the mother. Green describes Winnicott as '*the analyst of the borderline*', meaning that Winnicott's innovations in technique and the use of the analytic setting as a containing environment are necessary treatment approaches (as discussed in Chapters 2 and 8) (Green 1977a [1997]: 68, his emphases). Green's concept of archipelagos of more-or-less reality-oriented functioning surrounded by terrifying void space accounts for the pervasive sense of futility and the capacity for rapid and radical decathexis of the borderline patient (ibid.).

Bollas refines various forms of borderline character pathology as 'normotic illness' (1987), 'ghostline personality' and the 'anti-narcissist' (1989). In normotic illness a person achieves a superficial coherence through the adhesive cathexes of material objects or certain kinds of 'lifestyle' which can be 'bought' within a consumer society. They may become addicted to material acquisition, sports, gym or running, routine or certain kinds of institutions, or even alcohol or other drugs. Corporate man can easily subsist in this way. What is missing is a subjective sense of self or deep emotional cathexis of objects, interpersonal or cultural, and intense experience. The ghostline personality structure is schizoid, and masks a profound lack of subjective or potential space. In this constellation, objects are 'appropriated' in a lifeless way to construct an alternative inner world devoid of meaning or deep cathexis of others. The 'as-if' existence of the 'ghostline personality' bypasses the demands of the external world or relationships, external and internal. The anti-narcissist enviously attacks libidinal or 'true self' cathexes, internal and external, and makes a cult out of his own disguised cruelty, defeat of others' investment in him and refusal of life. This latter constellation describes one possible incarnation of Rosenfeld's (1971) 'destructive narcissist' (discussed in Chapter 5).

Kernberg (1975) theorizes 'borderline personality organization' as a form of ego pathology, whose splitting originated in primary process in early infancy. In consequence a 'transference psychosis' may arise, and require specific forms of analytic management (see Chapter 7). Kernberg argues such patients may present with chronic and diffuse anxiety, multiple phobias, a tendency to hypochondria and paranoid and polymorphously perverse sexual trends. He focuses on their lacks—of differentiation of self and object images, of anxiety tolerance, of impulse control and *developed sublimatory channels*' (ibid.: 23, his emphases). He posits that contradictory ego states are alternately activated as a means to avoid anxiety and there is a chronic tendency to eruption of primitive affect. Capacity for concern and realistic guilt are usually deficient, but the prognosis is better when these exist in embryonic form.

Post-Kleinians emphasize constitutional levels of envy and destructive aggression in the aetiology of borderline disturbance, and make little reference to environmental factors such as maternal deprivation or sexual abuse. They theorize borderlinity as deeply fragmented forms of narcissism, and focus on the more destructive aspects of this syndrome and the analytic difficulties or impasses which may arise (also discussed in Chapters 4, 5 and 8). Rosenfeld (1965) linked the tendency to act out with excessively aggressive turning away from the earliest object and heightened levels of paranoid anxiety. He emphasized destructive and violent levels of projective identification in borderline patients (Rosenfeld 1987), and both he and Bion (1967) stressed the difficulty in maintaining a capacity to think with these clients. Rey (1979) described the spatial dimension of lack of self/object differentiation: the way the self is experienced in unconscious phantasy to reside inside an object, internal or external, and consequent claustro-agoraphobic dynamics and dilemmas. Both Rey (1994) and Steiner (1993) highlight the negativity and destructiveness of the borderline analysand, and their problems with revenge, guilt and forgiveness. Britton relates the borderline syndrome to Rosenfeld's concept of thin-skinned narcissism, in which the transference is 'adherent' and the analyst's psychic space 'colonized'—another version of a claustro-agoraphobic scenario (Britton 2003: 147).

To illustrate the borderline syndrome, I will cite some features of a case I supervised.[6] 'Angela' was born to a sixteen-year-old mother in a third-world country ravaged by war. Her parents broke up when she was two, and she saw her father sporadically at unpredictable intervals after that. Her mother told her she was not wanted and she was passed around the families of various relatives. In one of these, she suffered a rape at age twelve from her uncle. She left home at sixteen and feigned independence but was in fact very dependent on a series of abusive relationships. When these broke down, she often took overdoses but was always found in time to have her stomach pumped.

She was referred to a low-fee psychotherapy scheme by her GP after she had taken a very serious overdose, precipitated by a friend's being out when she went to visit. In therapy she presented as an attractive compliant girl but her volatility rapidly became apparent. Her emotional pattern—idealization followed by intense paranoia and flight—was enacted in several jobs and in her therapy. Moments of closeness and understanding would result in high anxiety and retreat. She missed huge numbers of sessions intermittently, and behaved in a high-handed and omnipotent fashion, demanding changes of times at short notice and frequently not paying her bill. She was, of course, terrified of both closeness and rejection. She tested her psychotherapist's ability to contain her to the limit. Her psychotherapist's countertransference was as volatile and frightened as Angela herself. In uncharacteristic fashion, she sometimes felt that she must telephone Angela immediately and give her whatever she was demanding, lest she take another overdose.

Angela also challenged the containment she received from her therapist's contact with her GP. She moved to a different area and did not re-register for several months. When eventually she found a new GP, she complained to him about her psychotherapy and succeeded in manipulating him into advising her to finish it. Her psychotherapist never knew what to expect when she saw her, but over time learned to recognize her manic and paranoid swings and to time interpretations and phrase them in such a way so as not to exacerbate Angela's paranoia.

Despite these apparently unpromising circumstances, Angela remained in treatment for three years and there were marked therapeutic gains. She became able to attend more of her sessions and developed some capacity for insight. Her moods and employment stabilized to some extent.

PERVERSION

Within contemporary psychoanalysis 'perversion' denotes a specific structuration of subjectivity, not necessarily involving 'perverse' sexual practices. 'Perversion', in my use of the term, never implies homosexuality, although some homosexuals and many heterosexuals may have a perverse structure. Most psychoanalysts today concur there are homosexual and heterosexual components in all sexuality, whether or not these are repressed in practice.

Contemporary Lacanians present accounts of the aetiology and dynamics of a perverse structure following Lacan's expositions in *Seminars IV* (1956–7) and *V* (1957–8a). Lacan separated perverse structure from sexual practice: 'What is perversion? It is not . . . an atypicality according to natural criteria, namely that it more or less derogates from the reproductive finality of the sexual union. It is something else in its very structure' (Lacan 1953–4 [1991]: 221). Gurewich (2003) underlines this distinction: '. . . Lacan's return to Freud has allowed the structure of perversion to emerge not as a form of sexual aberration . . . but as a form of psychic functioning that can be traced back to the vicissitudes of the Oedipus Complex' (ibid.: 192).

Lacan thought the 'pervert' remains enmeshed at an early stage of the Oedipus Complex (Lacan 1957–8a; Dor 1985):[7] he identifies with the imaginary phallus—in fantasy the sole object of the (m)Other's desire (Lacan 1956–7). He has undergone alienation but not separation and refuses the paternal metaphor (the Name of the Father), with consequent implications for symbolization. The critical question for the 'pervert' then becomes whether or not to *be* the imaginary phallus, in contradistinction from the neurotic whose issue is whether or not to *have* the phallus in a symbolic sense (Lacan 1957–8a; Dor 2001).[8] As he has only incompletely entered the symbolic order, perverse fantasy involves being the object of the Other's *jouissance*: the Other is still experienced as omnipotent (not subject to lack) (Lacan 1960). This is the converse of a neurotic structure of fantasy in which there is an unconscious attempt to make the Other subject to one's own desire: '. . . the structure of perversion . . . is an inverted effect of the [f]antasy. It is the subject who determines himself as object, in his encounter with the division of subjectivity' (Lacan 1964a [2004]: 185).

A distinguishing feature of a perverse structure then becomes an attempt to ensure the *jouissance* of the Other within a belief system (alternative to the Law) in which he can continue to be the be-all and end-all for the Other and neither is subject to lack. The 'pervert' refuses symbolic castration and the Law, with a consequent strangulation of his own desire. Something which is already known or sensed (the mother's lack of a penis) must be disavowed (*Verleugnung*) with a concomitant split in the ego. Lacan (1975–6) punned on perversion as '*une père-version*' (father version): the perverse subject stages a distorted version of the law of the father (Van Haute 2002).

Contemporary Lacanians emphasize different aspects of Lacan's original formulations, and in some instances expand on them. Fink (1997) extrapolates from Lacan to provide a more systematic theory, much as Lacan did with Freud, whilst acknowledging '. . . to the best of my knowledge Lacan never formulates it as I am going to' (Fink 1997: 170). He stresses a lack of paternal function, either in the mind of the mother and/or from an actual father. In contrast to its complete absence in psychosis, in perversion some paternal function has been established but this is still insufficient to effect a neurotic level of recognition of lack and separation from the Other. The 'pervert' therefore remains enmeshed with a primitive phallic (m)Other. Whilst Fink sees this as an effect of deficient paternal function, Nobus (2000) prefers to place the onus on the child's 'unfathomable decision of being' ['*insondable décision de l'être*'] (Lacan 1946 [1999]: 177). It is, of course, likely that both mother and child will collude with the child's remaining fixated in her orbit in this way. Perverse sexual activity, if it exists, aims to set limits to *jouissance* and to establish the Law and the Name of the Father, as well as enacting some form of forbidden *jouissance*.

Hence, for Lacanians a perverse structure presents special challenges in treatment. The perverse patient must relinquish the *jouissance* derived from the staging or enactment of denial of castration, and submit to the pains of the discovery of loss, lack and separateness. The path from perversion to neurosis resembles Kleinian accounts of the journey to the threshold of the depressive position through the relinquishing of infantile omnipotence. For Lacanians, the mother's desire must be symbolized (or 'metaphorized') and the omnipotence of disavowal surrendered to an acceptance of castration.

Those with a perverse structure may struggle to supplement paternal function, to separate and to symbolize: '. . . this symbolization [of the father] is not as complete as that achieved in neurosis' (Fink 1997: 170), insights supported by Lacan's insistence on the necessity of symbolizing the phallus at the third stage of the Oedipus Complex (Lacan 1957–8a [1998]: 179–96). For Lacanians, the neurotic has entered the symbolic realm through metaphorization (as the 'pervert' has begun to), but whilst the neurotic uses this as the basis to negotiate Oedipal triangulation, castration and lack, the 'pervert' stalls at this point. One can infer from this that those with a perverse structure have difficulty with symbolizing certain aspects of their experience: there may be lacunae of inhibited symbol formation and a paucity or restricted range of representation. Kristeva (1993) argues that in perverse speech affects are split from discourse, and that the mobilization of a perverse scenario within the transference can constitute a precondition for translation into interpretive speech. Paternal function in the mind of the therapist can have a direct and immediate effect on this struggle, as in the following example.

'Howie', as I shall call him, the American heir of a chain of shopping malls, had been an idolized and maternally indulged only child. He felt as if his mother's well-being depended on his involvement with her, and whilst this provided him with a charmed life with many attendant gratifications and privileges, he was aware of the exclusion of his father from this set-up. His father was often away on business but, even when present, was ignored by Howie and his mother. His father had no close friends or relationships, including apparently in his marriage.

Howie was highly intelligent and quick to grasp complex and subtle psychological issues, but at the beginning of his therapy, there were curious absences of symbolization. Although he wanted to, he could not describe many aspects of his relationship with his mother. In marked contrast to his intellectual articulacy, he dreamt little and the content of his dreams was bald and unelaborated. For example, he had several dreams in which he was running across a dam, perhaps because his use of disavowal 'dammed up' his capacity to represent his experience and resulted in a precarious psychological balancing act.

Unlike his mother, I bore his relationship with his father, internal and external, constantly in mind and would allude to it regularly.[9] The session in which I suggested he might be like his father (in his tendency to withdrawal) produced perplexity and consternation. He felt more comfortable speaking and thinking about his relationship with his mother, even though he could not articulate anything emotionally specific about it. That night, he had his first vivid and detailed dream ever. In this dream, he was in his friend Simon's flat, which was entirely painted in white. He set off with a 1980s twin-spool tape recorder, and sat in the apex of a triangular-shaped bar, also decorated in 80s fashion. He was drinking a bottle of beer and a bottle of cherry brandy. The bar manager, who was black and also in 80s garb, told him he was drinking too much. Howie told him to 'piss off and mind his own business'. I was sitting a few feet away and I also told him he was drinking too much and that he should not be so rude to the bar manager. I was dressed in a contemporary fashion but I was about six feet four inches tall (I'm about five feet six inches in the flesh).

Howie's associations were as follows: Simon is an older man who helped him professionally. He loves beer and drinks it a lot (but, he said emphatically, not too much), but hates cherry brandy and never drinks it—it was too sweet and sickly, he said. It was the sort of thing his mother used to drink. His father liked beer too but, in Howie's opinion, his father lacked discrimination in drinking only American brands. I interpreted this dream as being set in the paternal realm (Simon's flat).[10] I pointed out my name was White, at which Howie giggled and immediately grasped the significance. I said I thought the many references to the 1980s indicated an attempt to record experience from his early childhood. I said the two drinks seemed to represent his ambivalent attachment to his mother—on the one hand, he loved it and, on the other, he found it too cloying. The fact that he was sitting in the apex of a triangle suggested he was beginning to allow both his parents a place in his mind, although they were still very separated. I suggested the bar manager might represent his father, and perhaps his blackness might be a way of communicating his outsider status. I seemed to be the sort of height I might look like from a small child's point of view and I seemed to be trying to instil a bit more respect for his internal father. My height in his dream also indicated the terrifying dominance another person would rapidly come to assume in any close relationship with Howie, as his sense of himself as a separate person was still so fragile.

Dor (1997, 2001) emphasizes the elements of defiance and transgression in the perverse patient's refusal of the paternal metaphor. Confronted with the necessity of renouncing his primal object, the 'pervert' renounces desire instead but his denial must be predicated on something he already knew. Therefore, he simultaneously tries to demonstrate that his law is the only way whilst reinforcing his knowledge of the law of the father. This struggle may involve him in ritualized sexual enactments in which an accomplice is a necessary witness to transgression. The analyst, because of his commitment to listening and to confidentiality, may be vulnerable to cooption into this role. Dor (2001) recounts a horrific case in which an analyst listened to increasingly lurid accounts of sexual enactments. After several months of this, his patient implicated some of the analyst's colleagues in these orgies, and in a final sadistic flourish, the analyst's own daughter. A more commonly encountered perverse twisting of the transference is exemplified by a patient who insisted that he could not afford to pay a full fee. At the end of his therapy he announced, with considerable satisfaction, that he possessed assets worth several million pounds.

Lacan considered the perverse elements in everyone's sexuality may be enacted in diverse forms of cultural life. In film, for example, voyeurism can be seen as a form of disavowal, where we suspend our disbelief for the duration (Lacan 1956–7). Metz (1982) argues that film blurs the boundary between imaginary and symbolic realms. Some feminist theorists apply Lacanian ideas on perversion to explore psychoanalytic and other 'masculinist' theories. Irigaray (1977, 1985), for example, argues that the phallic monism of much psychoanalytic theory is an expression of a masculine infantile theory which can only conceive of a lack of a penis by an absence, an idea adumbrated by Karen Horney as a form of masculine narcissism (Sayers 1991).

Although theories of perversion occupy prominent positions in some contemporary Independent and post-Kleinian thought, which I will now briefly recount, they do not take up central territory as in Lacanian theory. Borderline and narcissistic pathology, with their underlying substrata of lack of internal separation/individuation from their objects cover parts of the same ground but from different metapsychological perspectives.

Post-Kleinian concepts of perverse states of mind do not often include a sexual component, except in the sense in which some Kleinians consider all psychopathology to have a perverse basis (Meltzer 1973, 1992). Waddell and Williams (1991) argue perverse addictive states of mind to be the product of a gang mentality (Rosenfeld 1971). Here idealized omnipotent infantile sadistic part-objects gain dominance over the personality, prohibit loving dependence and vulnerability and promulgate a form of psychic propaganda which constitutes a reversal of normal value systems. Waddell and Williams contend that these states of mind correlate with funda-mentalist slogans, such as Big Brother's 'War is Peace' and 'Freedom is Slavery' in Orwell's *1984*. They claim the regressive sexual component here is less significant than the destructive narcissistic disavowal of need for others.

Meltzer thought infantile perverse sexuality was the cornerstone of both destructive narcissistic and perverse states of mind and used these two terms almost interchangeably. Early in his career (Meltzer 1966), he theorized a phantasied relation between a child's anal masturbation and intrusive projective identification into compartments of the internal mother: the second concept was developed much further in *The Claustrum* (1992) (discussed in Chapter 4). This form of projective identification constitutes an omnipotent perverse mechanism for avoiding the pains of weaning and separation, and the threshold of the depressive position and the Oedipus Complex, coterminous in Kleinian theory. A split involving the idealization of a manic envious destructive part of the personality creates confusion in preference to facing depressive reality and constitutes the precursor to delusional thinking. In sanity and creativity, Meltzer thought, a loving internal parental couple, united in fruitful intercourse, are internally established and gratefully acknowledged. For Meltzer, all mechanisms which evade this acknowledgment have perverse sexuality at their heart.

Other post-Kleinians do not centralize the perverse in the same way. Bion 'practically ignores perversion' (Bléandonu 1994: 281). Although Britton (1989) posits a connection between an internal phantasy of the primal scene and the way mental links are made or evaded, he does not investigate perverse sexuality or states of mind. Hyatt-Williams (1998) found in sadistic murder evidence of a perverse phantasy in which orgasm is equated with the destruction or annihilation of the idea of a baby. Here, the way generativity is attacked in a savage and sexually excited way is reminiscent of Meltzer's perverse alternative leader of the internal world, whose dominance consists in his ability to deny and attack the evidence of the primal scene and the mother's internal babies. Severe persecutory anxiety emanates from the dead babies murdered in unconscious phantasy inside the internal mother (Meltzer 1968).

Some contemporary Independent analysts conceive of perverse structures between the psychoses and the neuroses. Like Steiner's pathological organizations, these perverse formations may bind the personality against the threat of further disintegration or breakdown but also prohibit or constrict further development. Khan (1979), Chasseguet-Smirgel (1984) and McDougall (1978) emphasize environmental factors in the aetiology of perversion, in particular the tendency of a mother to over-indulge or 'idolize' her child (Khan 1979), and to focus on him to the exclusion of her husband and their sexual relationship. All three stress the role of sexual acting out in the maintenance of a perverse structure. All three link the significance of idealization and manic elements in perversion with narcissistic structures, and Khan emphasized the role of precocious ego development as an attempt to repair or preserve a narcissistic sense of self (ibid.).

For Khan, a deficit in ordinary good-enough maternal care can result in splitting the ego and also possibly mind and body. A 'collage' of bits and pieces of the parental environment, which might include aspects of bodily care and the mother's dissociated unconscious as well as archaic elements of primitive body-states, becomes a split-off aspect of precocious ego development. A corresponding 'collated internal object', the perverse equivalent of Winnicott's transitional object, may become re-enacted through ritual complicit sexualized scenarios. Here, sexual activity is used to ward off feelings of anxiety or distress (ibid.: 120–38).

Whilst Khan emphasized the predicament of the 'pervert', Chasseguet-Smirgel (1984) stresses his omnipotence and sadism. Through a comparison with de Sade and the Nazis, she demonstrates the perverse aim of collapsing genital activity into an anal–sadistic mass to deny the difference between sexes and generations. Through idealization of the anal–sadistic phase, the 'pervert' creates '. . . a pseudo-genitality in which objects, erotogenic sources and pleasures are adapted to the child's potential' (ibid. [1985]: 11). We all have a perverse core, she claims, which may be activated in fundamentalist movements or even in artistic creation. Chasseguet-Smirgel's 'pervert', like Meltzer's, takes perverse pleasure in creating chaos, turning things upside-down, and idealizing the sham and the false. In consequence true perversion cannot exist without thought disorder.

McDougall succeeds in integrating Lacanian insights into her conception of the 'neo-sexualities' (McDougall 1978). Like most other contemporary theorists, McDougall argued perversion as the result of turning away from an Oedipal scenario: it is 'circumvented' (ibid. [1990]: 41). The primal scene is denied through the invention of 'a counterfeit couple', and castration anxiety is mastered through a sexual staging or enactment. The primary defence is disavowal: devaluation of the father is countered with an ambiguous image of an idealized phallic mother. McDougall attributes the role of secrecy in perversion to the maintenance of a fictive anal penis (ibid. [1990]: 44). Psychic stability depends on the compulsive re-enactment of a perverse scenario to protect 'the pervert' from further collapse into merger with an archaic maternal imago and possible breakdown.

Drawing from Khan, Chasseguet-Smirgel and McDougall, Ogden (1996) shows how a perverse core of deadness masked by the pseudo-excitements of the erotization of the transference impacts on the analytic relationship. The task, as he sees it, is to recognize the 'lie/lifelessness' which constitutes the core of the transference/countertransference relationship (ibid. [1999]: 103). Only through the analysis of the missing generativity of parental intercourse can more authentically alive forms of communication begin to develop in the analytic couple.

Both Independents and post-Kleinians link the possibility of criminality, delinquency and anti-social activity with perversion (Costello 2002). Most frequently, this is assigned to the perversion of moral values implicit in the substitution of a fictive sexual scenario as a means of bypassing the pain and loss associated with Oedipal recognitions. In Lacan's (1932) work on paranoia, however, he related criminal behaviour to 'passage à l'acte' (acting out), in which there is a flight from symbolic functioning into the real and a corresponding destruction of subjectivity.

NEUROSIS

Neurosis, as a clinical concept, has been debated psychoanalytically in recent years. Some theorists claim advanced consumer capitalism promotes shallow narcissistic functioning, in which the ties of family and community may be less important than the ability to be mobile and sever connections without undue pain when necessary (Lasch 1979; Hoggett 1992; Richards (ed.) 1984) (see Chapter 5). Some argue the increased fragmentation of social units results in a devaluation of motherhood and a reduction in the supportive networks which enable women to provide the consistency of care their babies need to develop stable neurotic structures (for example Gerhardt 2004). The result, some maintain, is a preponderance of narcissistic and borderline personalities in treatment (Rutter and Madge 1976; Egeland and Stroufe 1981; White et al. 2001). Kristeva (1993) argues that private life and the 'soul' are constricted in late capitalist societies by a lack of personal time and space, leaving people without a deep sense of sexual, subjective and moral identity. The result, she asserts, is a 'deficiency of psychic representation' (ibid. [1995]: 9), which may manifest in narcissisms, false personalities, borderline states, psychosomatic conditions and forms of perversion.

However, whilst a tendency towards greed, shallowness and narcissism was argued in the 1980s, in the 1990s some analysts revised the theorization of neurosis (Kristeva 1993; Bollas 2000). Hysteria, in particular, was moved centre stage and now occupies some of the clinical ground previously given over to borderlinity. Bollas (2000) and Britton (2003), among others, have argued hysteria to constitute a distinct psychoanalytic syndrome, separate from neurosis. I will not engage with those arguments here, but will focus on those aspects of hysteria revisioned in contemporary theory.

All three schools consider one hallmark of neurosis to be the ability to symbolize experience and represent it verbally. For Lacanians, the neurotic person has entered the symbolic realm through 'metaphorization' (as the 'pervert' has begun to) but whilst the pervert stalls at this point, the neurotic person uses it as the basis to negotiate Oedipal triangulation, castration and lack. For post-Kleinians, a neurotic person can tolerate sufficient frustration to permit metabolization of emotion through mental processes and this is linked with a capacity to bear depressive pain and to recognize Oedipal realities. For all three schools, the primary neurotic defence mechanism remains repression (*verdrängung*)—a more modest and easily recoverable form of putting out of mind than the obliteration of psychotic foreclosure or the splitting of perverse disavowal. Lacan (1955–6, 1958a, 1960) deemed that what was repressed were thoughts pertaining to perceptions with which affects are associated. The unconscious, structured like a language, consists of these thoughts.

Lacanian concepts of different forms of neurosis are central to treatment strategy: as transference neuroses, the unconscious relation to *objet a* will determine the 'fundamental fantasy' (Lacan 1960–1) and the neurotic structure (hysterical, obsessional or phobic) (Lacan 1960). Obsessionality is conceived of as a defensive overlay of hysteria (cf. Freud 1926). Lacan thought *sexuation* was inscribed through neurotic structure, with the hysteric as feminine and the obsessional masculine, although he considered himself to be a hysteric (Schneiderman 1983). Hence, woman are psychically stronger than men because they have a less ambivalent relation to lack (Van Haute 2002).

In Lacanian theory, a hysteric person attempts to mitigate symbolic castration by unconscious constitution of herself as the object the Other desires. In relationships and in analysis, she tries to ensure the other's desire remains unsatisfied in order to retain her role as object (Lacan 1960–1). In the transference, she looks to the Other, the analyst, to supply answers in preference to exploring her own unconscious: '. . . the hysteric seek(s) the lack in the analyst's knowledge, the lacuna or gap; for this gives her the role of exception, living proof that she can supplement or complement the analyst's knowledge' (Fink 1997: 132).

> For example, the young woman described in Chapter 3 as 'Ruth' tried to conduct her sessions in question and answer form, produced a new problem every time something appeared to be resolved and struggled to manipulate me into speaking for her. She had not yet found her own desire. Until she began to articulate herself in therapy independently of my views, she was unwittingly enacting a deeply unconscious scenario in which her existence depended on my interest in her.

The obsessional, on the other hand, refuses to recognize the Other's existence or desire. If hysteria is characterized by unsatisfied desire, obsessional desire is impossible (Lacan 1960–1). Hence, they attempt to control their primary objects and refuse to recognize affinity between the object and the Other. In analysis they may try to neutralize the analyst as the Other (Fink 1997: 130).

> As an example, a 'self-made man' from a working-class background, 'Bill', had achieved prominence in political and professional arenas, but was struggling with his third unsatisfactory marriage. He characterized his problem himself, as he preferred to do, as a compulsion to be doing and a difficulty in being. He refused to come more than twice a week or to lie on the couch, which I think he viewed as liable to make him subject to my desire. He made progress in understanding his dilemmas, usually through formulations he discovered in 'self-help' books, and his marriage stabilized. But it remained a constant struggle to develop a strong relationship with him and he remained preoccupied with his ratiocinations and achievements.

The 'phobic', like the 'pervert' in Lacanian theory but to a less radical degree, struggles with insufficient paternal function: phobic objects are used to supplement it. Both Lacan (1956–7) and Fink (1997) cite Freud's (1909) account of 'Little Hans' to exemplify this phenomenon.

In some contemporary Independent and Lacanian theory, these conceptualizations are more varied. The history of hysteria as a diagnostic category has always been controversial. Many saw it as a response to repressive and restrictive social conditions by women who were rendered voiceless and had no other means of protest (Appignanesi and Forrester 1992; Showalter 1998; Mitchell 2000). Irigaray's (1974) disquisition on '*La Mystérique*' takes up Lacan's fascination with feminine *jouissance* as personified by St. Theresa. Her title incorporates mysticism, hysteria, mystery and femaleness. She sees hysteria/mysticism as a means to break out of identifications imposed on women in male discourse: 'In such ex-stasies, she risks losing herself or at least seeing the assurance of her self-identity-as-same fade away' (ibid. [1985]: 192). Hysteria as a diagnostic category must therefore be understood in the context of women's position within a patriarchal society which defines, mutes and confines them.

Conversion hysteria, in which distress or trauma is represented somatically, is constituted through post-symbolic bodily expression and is usually a condensation of difficult and conflictual unconscious areas of experience. It should not be confused with pre-symbolic psychosomatosis (see earlier in this chapter).

> An example is a young woman who was infertile and suffered from severe uterine cramps. In analysis, it became clear that she was expressing an 'unthought known' (Bollas 1987) about a still-birth immediately before her birth. Her mother had not informed her of this event, but had unconsciously communicated her extreme anxiety about childbirth.

Here, the somatic expression is that of a body overwritten with signifiers: linguistic mechanisms are literally incorporated. The body becomes a metaphor.

Bollas re-theorized hysteria twice. In 1987, he focused on dramatization of affect as a reaction to a mother who could not take in her child's feelings. In 2000, influenced by Lacan and Jean Laplanche, he centralized the parents' reaction to the emergence of sexuality in childhood. Conflicted sexuality, seductiveness and emotional withdrawal masked by theatrical attention seeking are still considered the signatures of hysteria, in men as well as women (Borossa 2001). Bollas (in Molino (ed.) 1997) posits a resurgence of hysteria in the United States as a response to a religious fundamentalism in which sexuality is still the unspeakable repressed force. Juliet Mitchell places a new emphasis on siblings as potential carriers of the first major narcissistic wound, that of replaceability, in early childhood, and on hysterical reactions to the birth of siblings: 'The hysteric becomes like the mother (and/or like her baby) in order not to lose her' (Mitchell 2000: 143).

Nasio (1990) focuses on the chronic dissatisfaction of the hysterical patient as a defence deployed from fear of being overwhelmed by too much pleasure. A surplus of affect which cannot be dissipated by repression may be redirected into somatic conversion. The hysteric person tries to prove to herself and to the world that pleasure is unsatisfied, and she may hence often play the role of the excluded one. A pervasive sadness is frequently encountered. Analysis can provide the containment necessary to reconcile the conflictual feelings and process the sexual excitement which could not be dealt with in childhood.

Kristeva (1993) prioritizes the role of countertransference in the treatment of hysteria. In her account, the bivalence of the hysterical psyche consists in '*exuberant affect*' (ibid. [1995]: 70, her emphases), either distressing or ecstatic, which cannot be symbolized and where sexuality is disavowed by sensualization. The analyst contains the overload of excitement the hysteric has displaced so that the 'revived hysteria' in the transference/countertransference relation '. . . can lead from an endogenous hunger-dissatisfaction to a pure appetite for words' (ibid. [1995]: 86).

Kristeva characterizes the obsessional by a preference for doing over saying and 'a *shortage of signs*' (ibid. [1995]: 46, her emphases). Trauma is deprived of affective cathexis, and psychic representation of affect is dissociated from verbal representation. She postulates the existence of a 'buried mother'—different from Green's (1983) 'dead mother'—in the obsessional psyche. This mother had masked her depression in an exaggerated activity level, so that language had to be formed in another world, split off from depression and demand. In consequence, there is a predisposition to fail, a difficulty in making choices, a reversal of desires and relationships which are disappointing, repetitive, and destined to failure. The task of analysis becomes to propose verbal and affective constructions and to elucidate the traumatic oral relationship with maternal depression.

Post-Kleinians (for example Steiner 1993) tend to focus more on areas of entrenched psychopathology, narcissistic or psychotic, in everyone, and less on neurosis as a defensive structure *per se*. Britton, however, claims in an extended study of hysteria that '. . . a central feature of hysteria is the use of projective identification by the subject to become, in phantasy, one or other or both members of the primal couple' (Britton 2003: 10). Hence, the defensive aim is to possess the object in the realm of love—an interesting correspondence with the Lacanian view—and everything significant becomes eroticized.

As we have seen, all three contemporary schools link the achievement of neurosis, or at least some neurotic functions in the personality, with the negotiation of Oedipal configurations, the greater degree of separation they enable and increased capacity to tolerate frustration and to symbolize. Post-Kleinians see successful resolution of the Oedipus Complex as indissoluble from and co-terminous with the depressive position, or as Britton put it: '. . . the struggle not to reject the banal goodness of ordinary life when contrasted with the hints of a lost ideal world' (Britton 1992: 39).

The links between neurosis and the acquisition of a sense of gendered identity are developed by recent Independent theorists as well as Lacan. Ogden (1987, 1989b) uses Winnicott's theory of transitional space to expand accounts of Oedipal processes but still implies we reach some sort of conclusion or closure. Benjamin's (1995, 1998) accounts of the acquisition of gendered identity and sexual orientation through Oedipal processes (discussed in Chapter 2) offer both a more radical critique and the possibility of 'post-Oedipal' configurations open to renegotiation throughout life. She argues for an 'overinclusive' account of Oedipal processes in which a child can both identify with and desire both parents (Benjamin 1995). In her retheorization, no one of the multiple internal configurations (of identifications and desire) this enables ever has to be entirely relinquished (or split off). In adulthood, then, the person can call on a range of gender identifications to meet different life situations and relationships, and Oedipal configurations may be revisited throughout life. This expanded view of the Oedipus Complex, which never reaches fixity or conclusion, calls for a review of theories of neurosis to incorporate more complexity, openness and fluidity.

In summary, for all three schools, in psychosis there is a failure to separate from the first other and enter Oedipal processes. In consequence symbolization is disturbed (in Lacan's terms 'imaginarized'), and the primary defence mechanism becomes foreclosure (Lacan 1955–6) or evacuative projective identification (Bion 1967). In perversion, some separation has taken place but a full Oedipal scenario is turned away from or circumvented (McDougall 1978), and some areas of symbolization are restricted or inhibited (Lacan 1957–8a; Fink 1997). The primary defence mechanism is considered to be disavowal by Lacanians and contemporary Independents, and omnipotent triumph by post-Kleinians. In neurosis, the Oedipus Complex has been engaged with and lack and/or castration are acknowledged. Post-Kleinians link the capacity to bear sufficient frustration to permit symbolization of affect with tolerance of depressive pain. Hence, symbolization is fully established, but there will be compensatory defensive mechanisms of various forms against lack and aloneness. The primary defence mechanism is repression.

Contemporary theorists of all persuasions recognize the potential for a constantly evolving self. Some form of neurotic structure provides the springboard for this. Britton's formulation of 'Ps (n) → D (n) → Ps (n + 1)' (see also Chapter 9) describes the continual necessary regression to less organized states of mind in order that new forms of hope, faith and thought based in concern may replace overly organized ways of thinking: 'Yesterday's depressive position becomes tomorrow's defensive organization' (Britton 1998: 73).

NOTES

1. Bollas' normotic and ghostline personalities and his anti-narcissist, McDougall's concepts of psychosomatosis and the neo-sexualities and Khan's re-theorization of perversion are discussed later in this chapter, and Ogden's autistic-contiguous position in Chapter 2.

2. Lacan's concepts of the real, the imaginary and the symbolic are discussed in Chapter 3.
3. Joyce, as one of the greatest writers of the twentieth century, cannot be reduced to a diagnostic supposition.
4. For Lacan's use of topological concepts, see Chapter 9.
5. From the French *suppléer*—to make up for.
6. For more extensive clinical examples of borderline patients, see White *et al.* (2001).
7. For Lacan's three stages of the Oedipus Complex, see Chapter 3.
8. In Lacanian terms, the symbolic 'phallus' does not refer to castration via the penis (except perhaps in a metaphorical sense as a pure lack), but rather to the symbolic father as a signifying element (Lacan 1958b [2001]: 316) (see Chapter 3). In perversion, the identification is with an *imaginary* phallus; that is to say, in a stage preceding the final sealing of symbolization through the paternal metaphor.
9. Lacan's concept of 'extimacy' challenged the distinction between internal and external (see Chapter 3).
10. In the following sequence of interpretations, although I follow aspects of Lacanian understanding, I am not using Lacanian clinical technique. Lacanian analysts never fill in the meaning for their analysands.

Chapter 7

Motivational echoes

Transference and countertransference in contemporary theory

It is a highly remarkable fact that the *ucs* of one person can act on that of another.

(Freud 1915b [2005]: 76)

The transference is a phenomenon in which subject and psycho-analyst are both included. To divide it in terms of transference and counter-transference—however bold, however confident what is said on this theme may be—is never more than a way of avoiding the essence of the matter.

(Lacan 1964a [2004]: 231)

[T]he idea of the transference neurosis is gradually substituted by the notion of the psychoanalytic process. This is seen as a form of organization, during the analysis, of the internal development of the patient's psychic processes, or as exchanges between patient and analyst.

(Green 1975 [1997]: 44)

La cellule analytique, même douillette, n'est rien de moins qu'un lit d'amour (The cell of analysis, even if it is comfortable, is no less than a [hot]bed of love).

(Lacan 1960–1 [1991]: 24)

As the crucible of the analytic relationship, the transference/countertransference matrix is where the subject's unconscious conflicts and psychopathology come alive in a powerful two-person drama. The analyst will be tested to the limit (at least some of the time) when his patient's projections find their 'match' in his internal world. He may have to grapple with a countertransferential or 'situational' illness, or a 'generative countertransference regression' (Bollas 1987: 204). He should need to rework his own unconscious constellations and conflicts so that something new may emerge from this potent admixture, hopefully for both parties. If none of this happens, the analysis or therapy will not have taken hold and will be unlikely to produce dynamic internal change for the patient. The three contemporary schools of psychoanalysis diverge considerably in their conceptualizations of this critical struggle.

The understanding and application of the twin concepts of transference and countertransference depend to some degree on the issues of differential diagnosis discussed in Chapter 6. Above and beyond this though, striking contemporary developments in their usage inform psychoanalytic practice today. The range of ways the analyst may use herself as a clinical instrument has greatly extended. The two concepts have become more closely intertwined, indissoluble in some instances, and their meanings more complex and subtle. The evolution of their meanings has been fraught with conflict, reversals and difficulties.

What is the transference? Freud's view that complexes from infantile instinctual relations and their inhibitions and frozen trauma are activated in the analytic relationship remains true today. His shift of perspective from a belief that repressed memories of actual events were revived in analysis (early 1890s) to an understanding of how an unconscious phantasy might be reinforced by a congruous event (later 1890s) is still an issue for some. Traditionally, transference was thought of as a recruitment of the analyst to carry her client's projections. The patient's communications from the past might convey insight into this, or their subjective experience of the therapist might constitute the transference, or the interplay between unconscious phantasy and past and present reality would construct the same distortions in analysis as in the patient's experience of her history (Caper 1999). Today, the picture is more multifarious and more fluid. The analytic relationship incorporates potentialities of the transference/countertransference matrix in both regressive and progressive forms.

Its regressive aspects include the likelihood that early internal conflicts, infantile complexes and instinctual impulses will be revived within the analytic relationship and a relational pattern in which the client is stuck may become the dominant mode of the analytic relationship for a period. There may be a need to return to earlier states of being to repair deep-seated psychic damage, as for example in the Independent emphasis on regression to dependence (discussed later in this chapter and in Chapters 2 and 8). However today the progressive potential of the transference, in terms of the opportunity to resolve and move on from these positions, is what is seen as critical. Indeed, a new emphasis on transference as a possible locus for actualization of dormant potentialities has become a vital ingredient of all three contemporary schools' praxis.

This emphasis on progressive potential incorporates a stress on the intersubjectivity of the analytic relationship, theorized in divergent forms by these three schools.[1] The analyst's role is not restricted to her ability to recognize and work with the transference and utilize her countertransference to this end but is involved in an unprecedented relationship with the analysand, which may, or even should, change the analyst as well. Ogden's (1994a, 1997) 'intersubjective analytic third', Lacan's (1952) early emphasis on the intersubjectivity of the analytic relationship, and Bion's (1962, 1965, 1970) concepts of 'reverie', 'transformations' and 'O', to name but a few contemporary innovations, extend the parameters of the analytic relationship and bring fresh intensity and immediacy to it.

The meanings of countertransference have also undergone a sea change from an indicator of the analyst's problems to the most potent source of deep unconscious information from the patient to, most recently, a fertile intersubjective field. Many contemporary practices incorporate the possibility of all three.

The erotic has always held a special place within transference/countertransference. Freud's courage in neither attributing his patients' infatuations to his personal charms nor, like Breuer, fleeing from their intensity, opened the door to transference. Despite its centrality, the theorization of erotic transference as a specific phenomenon has not always kept pace with conceptual advances in transference/countertransference overall. Mann (1999) argues the erotic has become a frozen, encapsulated area within psychoanalytic theory because of the difficulties and temptations inherent in negotiating the erotic within an intimate professional relationship.

Whilst an explicitly erotic transference may signal defensive or regressive possibilities—as a perverse binding of hostile impulses or an indicator of intense neediness resulting from extreme early deprivation, for example—in most of the conceptual developments discussed here the erotic is seen as an integral part of psychic development. Some see it as holding the greatest potential for unpredetermined growth. Searles (1959b) demonstrates vividly how erotic countertransference is a necessary aspect of enabling a client to become a fully fledged sexual adult. Ogden (1987, 1989b) and Benjamin (1995, 1998) emphasize the centrality of the erotic in processes of separation, individuation and moving on.[2] Lacan's (1964a) insistence on how sexuality and the drives push growth forward, and the Anglo-Saxon world's sometimes evasion of this, called for a re-incorporation of the body, albeit one that is overwritten with signifiers, into a radically revised version of the Freudian unconscious.

The use of transference interpretations has been greatly re-thought (Lacan 1953; Steiner 1993; Britton 1998). Their role as the principal mutative instruments in analysis has become less central for many contemporary theorists, and this shift is described at the end of this chapter and in Chapter 8.

I will now look at some significant moments in the history of the two concepts, before I explore in greater detail how the transference/countertransference matrix is being used in psychoanalysis today.[3]

SOME KEY MOMENTS IN THE HISTORY OF
TRANSFERENCE AND COUNTERTRANSFERENCE

Freud recognized the therapeutic potential as well as the problematic nature of transference phenomena from the outset, although he remained conflicted about and grappled with its import and function (Freud 1893–5). He moved from a position in which transferences from previous traumas or sexual wishes were seen as 'obstacles' which had to be 'removed' through interpretation and a manifestation of resistance (ibid. [2004]: 304) to a concept of 'transference neurosis' through which a patient's repressed conflicts about significant figures from her past were re-experienced in the analytic relationship (Freud 1920 [2003]: 87). Freud recognized '. . . whether she made this psychical repulsion the theme of her work in the historic instance or in the recent one connected with me seemed to make no difference to its success' (Freud 1893–5 [2004]: 305). He saw countertransference mainly as a problem for the physician who required further analysis (Freud 1915a).

Countertransference retained its problematic status within psychoanalytic theory well into the 1950s. As late as 1960, Annie Reich argued that countertransference was a manifestation of an analyst's infantile motivations and/or over-identification with her patient and an indicator of a need for further analysis:

> For the analyst's awareness of his undue emotional response warns him of an obstacle that interferes with his competent functioning and ought to be removed. *The counter-transference as such is not helpful, but the readiness to acknowledge its existence and overcome it is.*
>
> (Reich 1960: 392, her emphases)

Countertransferential experiences may still be a warning sign that something is amiss in the analyst's attitude to her patient: she may be over (or under) involved and in danger of losing an analytic perspective, for example. The constant monitoring of this possibility is sometimes forgotten in more recent enthusiasm for new sources of unconscious communication and information. An amusing anecdote about Melanie Klein illustrates this pitfall. In supervision a trainee reported a difficult session, and interpreted that his patient was projecting his confusion into him. Mrs Klein replied: 'No, dear, that's not it, *you* were confused' (Grosskurth 1985: 449, her emphasis).

Reich was responding to ways in which transference and countertransference had been re-conceptualized in the 1950s and 60s in a period of cross-fertilization between the Kleinian and Independent schools. Paula Heimann, originally a Kleinian and later a leading Independent, produced a groundbreaking paper, 'On Counter-Transference' (1950). Heinrich

Racker, an Argentinian Kleinian, published 'Transference and Counter-transference' (1968). Its influence percolated throughout the Kleinian and Independent groups and to some contemporary Jungians.

Up to 1950, countertransference was thought of as either an indication that the analyst was deviating from an analytic position because his transference to the patient had become entangled with aspects of his own history or infantile complexes, or as specific ego-dystonic experiences which might contain unconscious communication from the patient. Heimann argued that everything the analyst experienced in the course of the treatment should be considered countertransference, thereby enabling a more complex approach to the subtle intersubjective interplay between analyst and client. Of course, countertransference remained a potential signal of an analyst's problems.

Heimann's paper opened the possibility of a detailed scrutiny of every-thing the therapist experiences for unconscious countertransferential communications: '. . . the analyst's countertransference is an instrument of research into the patient's unconscious' (Heimann 1950: 81). Heimann stressed the analyst must '. . . *sustain* the feelings which are stirred in him, as opposed to discharging them . . ., in order to *subordinate* them to the analytic task' (ibid.: 82, her emphases). This new emphasis on the centrality of countertransferential experiences in many forms as vehicles of uncon-scious communication in no way gave licence for the enactment or expression of those experiences, in however subtle a form.

Racker (1968) outlined some specific and critical transference and countertransference constellations. A patient's tendency to 'confess' can cast a therapist in the role of 'moral superego'. The patient thereby risks becoming too identified with her censored 'bad' impulses whilst her analyst may be in danger of acting out the role of idealized (and persecutory) superego through interpretation of her client's ('bad') infantile feelings (ibid. [1982]: 159). Racker stressed interpretation of repressed impulses must include a recognition of defences against them or else a split arises in the transference relationship. He thought classical analytic technique involved too much frustration to be conducive to emotional closeness or positive transference.

Racker conceived of transference and countertransference as two aspects of a single unified phenomenon, which give life to each other and create the interpersonal relationship of the analytic situation, and he showed how countertransference gives critical information about what is alive in the transference at any given moment. The analyst's total response is hence decisive in the understanding and interpretation of the patient's uncon-scious processes.

Racker postulated a 'countertransference neurosis', corresponding to the 'transference neurosis', which may comprise identifications with the patient's transferred internal objects or undue persecutory anxiety in the face of the patient's aggression. However, '[h]e who on certain occasions does not lose his sanity, shows that he has none to lose' (Lessing, quoted in Racker 1968 [1982]: 64). He considered the idea that an analysis comprises an interaction between a sick one and a healthy one a gross distortion of truth: an analyst must always be ready to (silently) recognize his own part in the transference neurosis. His way of thinking prefigured the North American 'relational' emphasis on the analyst's role within an inter-subjective relationship.

Racker formulated two types of countertransference experience: 'concordant' and 'complementary' identifications (ibid.: 134–7). A concordant countertransference occurs when the analyst's feelings correspond to those of his patient, either in the past or the present or both, and signifies an identification. A complementary countertransference may be more difficult for the analyst and potentially more dangerous for the patient, as there may be pressure to feel like and act into either a significant figure from the patient's past or present or an internal object. To the extent that the analyst fails in concordant identifications, he becomes more prone to complementary ones, and this can result in a *folie à deux* in which both parties collude in a rejection of the patient's instinctual impulses and aggression.

THE TRANSFERENCE/COUNTERTRANSFERENCE MATRIX IN CONTEMPORARY PRACTICE

The forms in which transference and countertransference phenomena are used today vary enormously. For most contemporary Independents, the two concepts are indissoluble: the 'analytic third' (Ogden 1994a, 1997) and the 'analyst's act of freedom' (Symington 1983) (discussed a little later in this chapter) are but two examples. Independents and post-Kleinians regard sensitive attention to and skilled differentiation between different aspects and levels of countertransference as the key to understanding transference manifestations, although they deal with this differently. Independents place more emphasis on the analyst's involvement in the relationship and pay more attention to the external reality of the patient's history, whilst recognizing this is filtered through an intrapsychic domain. Contemporary Kleinians stress the intrapsychic dimension, following Klein's (1952b) account of how the minutiae of fluctuating internal interrelationships and early states of mind are revived in the moment by moment experience of the transference. Lacanians focus on a primitive dimension of transference in which a residual fantasy of the primal relationship is revived and must be worked through or 'traversed', but they do not use countertransference as a therapeutic instrument in the same way as the other two schools.

I will outline some different approaches from the three schools. The regressive and progressive potential of this powerful arena may co-exist within the same set of phenomena, but where necessary I will differentiate between these two.

Contemporary Independent approaches: Indices of aliveness and acts of freedom

Regressive forms of transference

For contemporary Independents, regressive transference and countertransference issues are central to work with disturbed patients: here, the major repair work is undertaken. Green, writing from France, describes it thus:

> [F]or writers of the English school, it is not a question of pushing affect back towards biology but, rather, of setting it in a framework of a primitive sensibility, the vestiges of which must be sought by the analyst in the analytic situation through the transference and counter-transference.
>
> (Green 1977b [1997]: 1)8)

With many patients, and particularly those with 'disturbances of the self', the need for a regressive transference and the management of very early states of mind and being in analysis is primary, requiring a modification of classical psychoanalytic technique (discussed more extensively in Chapters 2 and 8). Within a quasi-maternal psychoanalytic environment '. . . our reliability, our unintrusiveness, our use of empathic thought to meet the requirements of the analysand, are often more maternal than was the actual mother's care' (Bollas 1979 [1987]: 23).

The primitive sensibility Green refers to is evocatively described by Bollas as the search for a transformational quasi-maternal object relation in the analytic experience:

> A transformational object is experientially identified by the infant with processes that alter self experience. It is an identification that emerges from symbiotic relating, where the first object is 'known' not so much by putting it into an object representation, but as a recurrent experience of being—a more existential as opposed to representational knowing. As the mother helps to integrate the infant's being (instinctual, cognitive, affective, environmental), the rhythms of this process from unintegration(s) to integration(s)—inform the nature of this 'object' relation rather than the qualities of the object as an object.
>
> (ibid.: 14)

Even in severe disturbance, contemporary Independents stress the primary role of external reality in the origins and evolution of self, beginning with this same 'maternal environment' and eventually moving on to more complex and triangulated forms of relating. Although the intrapsychic dimension with its internal object and part-object interrelationships is the central focus, they stress how the self has been formed in a context of relatedness. In more disturbed states of mind, some turning away from the primary object towards narcissistic idealizations may have occurred, but nonetheless the idiom of the self always bears the traces of the human environment from which it could not originally distinguish itself (ibid.). Therefore, the analytic situation will recapitulate this primary environment, as well as its later elements, and in the management and interpretation of the transference the analyst will bear this constantly in mind—even when the traces of external reality in transference manifestations assume bizarrely psychotic forms.

Searles distinguishes between 'transference psychosis' and 'transference symbiosis' (Searles 1963, 1965, 1973, 1979). Drawing from Klein, Rosenfeld and Bion's work with primitive states of mind and severely disturbed patients, Searles details the extreme confusions between internal part-objects and external reality which embroil the therapist in transference positions where he may be so grotesquely misidentified as to tax his resources to the limit. He identifies four varieties of transference psychosis, which may co-exist in the same patient at the same or different times. The therapist may be unrelated to or even become an inanimate object or, as in the case I described in Chapter 4, an intergalactic enemy from outer space. The relatedness may be deeply ambivalent, including either 'a demeanour of stony and silent antagonism' (Searles 1963 [1986a]: 680) or relentless attack and persecution. The patient's psychosis may represent, in the transference, an effort to complement the therapist's personality or to help the therapist-parent become established as a separate and whole person, as when, for example, one of Searles' patients was trying to relieve his therapist/parent's depression with crazy utterances and behaviour. An ambivalent perpetuation of a symbiotic relationship or an apparently sadistic nullifying or undoing of the therapist's efforts to be helpful and thoughtful may render his task frustrating in the extreme.

What is new in Searles' formulations, and different from the Kleinians whose work he cites, is his readiness to recognize an element of reality in the strangest perceptions in the transference relationship, or non-relationship as it might well be, even when it threatens cherished assumptions about himself. He is also concerned to locate unusual behaviour in a past reality. So, for example, the severe apathy of a chronic hebephrenic patient is

> . . . that of a person who had felt it necessary to bank the fires of his own ambitions and devote himself to staying by . . . a psychotically depressed father, whose needs . . . took priority over the patient's own life as a boy and as a young man.
>
> (ibid.: 655)

Therapeutic symbiosis (Searles 1973), on the other hand, involves less overt confusion between internal and external reality, and between client and therapist, but still some need to function as an extension of another person or to complement areas of ego incompleteness in others. It represents a step on the way to more individuated functioning and towards adult responsibility for relationships but is still likely to be, at least covertly, highly ambivalent.

Other regressive forms of transference may include the various narcissistic possibilities discussed in Chapter 5, in which either a high level of idealization may need to be held for a period (Kohut 1971, 1977) or massive primitive rage and hostility managed and robustly interpreted (Kernberg 1975, 1986a, 1986b, 2004; Rosenfeld 1965). McDougall's (1989) understanding of psychosomatic phenomena, discussed in Chapter 6, also requires transference and countertransference experiences to be located at a pre-verbal and pre-symbolic level. Psychosomatic manifestations may become the most critical elements of the transference and may give the therapist the opportunity of putting into words, for the first time in the client's history, these primitive non-verbal signals. 'Unacknowledged representations, charged with affects of terror and rage, are also frequent elements in the precipitation of psychosomatic phenomena' (ibid.: 38).

Bollas (1987, 1992) suggests we also scrutinize countertransferential feelings for signs of deadness, dullness or flatness as indicators of entrenched psychopathology. Such 'feeling states' may alert the analyst to the possibility that she is being 'used' in an anti-developmental way. A 'conservative' form of object usage may indicate a defensive constellation designed to protect the child from experiences too traumatic or overwhelming to be symbolized, but it has huge therapeutic potential as the guardian of dissociated 'true self' experiences (Bollas 1987: 110–15). 'Terminal' object usage, as the product of invasive early parenting, defends against surrender to unconscious experience (Bollas 1995).

Transference and countertransference as a conjoint entity

The primary tool in the understanding of the patient's transference in all these scenarios is the analyst's countertransference. The analyst must generatively split her psyche so that while one part is open and available to all forms of projection and projective identification, another is able to observe and think about the impact the patient is having on her (Bollas 1987). The analyst must know herself well enough to be able to disentangle what belongs to herself, even when it seamlessly matches something in the patient, as a continual scrutiny. Often a silent processing of these experiences may be all that is required, or it may lead to a fully worked-through interpretation.

Symington (1983) argues that an analyst's unconscious shift of attitude can precipitate a way out of a transference/countertransference collusion or gridlock and hence enable the patient too to step out of her previous unconscious mindset. His argument prefigures the new emphasis on inter-subjectivity in Independent and American Relational thought (Stolorow *et al.* 1987) and proffers one of the first examples of an 'intersubjective moment' as equally mutative as a transference interpretation.

Symington gives a clinical example of 'poor little Miss M.' whom he assumed was not capable of paying more than a very low fee. When it dawns on him that maybe this was an unwarranted assumption 'lassoed into the patient's self-perception' (Symington 1983 [1986]: 253), he raised her fee. Miss M. henceforth became more self-confident and disentangled herself from some other relationships in which she was being patronized or used.

Hence, a distinctive aspect of contemporary Independent usage of the transference/countertransference matrix, as it is evolving now, is their emphasis on the irreducible elements of the unconscious interaction of two minds in analysis. The new focus on intersubjectivity, theorized differently by Benjamin (1995, 1998) and Ogden (1994a, 1997) (discussed in Chapter 2), means transference and countertransference need no longer be thought of as discrete entities. Ogden's 'intersubjective analytic third', a unique interaction created afresh in every session, incorporates the projective and inter-subjective interplay of dual unconscious communication, and by implica-tion, the analyst's as well as the patient's psychopathology. Ogden insists that the analyst's free associative meanderings contain information from the patient even, and perhaps especially, when they appear to be completely irrelevant—when one might think one's mind is simply wandering.[4]

An example of this dual contrapuntal process comes from McDougall's 'countertransference dream' while working with a severely phobic woman, 'Marie-Josée', in the grip of an intense homosexual transference (McDougall 1995). One night, when McDougall's husband was absent (as was her patient's), she dreamt about '. . . an attractive Asian woman, dressed in a provocative, sexy manner' (ibid.: 24), and felt, in the dream, that she '. . . must renounce all will-power and passively submit to whatever this exotic creature wants' (ibid.: 25). McDougall, unable to sleep after the dream, associates to a former patient who was Chinese. She gropes to remember her name and is shocked to discover it was 'Lili' as her own mother was called 'Lillian'.

> Through an intensive search of her childhood memories, she decides that she had denied her erotic feelings for her mother, and neither had these been explored in her two analyses. She remembers the evening when her mother was going to a party wearing a shimmering apricot shot-silk dress which seemed to change colour as she walked, and wishing that it could be she, and not her father, who was taking her mother to the party. Through this series of associations, she '. . . came to the astonishing conclusion that I was *envious* of Marie-Josée's possessive mother—always phoning, always proposing that they share cultural and other activities, forever inviting her to come home as soon as her daughter's husband was away' (ibid.: 27, her emphasis). She discovers that her patient's overt resentment of her clinging mother occludes a disavowed homosexual tie, thereby demonstrating her profound unconscious links with her patient.

Symington's (1983) 'act of freedom', Casement's (1985, 1990, 2002) (Langsian) 'unconscious supervision' and Green's (1975) 'analytic object' all focus on intersubjective unconscious interplay as a mutative factor in analysis. Searles (1958) description of how the schizophrenic patient is vulnerable to picking up and possibly acting out dissociated aspects of the analyst's unconscious can also be applied in some measure to less disturbed patients. Analytic neutrality here means continence: as the analyst's unconscious is inevitably part of the process, honesty, scrupulous monitoring and sustaining the feelings stirred up in oneself are more important than pretending to be an aloof 'blank screen'.

Bollas highlights certain aspects of the transference/countertransference matrix as a trans-subjective field. He claims the analyst is compelled into reliving aspects of his own infantile history in the countertransference, which serves as a 'potential space' in which the analyst may also need to tolerate some temporary loss of identity (Bollas 1987). Interpretation, if it is used, proceeds from worked-through subjectivity and not from any notion of authority.

Transference/countertransference as a progressive force

Although Phillips thinks '. . . it is as though, from a psychoanalytic point of view, the future can only be described as, at best, a sophisticated replication of the past; the past in long trousers' (Phillips 1994: 155), within the contemporary developments described here there is a refreshing and innovative emphasis on the analytic relationship as a matrix for new developments and for the unfolding of previously dormant potential. The revisioning of transference/countertransference as an intersubjective field, including the aforementioned 'analytic third' (Ogden 1994a, 1997) and 'act of freedom' (Symington 1983), enables the emergence of new constellations. Bollas theorizes how future selves and states of mind may arise through being '. . . *played* by the evocative effect of the other's personality idiom, a correspondence between two unthought knowns' (Bollas 1992: 189, his emphasis).

Future selves may also arise through the negotiation of Oedipal dynamics and tolerance of the greater aloneness and complexity thereby generated. Ogden's (1987, 1989b) account of Oedipal discoveries within a transitional space and Searles' (1959b) account of how erotic countertransference serves the patient's growth both demonstrate the uses of the transference/counter-transference matrix in the sexual arena (see Chapter 2). However, as Bollas emphasizes, the achievement of a sophisticated level of separation/individuation is difficult and precarious: '. . . the risks to such adventurers are high. Most people, in my view, find consciousness of this aspect of the human condition—the complexity born of having a mind to oneself—simply too hard to bear' (Bollas 1992: 242). For Bollas (1995), this complexity consists in the dissemination of the self and the freeing of a potentially endless process of invention and reinvention in generative relationships and solitude.

In summary, contemporary Independent analysts trace affect back to its primitive origins within the transference/countertransference matrix. Their sensitivity and sensibility enable an emergence of the traces of the first relationship. They stress the potential for 'true self' experiences to emerge in analysis—some of which may have already been developed to some extent, some may have been overdeveloped as compensation for a deficit in other areas, and some may have lain dormant and unknown up to this point. They use themselves as their primary therapeutic tool, even when this embroils them in disturbing experiences such as the need to acknowledge some reality in bizarre psychotic projections. It is only the limitations of the analyst, and those aspects of her personality and self experience she may have dissociated, that set limits to what can be contained and managed in the transference and what new areas of growth may be generated therein.

Lacanian approaches: Love, desire and the traversing of fantasy

Lacanians also seek the trace of the earliest relationship in the transference, but in fantasy—as the way *objet a* compensates for the lack discovered in and of the Other. Although some think Lacan paid insufficient attention to affect (for example Kennedy 1986), his formulation of *objet a* incorporated the desirous and drive-related wellsprings of primitive love, as we shall discover in the following account.

Like his contemporaries, Lacan (1960–1) considered transference to lie at the heart of psychoanalytic treatment, and his position on it was in constant evolution throughout his long career. Initially, he emphasized the intersubjective aspect of the transference/countertransference relationship and the unavoidable implication of the analyst in the analysand's transference (Lacan 1952). Slightly later, he distinguished between 'transference insistence' (or symbolic repetition), which he saw as the motor of psychoanalysis, and 'transference resistance' (or imaginary projection), which he saw as a narcissistic re-playing of archaic infantile imagos (Lacan 1954–5).

> [T]he efficacious transference which we're considering is quite simply the speech act. Each time a man speaks to another in an authentic and full manner, there is, in the true sense, transference, symbolic transference—something takes place which changes the nature of the two beings present.
>
> (Lacan 1953–4 [1991]: 109)

As from *Seminar VII* (1959–60), he differentiated transference from repetition. By *Seminar VIII – The Transference* (1960–1), he was arguing that transference could not be reduced to the repetition of a prior unresolved conflict. Transference creates something novel within the specific context of a relationship with an analyst who will play a part in shaping the form it will take (ibid.). The work of transference consists of far more than an opening and closing of an unconscious impulse; it insists in working through a modification of the analysand's subjective position (Harari 2004). In *Seminar XI* (1964a), both transference and repetition became two of Lacan's 'four fundamental concepts of psychoanalysis'—the other two being the unconscious and the drive. He pronounced '. . . *the transference is the enactment of the reality of the unconscious*' (ibid. [2004]: 149, his emphases), insisting that this reality was always sexual. Before I explore some of these fascinating ideas further, I will consider some transferential issues with psychotic and perverse analysands, and countertransference in Lacanian analysis.

Psychotic and perverse 'transference'

As psychotic psychological structure is an imaginarized version of symbolic functioning, such patients may be threatened with a psychotic break if their version of reality is called into question. Their '. . . certainty is radical' and founded on delusional belief containing 'enormous meaning' which '. . . has never entered the system of symbolization' (Lacan 1955–6 [1993]: 75, 85). When the delusion stabilizes, the subject becomes calmer and more able to function (ibid.: 86): '. . . the subject is only able in psychosis to reconstitute himself in . . . the imaginary allusion' (ibid.: 162). Therefore whilst, in work with neurotic patients, a therapist might indicate that she hears something which was not consciously intended, with psychotic patients the analyst must be careful not to introduce 'symbolic opposition' into the imaginary, or in other words not to triangulate (Fink 1997: 104). Transferentially, the 'delusional metaphor' thus created provides a frame of reference in which a psychotic patient can organize his own sense of meaning. This 'delusional metaphor' buttresses psychotic structure.

> For example, my patient 'Patrice' (described in Chapter 4), could not tolerate another point of view during the first two years of his therapy, in which he was frankly delusional. Interpreting his delusional system and transference would have made him feel more persecuted and paranoid and resulted in a vicious circle in which complete breakdown could have been the outcome. I therefore had to tolerate a transference position of functioning as an imaginary other, or an aspect of himself: I was seen as an intergalactic enemy from outer space. I had to interpret from within my transferential role and empathize with his terror of what I might do to him.

The question of transferential issues with perverse patients in contemporary Lacanian theory is fraught with ambiguity (see Chapter 6). Subsequent theorists (Fink 1997; Dor 1985, 1997, 2001; Nobus 2000) expand and systematize the clues from Lacan's own work (Lacan 1956–7, 1957–8a, 1960). You will recall the distinguishing feature of a perverse structure is an identification with the imaginary object of the (m)Other's desire, the imaginary phallus, and a refusal of the final stages of the Oedipus Complex. This results in an attempt to ensure the *jouissance* of the Other within an alternative belief system in which neither is subject to lack. Nobus (2000) suggests the analyst must not identify with the 'pervert's' image of him and must try to lever the 'pervert's' fantasy so that it becomes invested with desire at the expense of *jouissance*. Fink focuses on the *'lack of lack'* (Fink 1997: 177, his emphases): some paternal function has been established but insufficient to enable these analysands to symbolize their own desire. Within the transference, therefore, the therapist will need to grapple with introducing a notion of lack.

> Using the case I described in Chapter 6 as 'Howie', we can see how Howie's enmeshment with a phallic (m)Other led to distinctive phenomena in his transference to me. First, he found it difficult to accept the ordinary boundaries of an analytic relationship and my lack of availability outside and

flexibility about session times. On occasion he arrived at different times and had to be sent away. Although such boundaries are important with all clients, in Howie's case they were critical lest a re-enactment of the enmeshment take place in his therapy. In time, Howie began to symbolize such boundaries: he dreamt for example about an older female friend to whose house Howie and his friends would go after the pubs shut. She became known in the intimate shorthand which usually develops between therapist and patient as 'open all hours'.

Howie's struggle with symbolization is described in Chapter 6. There, I observed how my allusions to his father (unusual from Howie's experience with his mother) had the effect of producing a sense of confusion and a difficulty in articulating his thoughts initially, but later an increased capacity to symbolize. The place of a 'third'—in the form of clearly bounded substantial breaks from therapy, other patients whose place would take priority over Howie's if he arrived at the wrong time and a refusal to change session times at short notice—was crucial in establishing greater paternal function and separation. This 'third' had to be repeatedly instated and tested over time, but eventually it had the impact of permitting Howie to feel more separate and to risk attending his therapy at a greater frequency than once weekly, which had been all he could manage at the outset without feeling taken over by me.

In the transference, therefore, at first Howie behaved as if we were an extension of each other. Through the repeated establishment of boundaries which clearly demarcated our separateness, a space was created between us in which Howie could begin to see me as an interestingly separate person with a mind of my own and a stronger sense of his own ground, which he referred to as 'reclaimed territory'.

Countertransference in Lacanian analysis

Lacan considered countertransference to be the product of an analyst's imaginary embroilment with his analysand, in effect an identification: '. . . the counter-transference is nothing other than the function of the analyst's *ego*, what I have called the sum total of the analyst's prejudices' (Lacan 1953–4 [1991]: 23, his emphasis). Analysts who unwittingly enact an imaginary position may trigger narcissistic love, jealousy, competition and aggression. Nobus (2000) thinks this could lead to misdiagnosis of an underlying psychosis or borderline state in neurotic analysands.

Lacan (1958a) developed the concept of 'the analyst's desire': a form of purified desire for the analysand to engage in the process of analysis and to discover the roots of her own desire. He stressed that the analyst is concerned with the direction of the treatment and not with his patients' well-being or wherever their lives might lead. The analyst's desire can thus be compared with the 'desire' element in Bion's (1970) 'without memory and desire', in which the analyst does not require her patient to do or be anything in particular. Lacan thought the analyst's desire should protect him from imaginary embroilments in his countertransference.

Transference with neurotic analysands

Lacan (1960–1) introduced the concept of '*agalma*', a mysteriously potent internal source of attraction. His seminar on transference is a disquisition on Plato's *Symposium* (or *Banquet* in French) on the nature of love, and incorporates Lacan's shift of perspective from transference as an inter-subjective phenomenon to a 'subjective disparity' (ibid. [1991]: 11). Lacan related all the speeches at this banquet, described as '. . . a gathering of old queens' ('*vieilles tantes*') (ibid.: 163), to illustrate what love is not, until the moment when Alcibiades arrives drunk and '. . . brings us back to it [love] as it really is' (ibid.: 162). Lacan described Alcibiades as a sort of pre-Alexander and a cross between Kennedy and James Dean: he is a handsome warrior of conflictual reputation who is smitten with the old and physically ugly Socrates.

The secret of Alcibiades' unlikely infatuation is Socrates' *agalma* (ibid.: 167–82). Lacan recounted the etymology of this Greek word: its most superficial meaning is 'ornament'; through that it becomes precious jewels hidden in a box as a gift to the gods, then something which is admired but also envied and so tolerated with difficulty, and also a form of éclat or brilliance. Alcibiades' 'discourse of passion at its most trembling point' (ibid.: 171) was used by Lacan to link *agalma* with 'the partial object of desire' (*objet petit a*) (ibid.: 180–1). We are now in the realm of transference.

Lacan theorized the *agalma* sought in analysis as the '. . . subject supposed to know' (Lacan 1961–2, 1964a).[5] A neurotic analysand projects a notion of that which will complement their own lack onto the analyst, though not without conflict and ambivalence, and this provides the hinge, the lure on which transference is established. The 'subject supposed to know' is a projection of an illusory wholeness which is impossible to attain, an imaginary fantasy of a source of knowledge in an analyst who is not subject to lack. As part of the transformation of the space of demand into that of desire, in the process of which the analytic dialogue will move from an imaginary to a symbolic discourse, the analysand should eventually turn to her own unconscious as the 'subject supposed to know' (Fink 1997).

In his autobiographical account of the last month of an analysis which was principally Lacanian in orientation, *Wool-Gathering or How I Ended Analysis*, Dan Gunn (2002) cites his analyst's interventions very amusingly as '. . .', '. . .' and '. . .', with an occasional 'Hmmmm', 'Hmmmm?' or even 'Chhgmmm?', this latter a reference to his analyst's heavy smoking habit. He claims his analyst never interpreted a single dream and that all his interventions over the course of six years amounted to no more than two sides of A4 paper in small handwriting. Although there may be an element of caricature here, Gunn succeeds in graphically illustrating how he was forced to turn to his own unconscious processes, dreams and creativity as his principal source of knowledge.

As the space of demand is transformed into that of desire, the analyst comes to assume the position of *objet a* in the transference, so that the uncoupling of this neurotic relationship can proceed. Although Lacan equated the *agalma* with *objet a* in *Seminar VIII*, in his subsequent work these two concepts operate on different planes: the *agalma* is equated with a form of love (imaginary) and *objet a* with desire (symbolic).

Therefore, first, the demand (imaginary) to feel better, be rid of certain symptoms, sustain or improve one's relationships or to function more effectively must be replaced by the desire (symbolic) to get in touch with one's own unconscious processes. The analyst must come to represent unconscious aspects of the patient or, more precisely, the fantasy of the other within the patient. At a neurotic level of disturbance, the Archimedean point of analysis comes when the analyst is situated as cause of desire for the analysand, and he must then lever the transferential relationship so that the fundamental fantasy can shift: Lacan coined the neologism, '*hainamoration*' (lovehating or hateloving), to denote the passionate and ambivalent intensity of this enthralment (Lacan 1972–3 [1998]: 90). With the analyst as 'cause of desire', the analysand's basic psychological constellation or fundamental fantasy in relation to *objet a* can be re-worked within the transference (Lacan 1964–5).

As I outlined different forms of fundamental fantasy in Chapter 6, I will only briefly redescribe them here to illustrate their transferential impact. The hysteric patient lives a deeply unconscious fantasy that she is the object that makes the Other desire (Fink 1997). In the transference, she may produce a multitude of new symptoms so that the analyst is constantly seeking to understand her. The analytic task, therefore, becomes to turn the tables in the transference or to shift the 'hysteric's discourse' to an 'analytic discourse' (ibid.: 132), and to this end sustained silence, as exemplified in Gunn's analyst's '. . .'s, promotes the hysteric patient's separation from a fantasy of an Other whom she wants to desire her. She needs to find her own desire and cease to receive definition from an Other. Clinical examples of transference positions assumed by a hysteric patient and an obsessional patient are given in Chapter 6.

The fundamental fantasy of an obsessional neurotic patient involves a refusal to recognize an affinity between the object and the Other (ibid.) and an attempt to stand in the place of the Other (Lacan 1960). Hence, he tries to control the object. In the transference it can feel as if he obliterates the analyst and purloins interpretations as his own product. The analytic task is to hystericize the obsessional (Lacan 1969–70), meaning he must be confronted with the Other's desire, stopped from bulldozing his way through analytic interventions or acting as if the analyst is getting in the way of what he wanted to say (Fink 1997). An obsessional patient therefore requires more active interventions from the analyst, and perhaps not to be directed to the couch before a greater openness to the Other has been established. The obsessional patient discussed in Chapter 6, for example, would only consider ideas he took to be his own or gleaned from 'self-help' books. If I spoke, he simply carried on as if I did not exist.

A phobic patient struggles with insufficient separation from the Other. Paternal function is insecurely established in his psyche and an open relationship with another threatens a level of confusion, although as a less serious problem than in perversion or psychosis. One analytic task in the transference therefore may be to supplement paternal function, and resist transference pressure to act into functioning as an extension of a phobic structure, as exemplified in the part of 'Howie's' therapy discussed earlier.

Most contemporary Lacanians adhere to the traversing of these fantasy structures in the later stages of analysis. Like Freud's 'transference neuroses', Lacanian distinctions between different forms of neurosis are based on the way the Other is related to in the transference. Nasio (1992) emphasizes that the analyst becomes the cause of the symptom through the transference. The analyst's assuming the 'cause of desire' for the analysand enables change to take place. Lacanian 'strategies' as to how this might happen with different forms of pathology are new and add a different dimension to our understanding of transference.

Post-Kleinian approaches: Deep containment, projective identification and counteridentification, projective and rigid motion transformations

Much post-Kleinian theory and technique related to transference issues still rests on Klein's seminal paper, 'The origins of transference' (1952b). Here she outlined how the constantly shifting interrelationships and movements between objects and part-objects in the transference mirror the rapid vicissitudes of the infant's internal world and early confusions between internal and external reality:

> I hold that transference originates in the same processes which in the early stages determine object relations. Therefore we have to go back again and again in analysis to the fluctuations between objects, loved and hated, internal and external, which dominate early infancy . . .
>
> Altogether, in the young infant's mind every external experience is interwoven with his phantasies and on the other hand every phantasy contains elements of actual experience, and it is only by analyzing the transference situation to its depth that we are able to discover the past both in its realistic and phantastic aspects.
>
> (ibid. [1975b]: 53–4)

In Kleinian terms, unconscious phantasy is a mental representation of somatic instinctual processes which become confused with perceptions and memories (Isaacs 1952). Therefore, both present perceptions in the transference and memories of the past are subject to the same psychological processes and distortions.

The primary post-Kleinian orientation therefore lies is in the way the patient constructs the transference relationship in unconscious phantasy. Most or all interpretations centre round the patient's use of the analyst in the transference. This approach, at worst, can run the risk of what has been dubbed irreverently a 'me too' style of interpretation, and the kind of *folie à deux* Racker warns against (discussed earlier in this chapter). At best, this understanding is applied in a more sophisticated manner. Joseph (1985), for example, describes how every minute aspect of interaction with the patient is a manifestation of transference, including the way a therapist may unconsciously re-enact her patient's projected issues through 'parallel process' in supervision.

Regressive manifestations of transference

All post-Kleinians consider projective identification the primary route of unconscious communication between patient and analyst, and sometimes the terms projective identification and transference are used almost interchangeably (Caper 1999). For Kleinians and post-Kleinians, projective identification describes the process through which aspects of one's own feelings or impulses are experienced in others (Klein 1946, 1952b, 1955; Rosenfeld 1965, 1987; Bion 1967). The forms this can take range from a benign type of communication, such as Bion (1962) described in the early mother/infant relationship, to very hostile and intrusive forms of psychological assault (Hinshelwood 1994). In its more extreme destructive forms, powerful pressure is exerted on the recipient to identify and 'act in' to the projection. Aspects of oneself are then experienced as being in the external world, a phenomenon Britton describes as 'attributive projective identifications' (Britton 1998: 6). Hence, projective identification can be seen as a bridging concept in the internal/external reality debate around transference issues.

Bion's (1962) concepts of 'reverie' and 'container/contained' (described in Chapter 4) facilitated analytic receptivity to projective identification as a means of communication. In severe disturbance, splitting and fragmentation are inevitably accompanied by extremely forceful and hostile projective identification, often of aspects of the self confused with part-objects in primitive forms. Bion's (1967) work focused on the analyst's capacity to contain and ultimately detoxify these noxious, damaging states of mind, a process Caper (1999) describes as 'analytic *alpha* function'.[6] This approach has two great strengths. First, it permits of deep and taxing work with very damaged patients, and second, it enables the tracking of very fine movements from states of great to slightly lesser disturbance in terms of the width of splitting, the nature of the part-objects, and the relative violence of the projective identifications.

For example, my patient 'Patrice' (described in Chapter 4), moved from seeing me as an intergalactic enemy from outer space in the transference to a Conservative government agent sent to spy on him. Both these projections could be seen as equally delusional. However, the fact that a Conservative government agent might be part of our shared reality and closer to home, and more importantly the fact that being the recipient of the later projection was far less disorienting and disturbing, were both indications that an integrative movement was taking place.

Bion (1965) also distinguished between 'rigid motion' and 'projective' transformations in the transference. In keeping with his preference for mathematical abstract terms as empty 'unsaturated' concepts without an existing penumbra of meaning, these terms were originally used in projective geometry to distinguish degrees of deformation within spatial movement. Bion deployed them to differentiate between neurotic and psychotic forms of transference, regardless of the level of psychopathology of the client. Rigid motion transformations, which, as Bion pointed out, correspond to the term 'transference' as Freud used it, imply little deformation (ibid.), and are discussed slightly later under progressive aspects of transference. I will illustrate the properties of 'projective' transformations with a vignette from my patient 'Ewan', also discussed in Chapter 4.

Early in Ewan's therapy, he was not able to sustain either his feelings or a capacity to symbolize during breaks. After a three-week Easter break, Ewan arrived at his first session late and in a strange, disconnected and vague state. He seemed unable to think or to remember any of what we had talked about and made sense of prior to the break. He had been sleeping with his ex-girlfriend, whom he had no intention of going back to. He attributed his resumption of the sexual relationship to 'lust'.

   Because we were accustomed to Ewan's 'losing his feelings' during breaks, I was able to interpret his entire mental state as a reaction to separation and loss. Then, he was able to make a link with his attitude towards his mother, to whom Ewan was still not speaking because of his deep grievance about her perceived preference for his siblings in early childhood.

Ewan's reaction to my break was a 'projective transformation' because the distortion of his feelings through splitting, projective identification and confusion rendered them virtually unrecognizable and badly affected his capacity to think (Bion 1965: 31). At this point in his therapy, he had not yet securely established a good-enough internal object to enable him to tolerate absence and frustration, in Kleinian terms.

Transference and countertransference as a conjoint entity

Heimann (1950), while she was still a Kleinian, opened the potential of countertransference as the primary vehicle through which to experience and come to understand deep unconscious communication. Despite her contribution, post-Kleinians do not conceive of transference/countertransference as an intersubjective phenomenon in the same way as many of today's Independents. Whilst everything the analyst experiences is minutely scrutinized for countertransferential information about the patient, the analyst's personality and pathology are not deemed essential aspects of a newly created 'analytic third' (Ogden 1994a). If the analyst senses some countertransferential embroilment, it is as problematic in Kleinian as in Lacanian terms.

   León Grinberg (1990) theorizes 'projective counteridentification' as a situation in which an analyst unconsciously identifies with her patient's projective identification but her impartiality is not interfered with. Using Racker's (1968) concept of 'complementary countertransference', Grinberg posits that projective counteridentification only truly emerges when an analyst's neurotic residues are not reactivated by conflicts introduced by her patient, but she still takes upon herself the intensity and quality of her patient's projective identification. She remains able to think about what is happening to her, but on a 'razor's edge' which must lead beyond projective counteridentification if it is to be metabolized and used in the service of moving both parties in the analytic couple on (Grinberg 1990: 96).

Progressive aspects of transference/countertransference

On the whole, post-Kleinian views on progressive movements within the transference involve shifts to depressive processes with their concomitant concern, reparative impulses, increased levels of integration and separation, and improved capacity to symbolize and triangulate. Huge amounts of thought have been given to the differentiation between paranoid/schizoid and depressive processes in the patient (for example Joseph 1978). Bion's theorization of a necessary fluctuation between these two modes of experience lent different emphases to their uses in transference. The example of a projective transformation given earlier shows how regressions to paranoid/schizoid processes may be part of a reaction to specific anxieties such as separation and interpretable as such. Bion's complementary concept of 'rigid motion transformations' illustrates how such anxieties might be managed in a depressive and symbolic dimension.

> My patient 'Kevin' (discussed in Chapters 4, 5 and 9) left a message on my voicemail asking me to call him on my first day back from the same three-week Easter break. When I called, he seemed relieved but the purpose of his request was unclear. In his first session, he commented that he had felt a great intensification of longing for an ex-girlfriend although he knew he did not want to resume the relationship. He said: 'It wasn't difficult to tell that I had displaced my feelings about missing you onto her.'
>
> During the break, Kevin had had a dream in which a particularly valued friend had been run over by a truck, but had survived the accident. He had been anxious about whether I would come back from my break, and also about whether the resources he had internalized from his therapy would survive his anger at my absence.

In this rigid motion transformation, Kevin's feelings of loss, anxiety and anger remained intact and invariant. I was represented symbolically by the ex-girlfriend and the valued friend. He retained his capacity to think.

Bion's (1962, 1970) concepts of reverie and faith, and his emphasis on the inhibition of memory and desire in the analyst, make it possible for unexpected and new developments in the transference to become the most significant factor (see also Chapter 8). His concept of 'transformations in O' (discussed in Chapter 9) enables profound psychic shifts to arise from unanticipated and deeply unconscious states in both patient and therapist. Indeed he claims that the only resistance is to O, the imminence of reality and becoming that reality (Bion 1965). His orientation towards the unknown, new and not yet evolved in every session transmutes the meaning of transference into a dimension which may include unprecedented developments in the psychic evolution of the patient at least as much as any repetition or re-activation of pathology.

THE VEXED ROLE OF THE TRANSFERENCE INTERPRETATION IN CONTEMPORARY PRACTICE

James Strachey's (1934) landmark paper, 'The nature of the therapeutic action of psychoanalysis', cemented the role of the transference interpretation as the principal mutative instrument for several decades. Today, a wider range of clinical interventions are deemed desirable by many theorists.

Lacan (1953–4), whilst praising the rigour of Strachey's paper, criticized the circularity of its argument: the analyst is perceived as the patient's hostile superego and he must therefore wait for a time when the patient's id impulses are at their most intense to make an interpretation which can modify its harshness. For Lacan, Strachey's insistence on the perception of analyst as superego fell into the trap of imaginary transference, and ignored the possibilities inherent in a symbolic relationship which incorporates desire. He thought interpretation should be subordinated to reduction of the transference and:

> If the transference takes on its virtue from being brought back to the reality of which the analyst is the representative, and if it is a question of ripening the Object in the hot house of a confined situation, the analysand is left with only one object, if you will pardon the expression, to get his teeth into, and that's the analyst.
>
> (Lacan 1958a [2001]: 271)

Instead, interpretations, if they are made, are intended to be heard as coming from within a particular transferential position, as opposed to an interpretation of it. Lacan also suggested a range of interventions designed to confuse the ego and promote access to unconscious processes.

Like the Lacanians, contemporary Independents (following Winnicott) consider it more efficacious if the patient can find their own way out of a transference gridlock, move themselves on or make their own interpretation. This kind of moment, as Winnicott (1969) said, may arrive creatively and with great joy. The analyst's need to be clever may pre-empt this possibility.

Post-Kleinians still focus more on transference interpretations than either of the other two contemporary schools, although the ways they may be thought about and used have been modified, particularly in their emphasis on the patient's reaction to interpretation (Steiner 1993; Britton 1998). Bion's work opened the possibility of more enigmatic interventions and the transformative properties of unconscious processes themselves.

All these innovations in technique will be explored in the next chapter.

NOTES

1. Lacan later revised his theory of intersubjectivity. In *Seminar VIII* (1960–1), he introduced the concept of '*agalma*' or a mysterious object of desire linked to *objet a* with a consequent 'subjective disparity'; later still, he focused on *objet a* as the cause and object of desire (Lacan 1964a) (see later in this chapter).
2. Searles, Ogden and Benjamin's accounts of the uses of the erotic in the service of development are discussed in Chapter 2.
3. Excellent accounts of the history of transference and countertransference can be found in Symington (1986), Mann (1999) and Nobus (2000).
4. Another example of this process is given in Chapter 2.
5. '*Le sujet supposé savoir*' is translated as 'the subject supposed to know' by Sheridan and Gallagher. Nobus (2000) translates this as 'the supposed subject of knowing', thereby emphasizing that the subject as well as the knowledge is 'supposed'.
6. Caper's distinctions between 'synthetic' and 'analytic' *alpha* function, and between holding and containment, are discussed in Chapter 8.

Chapter 8

Surprise, humour and non-interpretation

A new look at psychoanalytic technique

[T]he whole notion of technique, at its most extreme, is complicit with fantasies of superiority.

(Phillips 2002: 31)

Our own technical interventions, I think, are . . . part of the unconscious work occurring usually, spontaneously and freely within us.

(Bollas in Molino (ed.) 1997: 25)

A session is a potential space . . . both persons are dreaming each other . . .

(Bollas in Molino (ed.) 1997: 37)

While all the above remarks are true, not to reflect on what we actually do and say with our patients can be dangerous, as if our unconscious intuitive processes could be infallible. We cannot separate issues of technique from the theories of the psychoanalytic paradigm, although whether theory determines what we can observe (Einstein 1971) or efficient practice precedes theory (G. Ryle 1949) is worth consideration.

In the two previous chapters, we saw how the three schools' clinical approach is partly determined by diagnostic criteria. For all three, major technical issues in work with very disturbed patients are critical. Equally importantly, the fabric of the transference/countertransference matrix germinates interventions rooted both in conscious reflective practice and in intuition honed by immersion in theoretical and clinical experience. The wisdom of the unconscious, the ultimate Lacanian 'subject supposed to know' (Fink 1997: 30), can be neglected only at peril of over-systematizing versions of psychoanalysis. Different patients elicit and need different forms of intervention from us, in ways that go beyond any embroilment in countertransference.

Whilst technical issues cannot be dissociated from the body of thought of their practitioners, specific innovations in technique do now distinguish and inform the therapeutic practice of the three schools. I shall devote this chapter to a discussion of these developments, and I shall also look at some aspects of clinical practice which emerged from tradition and have persisted in either conscious or unexamined form.

Process models of mind and psychic growth are now starting to permeate psychoanalytic thought and impact on clinical practice. Today, greater weight is given to a range of clinical interventions which may act as spurs to a shift to a new and surprising perspective and have an unconscious impact. The use of the transference interpretation as the principal mutative instrument has in varying degrees shifted to an emphasis on tools which stimulate the patient's own capacity for fresh and unprecedented apprehension.

The three schools converge over many issues included in the treatment of psychosis and other forms of severe disturbance, and agree that it is usually undesirable to spell out too much to the patient (with the possible exception of some contemporary Kleinians). However, there are unbridgeable divergences of opinion over such issues as the uses of countertransference and the timing and significance of non-interpretation. For the most part, there is now less of an appeal to the ego in all three contemporary practices, except in psychotic conditions or severe 'disturbances of the self', where insufficient capacity to oversee and mentate affective experience is likely to be an issue. Less emphasis on conscious recognition and understanding, and more appeal to powerful unconscious currents capable of promoting life and liveliness, creativity and change, may appear in unpredetermined developments. Greater emphasis on the intuitive, the spontaneous and the unconscious intersubjective interaction now supplements the consciously worked-through interpretation.

Issues of timing are critical for the three schools, but used in the service of different metapsychologies. All three broadly agree on central technical issues such as the boundaries of the analytic frame and the analyst's 'neutrality'. Non-disclosure of personal data enables the use of the analyst as a projective screen for all three schools, although they diverge over the ways in which an analyst may use her own subjectivity as a therapeutic instrument. All three concur on an analytic attitude of free-floating attention or reverie to maximize access to unconscious processes. Bollas' (1987) 'generative split' enables the analyst to observe how she is being affected (or projected into) by her client and her contrapuntal free associative processes.

Within the convergences of thought, radical differences exist: Bion (1970) and Ogden (1997), for example, place different emphases on what analytic reverie involves. The predominant analytic mode remains, within an attentive attitude, silence, although the uses and meanings of silence take on subtly different hues depending on the clinical context. Divergences in the uses of timing are major. Lacanians, famously, are the only contemporary psychoanalytic school to dispense with the invariability of the fifty-minute session (see later in this chapter).

CONTEMPORARY INDEPENDENT TECHNIQUE

> It seems to me that what the comedian, the lover and the mystic all keep very close to is a notion of the erotic . . . something that's to do with a certain kind of ease . . . getting a joke, for me, would be the model of a good interpretation.
>
> (Phillips in Molino (ed.) 1997: 133)

As we saw in Chapters 2 and 7, contemporary Independents emphasize the value of a period of regression to dependence for analysands with 'disturbances of the self': that is to say, people whose difficulties stem from very early in life and are manifest in their sense of themselves, their capacity for 'going on being' themselves and their interrelationships with others (Winnicott 1956: 303; 1962). These clients might be classified as narcissistic, borderline or as a specific form of 'character pathology' such as normosis (Bollas 1987), false self (Winnicott 1960) or 'as if' personality covering a fragmented instinctual self (Sandler and Sandler 1998). Regression to dependence may also be needed where a client's psychopathology includes lacunae of encapsulated non-relatedness (Green 1983; S. Klein 1981).

Drawing from Winnicott (1954b) and Balint (1968), Independents emphasize a quasi-maternal containment to enable a regression to very early unorganized states of mind in order to repair something which may have been missed or disturbed in early life. The ways this regression and its containment have been theorized are discussed in Chapters 2 and 7. I will briefly recapitulate here.

Within an attitude of 'primary maternal preoccupation' (Winnicott 1956), the analyst must use her countertransference in such a way that states of mind or being which are wordlessly transmitted or projected from the patient can be tolerated, held and digested for as long as is necessary to return them in a thought-through fashion without impingement or trauma. Much of the work may initially take place without interpretation. Often, all that is needed is for the analyst to bear and digest her patient's state of mind for long periods of time, whilst providing empathic attunement. In this way the analysand may gain an experience of 'going on being' undisturbed and unimpinged on in the presence of another, which may eventually enable him to bear and articulate his own states of being.

For this to be possible, a 'facilitating environment' is necessary, including the provision of a treatment setting which is stable, psychologically and physically comfortable and uninterrupted, and an ever-mindful and non-reactive emotional environment (Winnicott 1954b). This treatment methodology is only really effective in high-frequency analysis, four or five times a week, although it has been adapted for use in some public sector treatment settings where a damaged client group requires skilled, sensitive and adaptive clinical practice (White *et al.* 2001). The primary Winnicottian technical principle adopted by contemporary Independents is that the analyst must adapt to the patient, and never the other way around.

Some more recent theorists elaborated and extended the primary technical considerations introduced by Winnicott. Green (1977a) points out that borderline patients may have difficulty with symbolizing and the 'as if' dimension of treatment, and so for the patient the analyst and the treatment setting may literally become the mother for a period, become the primary object or other of the patient's experience, although, of course, the clinician must never lose sight of the 'as if' dimension of treatment. Khan (1969) described three modes of existence: being, knowing and experiencing, which may evolve in this kind of treatment setting and the critical importance of timing and 'not-interpreting': '. . . the basic ego-strength and complexity of psychic functioning has to establish itself in the patient before he can arrive at the point where the non-interpretation of the analyst crystallizes the experience of being in the patient' (ibid. [1996]: 205). Bollas (1979, 1987) and Milner (1969) theorized this form of treatment with extended clinical examples, and Searles (1965, 1986b) wrote vivid and graphic analyses of regression to dependence with frankly psychotic and very disturbed borderline patients. He said: 'The repetition compulsion is, in my view, an unconscious attempt not merely to "relive" an earlier experience, but to *live* it for the *first* time—to live it, that is, with full emotional participation' (Searles 1986b: 8, his emphasis).

Whilst regression to dependence has always been central for very damaged patients within Independent technique, recent Independent theorists place equal emphasis on how a client's moving on to differentiated relating can be enabled (Ogden 1987, 1989b; Bollas 1992; Benjamin 1995) (see Chapter 2). Accounts of how and why movements towards separation, individuation, triangulation and greater complexity of subjectivity are come by vary immensely. Benjamin's (1995) theorization of the beginnings of differentiated relating within the maternal dyad has profound implications for technique. As we saw in Chapter 2, she centralizes what goes on in the mind of the mother in early infant development, and, by implication, in the mind of the analyst with her patient. Through the mother's capacity to withstand the infant's aggression, the very small child comes to discover her as a separate person with a mind of her own. If the mother (or the therapist) caves in, or retaliates, or withdraws, she cannot be experienced as other but only as an aspect of the child's omnipotence. Benjamin's version of Winnicott's 'use of an object' stresses real contact with real people coming about through aggression and resilience. Benjamin (1995, 1998) and Ogden (1994a, 1997) stress the intersubjective process, with its constituent crystallizing moments, as formative and mutative: 'where objects were, subjects must be' (Benjamin 1998: xii).

An example comes from 'Edward's' therapy, a man who was creatively successful but unaccustomed to the analytic method. His attitude to his dreams had up to this point been dismissive. He recounted a dream in which he went into a Vietnamese restaurant, and was about to move onto something else as he thought its meaning was of no consequence (he liked Vietnamese food etc.). I asked him for his associations. He looked blank, and so I helped him along a bit: 'What does Vietnam mean to you? (knowing his political sympathies) It got bombed the hell out of . . .?' He suddenly jumped out of his seat: 'It had a civil war! It was divided against itself . . . just like me. God, is the unconscious really that clever?'

Therefore, whilst with patients with 'disturbances of the self' contemporary Independents prioritise minute attunement to promote an 'illusion of oneness' (Milner 1952 [1987]: 100), at a later stage and with less disturbed clients, they deploy a many faceted promotion of increasing degrees and differing forms of becoming more separate. This is always a very gradual process.

Ogden, as we saw in Chapter 2, sets his recognition of separateness, difference and alterity within the mother/infant and analyst/patient dyad, but within a re-conceptualization of Oedipal processes as occurring in a transitional arena. With different paths for boys and girls, Ogden grounds the onset of the Oedipus Complex in the recognition of another in the mother's mind. This 'transitional Oedipal relationship'—the mother is experienced as both me and not-me simultaneously—is of equal technical importance to Lacan's description of 'paternal function' as existing primarily in the mind of the mother and perhaps supplemented by an actual father or significant other. Its implications require the analyst to bear some form of other in mind to create necessary boundaries and space, once the patient has moved beyond the point at which interpretation of infantile dependence is appropriate. For example, a holiday break from therapy may not just be experienced as a difficult absence, but might provide intriguing possibilities of fantasied triangular relating.

For example, the patient I described in Chapters 6 and 7 as 'Howie' had been a closeted and indulged 'Mummy's boy'. Neither his father nor anyone else was allowed to intervene in his claustrophobically enmeshed relationship with his mother. Near the beginning of Howie's therapy, I made an interpretation about the interruption of his therapy by the holiday break. He let me know very quickly he hated such interpretations—it felt as if I were trying to bind him into his therapy for ever. I discovered with this patient that it was more helpful to him to make triangulated interpretations around break times. For example, on one occasion, Howie said: 'It's a very long break.' I replied: 'It is a long break and in some ways you will struggle with that. But it must also be a relief to you to know that there is someone or something who can take me away from you.'

These versions of access to triangular space expand the scope of subjectivity, and intersubjectivity. They decentre growth processes and relocate them potentially in any relationship in which difference can be recognized and utilized. As discussed in Chapters 2 and 7, Ogden's 'analytic third' denotes a new form of consciousness generated by the unique psychic combination of a particular analyst and analysand. From here on, a transference interpretation becomes just one of a range of interventions and intersubjective moments which may bring about change, development and aliveness. Surprise in many forms, a good joke or even a pointed piece of fun or mischief, the introduction of an unexpected perspective, even a piece of provocation or sarcasm, or the analyst's speaking from a place the patient has not anticipated, can all keep the process alive and both parties in the analytic couple moving on.

A brief example comes from the therapy of the patient I call 'Claudia' (discussed further in Chapter 9). Claudia had managed her early deprivations in a merged relationship with her husband and daughters, in which she effectively functioned as an extension of their needs. In breaks from therapy, she would usually 'adopt' another very needy person and fill up the emptiness in herself by projecting it into this temporary adoptee and ministering to her every need. A prime candidate for this role was her mother-in-law, Gladys.

Claudia had been planning to invite Gladys to share the family holiday during my summer break. In sessions she complained in anticipation of her mother-in-law's demands and intransigence. Claudia then had a dream in which Gladys was monstrously obese and covered in a cape-like garment, which she lifted to reveal huge pendulous breasts. I said 'You're flirting with Gladys to fill up the break', an intervention which also alluded to the mildly homoerotic aspect of the transference which can be a feature with emotionally deprived clients.

Psychoanalysis, although deeply serious, no longer requires a 'po-faced' attitude. Coltart (1986) emphasized the role of uncertainty, spontaneity and humour as potentially mutative aspects of the analyst's style. Like Ogden, Searles, Eigen and Symington, she privileged the unexpected as an indicator of development and stressed not so much the analyst's neutrality (although this is very much taken as read) as their delight in the process. She aimed, she said, not for shallowness, but lightheartedness, within a meditative state of mind (Coltart in Molino (ed.) 1997).

Searles' technique is radically honest, almost shocking, in particular his rigorous scrutiny of countertransferential areas many might prefer to disown. He thinks it important to tailor the tone and form of the inter-pretation to meet the patient's state of mind:

> For example, when the patient is in a phase of exploring predominantly oral conflicts, interpretations may need to be made in a spirit of feeding; when he is in a predominantly anal phase, in a spirit facili-tating of increasingly well-controlled catharsis; when he is in a phase of exploring genital-sexual conflicts, in a spirit of well-sublimated sexual interaction with him.
>
> (Searles 1986b: 14)

Contemporary Independents think very carefully about the timing as well as the nature of interpretation. Interpreting too early can impinge on an analysand's gradually evolving capacity to be herself, and to bear and articulate her own feelings. Searles pointed out a premature interpretation of a lack of self/object differentiation may be 'suicidal-despair-engendering' (ibid.: 19) in that it can highlight the difficulty in maintaining a sufficiently separate sense of self before the patient has had time to develop it. In consequence most Independents, like Winnicott, emphasize the importance of non-interpretation, not just with regressed patients but as an essential aspect of timing: knowing when to let a patient be and deploy his own creativity. Phillips thinks: 'A clinical preoccupation with "how to let oneself be used, become the servant of the process" implies that interpretation might become a sophisticated form of interruption, the way the analyst insists on being important' (Phillips 1993: 69). As Searles points out, though, silence may be experienced by the patient in a multitude of different ways, and may communicate a gamut of emotions from intense empathic interest to critical condemnation, from intent presence to deadly self-absorption—even con-stant and intrusive interruption (Searles 1986b: 15–17). For Searles, the 'emotional atmosphere or climate of the sessions, day after day and year after year' and the analyst's unconscious attitude furnish the critical thera-peutic and technical factors (ibid.: 4).

Independents also emphasize interventions which facilitate evolving self states at different stages of analysis. For example, Harold Stewart (1992) lists four 'agents for psychic change' aside from transference interpreta-tions: 'extra-transference interpretations', 'reconstructions', 'therapeutic regression', and 'techniques other than interpretation to overcome thera-peutic impasse' (ibid.: 139). 'Extra-transference interpretations' refer to transferences to other people and situations outside the analytic setting. As part of the Independent emphasis on realities outside the consulting room, they think: 'A "transference only" position is theoretically untenable and could lead to an artificial reduction of all associations and interpretations into a transference mould and to an idealized *folie-à-deux*' (Blum 1983: 615, quoted in Stewart 1992: 130).

An example comes from a patient I call 'Clara' who described her experience of a previous analysis. Clara, whose parents were both disturbed, had befriended an 'Auntie' who lived next door in a tight-knit East London community. At eighteen months, Clara would slip through the hole in the fence to talk to 'Auntie Belle', who remained a life-long friend until Clara was in her forties and Belle died aged ninety-three.

Clara, understandably upset, reported Belle's death in her analysis. Her analyst interpreted her anxiety about his survival. Now, whilst Clara's father had been suicidal and she was anxious about most people's survival, Belle had been one of her first experiences of a non-intrusive, responsive, friendly relationship (the other was her maternal grandmother). Clara needed these benign primary objects and had been unusually resourceful at an early age in discovering and making use of them. Her previous analyst's interpretation ran the risk of annihilating the varied relationships she had been able to create and restricting her experience to her disturbed parenting.

'Reconstructions' concern those aspects of a patient's history which may be unconsciously re-enacted in the present. In Clara's case her analyst could have acknowledged her resourcefulness in making use of other relationships including her analysis, and saved the interpretation about her anxiety for situations with a clear correlation. She was frightened of returning home after a holiday, for example. In adolescence she had come back from a week away with a friend's family to discover the front door open and a half-cooked pan of chips on the stove. She knew immediately her father had taken an overdose.

'Techniques other than interpretation to overcome therapeutic impasse' result from the extensive literature on clinical modifications with narcissistic and borderline patients, discussed in Chapter 5 and later in this chapter. Stewart cites Rosenfeld's (1978) example from a merged, delusional trans-ference psychosis when he '. . . sat the patient up, encouraged him to go over his criticisms and grudges towards his analyst, and gave no interpretations, simply adopting an entirely receptive, empathic listening attitude towards

him' (Stewart 1992: 136). Stewart also cites his analysis of a silently murderous schizophrenic patient in which, after he had borne his massive
hostility for several months, he eventually said he could stand it no longer
and that if he did not begin to speak by the end of the week, he would
terminate his analysis. My own experience is that, even with very disturbed
patients, such expressive uses of the countertransference are not needed. I
worked with a murderously silent severely borderline patient, and found
that with him, as with many patients, there was an unconscious recognition
of when I was about to reach the limits of my endurance and a corresponding analytic shift (cf. Symington 1983). Expressive countertransferential interventions should only ever be used in exceptional circumstances
by very experienced psychotherapists, who are fully aware of the dangers of
self-disclosure, and the ways this may interfere with the transference. The
client may become fearful of their therapist's vulnerability or even fragility:
self-disclosure on the part of the therapist often communicates a self-
protective stance. The painstaking, detailed monitoring of the transference/
countertransference matrix and an overall analytic attitude of restraint
should never ordinarily be broken.

Ogden (1994b) develops the concept of 'interpretive action' to supplement the verbal transference interpretation. 'Interpretive actions' might
include the expression on the analyst's face, the way the fee is set, the
announcement of the end of the analytic hour, the analyst's tone of voice
and non-verbal responses to the patient such as laughter. For example, the
patient I call 'William' (in Chapter 9) had a dream during a break that he
came to visit me in a large clapboard house with a verandah and a swimming pool. Both in his dream and in the session I laughed—an unconscious
intuitive recognition on both our parts of this client's tendency to idealize
and exaggerate the wonderful lives of other people in comparison with his
own. Such interpretive actions can be both a swift means of conveying
understanding and a form of analytic management.

Casement (1985, 1990, 2002) focuses on unconscious 'supervisory'
comments from the patient about her experience of analytic interventions.

An example comes from 'Clara's' therapy. She had a capacity to elicit punitive
and persecutory reactions from others as a consequence of an introject of a
pathologically critical mother, who seemed to experience everything Clara
attempted as a separate person as an attack on their relationship. Clara's
previous analyst had become persistently and punitively critical when she
began an intense love affair in the middle of her analysis. Whilst this could
have been splitting the transference, her analyst's response fell into the trap
Racker (1968) warned of when he wrote of the danger of the analyst's

becoming overly identified with a 'good' moralistic superego and interpreting the patient's 'bad' libidinal impulses. Clara told her analyst she felt his attitude was becoming like her mother's. Her analyst replied that she should stop trying to supervise him. If he had taken Casement's ideas on board, he could have reflected on a possible countertransferential entanglement, and disengaged himself sufficiently to become able to think about why he was interpreting Clara's relationship in a condemnatory way.

Bollas (1989) describes a range of psychoanalytic techniques to enable the crystallization of transitional moments of beginning to relate to and introject resourceful, interesting objects. As well as stressing the importance of non-interpretation, hesitation and 'minimal analytic presence' (ibid.: 98), he suggests the analyst may need to celebrate his analysand's ego abilities and expanding repertoire of affects as part of enabling his client to 'use' him as an object. He makes a plea for differing styles with different patients and the recognition of '. . . the unique idiom of each person' (ibid.: 109).

A patient in analysis with a practitioner of contemporary Independent orientation is likely to feel considered, attuned to and that her states of mind are met. A sometime omission of interpretation could feel baffling to the client, initially at least, but this could in turn lead to her feeling she has more resources with which to elaborate and think on her own dilemmas than she might previously have recognized. For those in acute or prolonged states of dis-ease with themselves, the Independent approach will feel holding, reliable, predictable and safe in that the client will not have interpretations foisted on her beyond her ability to make use of them at the time. For those psychologically ready to risk a more adventurous exploration of their internal worlds, the experience may be unpredictable, even sometimes heady, startling or fun. Although the analysand is likely to sense that her aggression is met, she may not always feel her destructiveness is confronted vigorously, and she might feel she has been overly left to her own devices or allowed to get away with things. At best, though, she is likely to have a creative, enriching experience, which enables her to make fuller use of her life.

CONTEMPORARY LACANIAN TECHNIQUE: A RED HERRING?

The principal Lacanian clinical aim, for neurotics at least, is to reveal the unconscious through slips and gaps in language. As language or, more precisely, the signifier and the signifying chain, structure experience, reflective subjectivity can be developed through symbolization, but by the same token, that which is unconscious is created by the constricting impact of language on experience. Lacanian analysts abstain from filling in the meaning of their interpretations so as to avoid acting into the imaginary role of 'subject supposed to know' (discussed in Chapter 7). They aim to intervene in the client's own signification and use of metaphor so that it can be modified, claiming that other techniques of interpretation involve substituting the analyst's metaphor for the client's (Nobus 2003). Nathalie Charraud (2000) demonstrates how hitting a point of convergence of signifiers (with multiple meanings) helps to unstick the fixed meaning of a signifier in relation to an object and hence also to free up the client's unconscious position.

Both Burgoyne (1997) and Fink (2004) cite Lacan's commentaries on a case described by Kris (1951), where the patient, a scientist, was convinced he was plagiarizing a colleague's work. Kris, after checking the evidence himself, decided that the reverse was true (Lacan 1953–4, 1954, 1955–6, 1958a). Burgoyne stresses that the analyst should interpret relatively little and demonstrates how attention to the German word '*gross*' (big) in this patient's chain of associations could have loosened some of Kris' patient's fixed significations. His use of the words grandfather (*grossvater*) (an eminent scientist), big fish (the patient competed with his father as to who could catch the biggest) and brains (*grosshirn*) linked stealing, eating and plagiarizing. This alternative play on words as an intervention would have introduced a notion of lack and hence brought desire into play. Fink focuses on Kris' literal approach to the question of plagiarism—his interpretation played into the imaginary relation between analyst and patient and aimed to bring the patient's perception of external reality into line with Kris' own. As Kris ignored the question of symbolic lack, the patient went out to eat fresh brains after the session, perhaps as fresh brains had been missing in the session. Fink stresses how Kris' practice standardizes the perceptions of his patient; Lacan calls this 'engineering' (Lacan 1954: 395). '[E]go psychology . . . lops off the entire symbolic dimension' (Fink 2004: 62). Traditional Kleinian interpretation is also taken to task for overstressing the imaginary dimension (Fink 2004: 52–62). The case of 'Clara', earlier in this chapter, is a clear example of an analyst interpreting in imaginary mode.

Therefore, Lacanians play upon the multiple ambiguities and double or treble meanings inherent in their analysands' discourse. This understanding enlivens psychoanalytic technique, has had some impact on contemporary Independent style, and is discussed later in this chapter. A brief clinical illustration will show how closely Lacan followed Freud in this respect.

My patient 'Howie', whom you will remember from Chapter 6 as struggling with the symbolic aspect of registering meaning, began a relationship with a woman I shall call Siobhan. Howie's previous pattern in relationships had been to start an affair or go off with someone else when it began to encounter difficulties. He wanted to keep this relationship, and was keen not to repeat the pattern.

His girlfriend's father, with whom she had a vexed and ambivalent relationship, had a heart attack. Siobhan became more clingy, and Howie found it very difficult to cope with this behaviour as it reminded him of the suffocatingly exclusive attentions of his mother. He had a series of dreams in which he was flirting or kissing or about to go to bed with a number of women with red hair. He wondered aloud in the session why this was so—he was not aware of being attracted to any of them and did not like some of them. The main women in his life, he said, were either blonde (his mother, me) or brunette (Siobhan). I said: 'Maybe it's a red-hairing.'

At a psychotic level of disturbance, though, a different analytic approach is required. As you will recall from Chapters 3 and 7, the need to strengthen the delusional metaphor means the analyst cannot position herself as an 'Other' in the symbolic dimension or introduce another perspective or point of view: 'In delusional speech the Other is truly excluded . . .' (Lacan 1955–6 [1993]: 53). She therefore acts and speaks as if she were an other in the psychotic's imaginary world, with the aim of buttressing this, his only mode of functioning:

> The symbolic order, missing a crucial element (the Name-of-the-Father) cannot be structurally repaired . . . it can, however, be propped up or 'supplemented' (to use Lacan's term) by another order . . . it is the imaginary that is relied upon to cover the hole in the symbolic . . . The goal, superficially stated, is to return the imaginary to the stable state that characterized it prior to the psychotic break.
>
> (Fink 1997: 101)

A clinical example of this process is given in Chapter 7.

Green thinks that, if someone tells you they are a Lacanian, you do not know what this will entail in practice.[1] Most contemporary Lacanians, who broadly speaking follow the technical principles established by Lacan, would not agree with this. Lacanians begin work with a 'pre-analysis' of one or two sessions a week with the patient sitting up for up to a year (Fink 1997), although some claim a few weeks are all that is needed (Hill 2002). This 'pre-analytic' phase has a dual purpose: it gives the analyst the opportunity to arrive at a more considered and deeper diagnostic picture than could be derived from a more superficial reading of symptomatology and gives the analysand the opportunity to become acquainted with the analytic method before they engage at a more intense level.

We saw in the previous chapter how Lacanian approaches to transference within differential diagnosis rely on a conscious manipulation of deep transferential variables. Within this context, the clinical emphasis is always on the primacy and the therapeutic efficacy of working with the unconscious. As always in Lacanian praxis, a dialectical tension exists between careful diagnostic procedures and intentional 'strategies' of transference, and the surprise-filled, lively affair that is Lacanian analysis in practice, moment to moment: '. . . the analyst is less free in his strategy than in his tactics' (Lacan 1958a [2001]: 254). This tension reinforces the dual movement of subjectification propounded by Lacan (discussed in Chapter 3) in which dispersal of meaning is as important as symbolization. The analyst maintains an attitude of free-floating attention which Lacan described (in relation to the value of supervision) as a second subjectivity, or '. . . having ears *in order not to hear*, in other words in order to pick up what is to be heard' (Lacan 1953 [2001]: 50, his emphases).

Lacanians take resistance very seriously, although they stress that it belongs mainly to the analyst. They believe a client's demand may not initially be for deep change, as she may come into treatment because of a life crisis or because her defence structure is not functioning as effectively or providing the same gains as previously (Fink 1997). Analysands do not necessarily arrive motivated to sustain the rigours of a long and deep analysis. Therefore, the emphasis is placed squarely on the analyst's desire (discussed in Chapter 7)—a purified form of desire for the analysand to remain in analysis and develop their own passion for discovering the unconscious (Lacan 1964a). The analysand learns to takes the satisfactions and excitements of the free associative process in preference to those provided by their symptoms or even the relief of their symptoms. The analyst's desire is never for the analysand to improve in any way or to do or not do anything in particular with her life. Neither is the analyst's desire associated with her countertransference, which must be rigorously scrutinized. The initial aim for the neurotic analysand, and the eventual aim for the perverse one, is to transform the space of demand into the space of desire, which, as you may recall from Chapter 3, is a quest that can be set perpetually in motion. In effect, the analysand finds a new position in relation to her suffering.

The analyst tries to keep the patient in treatment, even to the point of letting him know in subtle ways that they want him to come (Fink 1997). In Pierre Rey's account of his analysis, Lacan ended sessions with the phrase '*À demain*' (See you tomorrow) (Rey 1989: 64). Lacanians believe an analysand will leave when the analytic process has succeeded to the extent that they are sufficiently independent to make this decision of their own accord. Their emphasis throughout lies in promoting this independence, very differently from Independent and Kleinian uses of regression to dependence. To this end, Lacanian analytic technique aims to catch the analysand off-guard, to come at their material from a new and surprising angle and to open more questions than answers. As we saw in the previous chapter, the classical transference interpretation is seen as a vicious circle which ties the analysand to her analyst's discourse as to that of the Other from whom she must separate and whose lacks she must discover. Instead, therefore, a range of interventions encourage the analysand to question herself and break up easy or over-systematic forms of understanding: '. . . the art of the analyst must be to suspend the subject's certainties until their last mirages have been consumed' (Lacan 1953 [2001]: 47–8). Lacan gave some of these interventions grammatical names, in accordance with his precept that the unconscious is structured like a language (Lacan 1953, 1958a, 1964a).

For example, 'punctuation' refers to the analyst's use of phrases like 'huh' or 'a-ha' or repeating or emphasising a word or a sentence of the analysand's own. The analyst uses the analysand's own language, but returns it in such a way that the analysand is able to hear it differently (Hill 2002). This method emphasizes linguistic tropes and the ambiguity and sliding meaning of the signifier, dependent on its context of usage. It also shifts the focus from the analyst's knowledge to the analysand's unconscious, to the development of their subjectivity and their ability to move from fixed positions to differing perspectives.

A brief example comes from 'Edward's' therapy. He was trapped in a relationship he dared not question for fear of his partner's repercussions. A friend, he said, had called him a coward. 'Coward, or cowered?', I replied.

More controversially, Lacan used the technique of 'scansion', another grammatical term, which relates to the communication of meaning through the rhythm of verse. In Lacanian usage, scansion involves stopping the session at a significant point, usually at an implicit question or ambiguity. Lacan drew from Freud's distinction between the time for understanding and the moments of concluding, which confer retroactive (*nachträglich*) meaning on any event. Lacan (1964a) thought the presence of the unconscious is always fleeting, and so ending a session abruptly at a point where the unconscious has erupted underscores the significance of what may have revealed itself (Harari 2004). He claimed that Freud: '. . . annuls the *times for understanding* in favour of the *moments of concluding* which precipitate the meditation of the subject towards deciding the meaning to attach to the original event' (Lacan 1953 [2001]: 53, his emphases). Hence, the 'precipitation of subjectivity' in the sense of haste or breach or spark flashing is maximized, and symbolization (the other aspect of the precipitation of subjectivity) is left to the analysand.

Scansion does not necessarily result in shortened sessions, although it often does. Freud did not always keep to a strict timetable, although his tendency was to lengthen rather than shorten sessions (Freud 1913 [2002]: 49). Lacanians claim this practice not only underscores unconscious significance through surprise, but frustrates a demand for knowledge from the clinician and promotes the client's desire. It helps to shift the locus of the 'subject supposed to know' from the analyst to the analysand's unconscious: 'The suspension of a session cannot *not* be experienced by the subject as a punctuation in his progress' (Lacan 1953 [2001]: 108, his emphasis).

The analyst remains as invisible as possible and constantly shifts her ground. According to Pierre Rey, Lacan also kept him off-guard by changing the time of his appointments to ones that were deliberately difficult for him, such as six in the morning for a man who was a habitual late riser (Rey 1989: 67–8). For Rey, these kinds of privations and challenges had the effect of his prioritizing his analysis above all else in life. He was never allowed to slide into an easy or comfortable position in relation to it.

Lacan thought that the ego needs freeing up, as it promotes imaginary or narcissistic identifications, and makes access to the unconscious and the liberation of desire more difficult: 'The unconscious completely eludes that circle of certainties by which man recognizes himself as ego' (Lacan 1954–5 [1991]: 8). Instead, the Lacanian analyst tries to confuse the ego to promote unconscious desire. Therefore interpretations often function as enigmatic enunciations and become a conundrum rather than a source of knowledge as part of the transmutation of the analysand's discourse from the imaginary register to the symbolic (Nobus 2000). Again, the aim is to move the analysand on from positions of fixity and certainty. Any notion of correctness is anathema in Lacanian analysis,[2] although meaning must be crystallized as well as dispersed. This dual process, as I have said, resonates with the double meaning of the 'precipitation of subjectivity', and also accords with Bion's (1965) conceptualization of a necessary fluctuation between paranoid/schizoid and depressive processes in thought and Bollas' (1995) emphasis on the function of free association in the disorganization of overly coherent meaning.[3]

Lacan invoked some of the principles of Eastern religious practices to underscore the fleeting nature of any knowledge and the necessity of confusing or bypassing the ego to gain access to the unconscious. He stated his intentions thus at the beginning of *Seminar I*:

The master breaks the silence with anything—with a sarcastic remark, with a kick-start.

That is how a buddhist master conducts his search for meaning, according to the technique of *zen*. It behoves the students to find out for themselves the answer to their own questions . . .

This kind of teaching is a refusal of any system. It uncovers a thought in motion . . .

(Lacan 1953–4 [1991]: 1)

In *Dhyana* or *Zen* Buddhism, the practice of a rigorous discipline such as archery can lead to renunciation of self or ego so that one becomes a channel for the unconscious or spirit: '. . . a kind of awareness which shows no trace of ego-hood and for that reason ranges without limit through all the distances and depths, with "eyes that hear and with ears that see"' (Herrigel 1953 [1985]: 64). Lacan also referred to the concept of 'resonance' or the power of words to invoke something they do not actually say, like the Hindu concept of '*dhvani*':

[T]he analyst can play on the power of the symbol by evoking it in a carefully calculated fashion in the semantic resonance of his remarks . . . In this regard, we could take note of what the Hindu tradition teaches about *dhvani*, in the sense that this tradition stresses the property of speech by which it communicates what it does not actually say.

(Lacan 1953 [2001]: 90)

This semantic resonance and Lacan's insistence on the linguistic structure of unconscious mechanisms lend themselves to the use of verbal play as an intervention, such as the 'red herring (hairing)' at the beginning of this chapter.

Another example comes from 'Claudia' (mentioned earlier in this chapter and in Chapter 9).

At the beginning of her therapy, Claudia had been very depressed. As her therapy progressed, she woke up, became more alive and robust, and began to be able to identify some of her own desires. At this point she had a dream in which the lawn at the back of her house was covered in black balls, which she associated with the balls and chains on prisoners' legs. She also said she had been typing recently and the balls reminded her of punctuation marks, full stops. I said: 'End of sentence.'

Jokes have an especially privileged role: '. . . humour, in the malicious grace of the mind free from care (*esprit libre*), symbolizes a truth that has not said its last word' (Lacan 1953 [2001]: 66). These techniques, as I have said, mean the analyst rarely, if ever, fills in the meaning for the analysand who constructs her own sense of what is going on as in a contemporary artistic or cultural experience. Lacan, like Bion (1970), Symington (1983), Bollas (1992) and Ogden (1994a, 1997), stressed the unexpected, new and not yet evolved in every session.

As in Independent technique, a startling new perspective may be generated by a range of interventions: a joke, a piece of provocation, an enigmatic utterance, repeating something the patient says in such a way they can hear their own words differently, a double entendre, a pun, laughter, sarcasm, irony, and so on almost *ad infinitum*. There are as many forms of intervention as human ingenuity and the resources of the unconscious permit. The analytic session now has the scope not only to be great fun but also for both parties to use it in the most creative and original way of which they are capable. Lacan himself exploited the new freedoms he introduced in a dazzling and unpredictable fashion. At least four of Lacan's analysands wrote about their analyses (Schneiderman 1983; Rey 1989; Giroud 1990; Godin 1990), and several verbal accounts exist (Roudinesco 1982).

Lacanian writers make less use of clinical illustrations than other contemporary schools. The main exceptions here are Nasio (1990, 1992), Kristeva (1993, 1996) and Fink (1997). Dor (1985, 1997) uses little clinical material, but demonstrates how minute attention is paid to the verbal structure and multiple significance of the analysand's discourse.

Nasio (1992) contributes a modification of Lacanian technique in line with Lacan's (1952) early emphasis on the intersubjectivity of the analytic relationship and Ogden's (1994a, 1997) 'intersubjective analytic third'. He contends that the unconscious is brought into existence in the relationship between analyst and patient:

> [T]he analytic relation will progressively cease to be a relation between two persons as it becomes a unique psychical place that includes conjointly the analyst and the analysand, or rather, the place of the in-between which envelops and absorbs the analytic partners.
>
> (Nasio 1992 [1998]: 98)

He also tells us he works more from his feelings, fantasies and associations than from knowledge or theory, and sits close to his patients (Nasio 2002). The physical ambience of his consulting room, '. . . in gold and orange tones which make the space light and transparent' (ibid.: 15), he claims, improves his capacity to listen. He attends to non-verbal signals: to the things the client brings with them, how they smell, the expressions of their face and eyes and their body language. Nasio contains his patient's projections, describing this as 'suffering with her'. This, he says, is the only way to really get to know someone and to treat them effectively (ibid.: 13–16). This emphasis on containment seems to be unique to Nasio and Kristeva: many other Lacanians do not recognize the concept.

Neurotic clients of Lacanian analysts can expect an unpredictable, stimulating, thought-provoking, sometimes bewildering experience. Although a necessary aspect of treatment, the level of analytic abstinence may feel frustrating. Gunn's (2002) account of his analysis involves huge exasperation about his analyst's lack of intervention and attempts to devise ploys to force his analyst to make an interpretation or a pronouncement. Nonetheless, Lacan's analysands' verbal accounts describe feeling completely heard and taken in by him (Roudinesco 1982).

The multiple ambiguities of speech and language are likely to be a major feature, as are unexpected and surprising interventions such as ending the session at an unanticipated point. Humour and laughter will feature. Gunn ends his analysis feeling intensely liberated (and symptom-free) but he concludes that it has been a huge joke. One can infer from this that joke is intended in the sense that comedy in classical drama provides a more profound resolution than tragedy, but also that his analysis worked at such a deeply unconscious level that its impact, although unquestionably massive, could not be traced to specific events or interchanges.

Lacanian analysands should not expect easily reducible understanding. As the mutative impact of their analysis will operate at an unconscious level, its effects may be apparent but not explicable. People who are severely disturbed may experience a Lacanian analysis as containing and supportive: its aim in these cases is to strengthen their existing means of functioning. Everyone else, though, may expect to feel caught off-guard. Clients who feel they need support or containment during a Lacanian analysis should look for other means of obtaining it.

POST-KLEINIAN TECHNIQUE

> The "act of faith" (F) depends on disciplined denial of memory and desire.
>
> (Bion 1970 [1984]: 41)

Traditionally, Kleinian technique is more actively interpretive than the other two schools, with less emphasis on timing and non-interpretation. Although Bion's influence modified this tendency for some analysts, most post-Kleinians still stress the centrality of the transference interpretation. Many consider everything their patient says or does, including enactments outside the analysis and reportage of events in external 'reality', as transference communications (Joseph 1985). At worst, this approach may restrict intersubjective possibilities. At best, it can promote a vivid and in-depth understanding in both patient and analyst which really brings to life the way the patient's internal world is operative in the here and now of the session. This, one of the greatest strengths of Kleinian technique, enables the tracking of generative events in the living theatre of meaning of internal objects and part-objects.

> For example, the patient discussed in Chapters 4, 5 and 9 as 'Kevin' began his therapy in a terrifyingly disintegrated state and had nightmares about being in a war zone with processions of maimed, mutilated and hobbling refugees. These 'refugees' probably represented parts of himself and his internal objects damaged by the destructive narcissistic organization dominant in his internal world at the time (Rosenfeld 1971). At a later point in his therapy, Kevin dreamt about another procession of refugees but this time proud upright Ethiopians. His association was that they were like him, very tall and slender. Post-Kleinian understanding (for example Meltzer 1973) enabled us to see that even though there were parts of himself still in exile, as it were, they were whole, undamaged and by this time extremely dignified.

Many Kleinians believe that, whatever the patient's background and history, the primary analytic task is to effect transformation in their internal world as it manifests itself in the transference in the session, and all other technical considerations are secondary to that.

A strong emphasis is placed on discerning at every point in the session whether the patient is functioning in depressive or paranoid/schizoid mode (Joseph 1978), and how projective identification is being used by the patient to deposit unwanted mental contents and affects into the analyst (see Chapter 7). The strength and quantity of projective identification is determined by the level of unbound hostility, aggression and envy, which Kleinians deem primary factors in the aetiology of serious disturbance (Rosenfeld 1965; Bion 1967). This attention to paranoid/schizoid processes and discernment of the level of projective identification leads to the interpretation of psychotic and narcissistic areas in everyone.

Whilst the Kleinian focus on aggression, hostility and destructiveness may seem (and be) harsh at times, it can be indispensable in the treatment of serious disturbance where internal and external reality have become confused. The patient may fear they have caused their own traumatic experiences, and may test the analyst to the hilt to establish her capacity to withstand and contain destructive assault. Kleinian technique is particularly strong on the deciphering and management of destructive aggression, backlashes, impasses and negative therapeutic reactions (Rosenfeld 1971;

Steiner 1993) (see Chapter 4), and may hence provide more active and vigorous containment than the gentler Independent or Lacanian approaches.

Some of Bion's innovative concepts have been developed in post-Kleinian writings on technique. 'Container/contained' (1962) explores the way a benign capacity to tolerate unbearable feelings and process them into thought derives first from the introjection of maternal 'reverie' and later from other thoughtful relationships including the analytic one. Bion thought an internal container established early in life can continue to grow in strength and flexibility. A powerful ability to think, able to develop throughout life, can be internalized from analysis and is one of its primary aims. This formulation has enabled a practice of deep psychological and emotional containment which has rendered the analysis of very disturbed or defended patients far more possible.

Caper distinguishes between holding and containment, drawing from Bion's distinction between benign and pathological projective identification and his work on 'container/contained' (Caper 1999; Bion 1962, 1967). Caper defines 'holding' as the transformation in the analyst's mind of a raw sensation projected into him, which can be thought about and given an emotional name, much as a mother holds and meets her baby's states of mind: he calls this 'synthetic' *alpha* function (Caper 1999: 145–6). Containment or 'analytic' *alpha* function, according to Caper, is a far more taxing process in which the analyst receives and tolerates very toxic projective identifications or 'anti-*alpha* function', often met with in severe disturbance. From this arduous and disturbing level of containment, such projections may be detoxified, and unbearable states of mind rendered bearable (ibid.: 146–9).

A necessary aspect of the process of thinking, according to Bion (1965), is a fluctuation between paranoid/schizoid and depressive processes (Ps↔D) (see Chapter 4). A temporary regression to a disorganized (or benignly paranoid/schizoid) state enables the emergence of a new idea or 'selected fact' (Bion 1962). Britton (1998) explores this concept in relation to what goes on in the mind of a therapist with her patient. The 'selected fact' then becomes a means of discerning whether the therapist is genuinely containing her patient's projections in a state of reverie in such a way that a new and facilitative thought may be possible, or whether she is bypassing this process to superimpose her own 'preconceptions' (Bion 1962) on her patient. Britton stresses '. . . the analyst's mind, primed with its theories, is waiting as a container for its imageless expectations to be fulfilled by the experience and material of the patient, rather than that a theory is looking for a patient!' (Britton 1998: 106). Britton's emphasis on three necessary movements— from Ps to D, from uncontained to contained and from preconception to conception—is a useful aide to differentiating when a knowledge of theory may be being misused, as is his emphasis on closely following a patient's material in response to interpretation. If a spirit of enquiry is fostered, it is likely that the analyst's intervention has been genuinely facilitative, whilst a sense of persecution or compliance may indicate either that the analyst has insufficiently taken in her patient projections or that a pathological object relationship is being unconsciously re-enacted.

Rey's theorization of the claustro/agoraphobic dynamics encountered in psychotic, borderline and narcissistic patients (introduced in Chapter 4) is crucial in analytic management or 'interpretive action' (Ogden 1994b). Because self and object are confused, intimacy and closeness to the analyst may feel suffocating and result in flight of some form. By the same token and because of lack of internal resources, separation from important others can also feel terrifyingly isolating or abandoning and cannot be borne. The analyst may therefore need to tolerate some distance, or perhaps even coming and going, until her patient feels strong and secure enough to engage in a closer therapeutic relationship. Sometimes it may be easier to implement this in institutional settings where clients may be held in mind but allowed periods of absence (White *et al.* 2001).

> An example comes from the young borderline woman, 'Angela', described in Chapter 6. Angela would often miss the second session of the week after moments of closeness or understanding. At the same time she had an absolute intolerance of being alone. She had made a serious suicide attempt when a friend had been unavailable at the precise moment she felt she needed her. Her therapist needed to tolerate Angela's absences as part of an interpretive action. To interpret her lack of self/object differentiation might have been 'suicide engendering' (Searles 1986b). Gradually, as Angela came to develop a stronger and more individuated self, she became able to attend more of her sessions.

Steiner's (1993) 'psychic retreats', or 'pathological organizations', embroil the analyst in an externalized impasse where 'real' or lively emotional contact is inhibited (see also Chapter 4). Steiner claims vigorous interpretation of the patient's defensive manoeuvres will result in retrenchment of the retreat as the patient may experience her analyst as shoving her own unbearable anxieties back into her. He suggests 'analyst-centred interpretations' as opposed to 'patient-centred interpretations' are more likely to give the patient a sense of being understood (Steiner 1993: 131–46). As a crude example, 'You are afraid that I was feeling hostile to you just now and may be trying to belittle you' is more freeing than 'You are trying to project your unconscious hostility and feelings of inadequacy into me.' Such interpretations, Steiner asserts, are more likely to enable the patient to feel understood so that a tentative and partial emergence from the retreat may be possible, although liable to be replaced with another set of defences which then require further disentanglement (ibid.). Following Steiner, the complex and intricate dismemberment of the labyrinthine defensive constructs involved in pathological narcissistic organizations becomes more possible.

In his later work, Bion (1970) amplified the analytic use of reverie into 'faith' and intuition so that new and unexpected developments in analysis could take priority, with enormous implications for clinical practice. He developed the idea of 'impartially suspended attention' (Freud 1912b [2002]: 33) through that of 'Negative Capability': '. . . when a man is capable of being in uncertainties, mysteries, doubts, without any irritable reaching after fact and reason' (Keats 1817, quoted in Bion 1970 [1984]: 125). Bion proposed the analyst should temporarily suspend memory and desire to maximize receptivity to 'O' or reality as yet unfiltered through mental processes (ibid.). He did not advocate that one should forget one's patient's material nor refrain from taking notes: 'what is ordinarily called forgetting is as bad as remembering' (ibid.: 41). He intended the therapist to free her mind from 'saturated' (or knowing) elements to the greatest extent possible in order to sense or intuit those aspects of her patient's unconscious reality (or 'O') that may be just out of reach (see also Chapter 9).

Britton (2003) investigates the benefits and misuses of humour in technique by distinguishing between a good joke and jokiness. A joke, he contends, may contribute to softening superego-based observations of the self, whilst jokiness often has a manic and defensive, even desperate, feel and function.

Patients of Kleinian analysts may expect a solid, robust, deeply containing experience. Their analysis will be reliable, predictable and usually at a high weekly frequency. Often more will be interpreted and at greater length than by analysts of Independent or Lacanian persuasion. Any manifestation of destructive impulses will be tackled immediately, which some may experience as persecutory. Such an intensive level of interpretation may result in a less playful approach, although many report it as very holding.

The primacy given to the transference and transference interpretations can provide an intense, deep level of relationship, although some may find it irritating that no realities outside the consulting room are considered and may experience such an exclusive focus on the analytic relationship as claustrophobic or restrictive. Post-Kleinian analysts influenced by Bion may interpret less and allow more space for the unexpected.

MONEY, KINDNESS AND SOME COMPARATIVE ISSUES

Contemporary theorists rarely mention money, despite Freud's (1913) observation that powerful sexual factors are at work in the way we value it. In private practice, the way the fee is established or negotiated is integral to the work, but as there is so little information, we cannot discern how representative it is. Coltart (1993) suggested we set the fee at the top of the market rate with patients who can afford to pay as a way of safeguarding some space for low-fee patients. Lacan's ex-analysand, Pierre Rey, claims Lacan established his fee at the upper limit of his analysands' capacity to pay (Rey 1989). Rey interprets this, generously, as a deliberate technique designed to impact on the analysand so that he cannot take his analysis for granted. On the other hand, Meltzer took the principled stand that one should '. . . refuse the sinecure conferred by overcharging on the basis of the supposed high opinion of one's colleagues' and that it is unfair to junior analysts to refer on 'difficult, unattractive and poorly paying patients' (Meltzer 1992: 156).

Few analytic writers mention kindness, a quality I consider to be paramount (not sympathy or reassurance). Meltzer claimed:

> [I]n analyses that really went the distance, as it were, when you ended up loving your patient and they loving you . . . the ending of an analysis of that sort was very much like a beloved child going out into the world.
>
> (Meltzer 2000: 7)

Searles would agree with Meltzer's sentiment. Interestingly, Lacan mentions kindness, albeit in passing—'Kindness is no doubt as necessary there as anywhere else . . .' (Lacan 1958a [2001]: 283)—whilst stressing the inappropriateness of an analytic desire for the patient's well-being. The analyst's desire, in his view, must be purely for contact with the analysand's unconscious.

The technique of these three contemporary schools accentuates different aspects of the analytic process. Clinicians may want to take account of this when referring and when adapting their approach to the needs of different clients. Lacanians may sometimes do damage by providing inadequate containment or consistency. Some post-Kleinians may harm their patients through an over-use of transference interpretations, an over-emphasis on infantile mechanisms and/or an over-interpretation of aggression and destructiveness without regard for the patient's history. Some post-Kleinians pay insufficient attention to processes which are not part of the depressive position but which nonetheless enable people to separate, individuate and move on, such as the uses of benign aggression and intersubjective processes and moments. Post-Kleinians can sometimes suffer from an insufficiency of paternal function and a tendency to conduct analyses in the maternal realm. Contemporary Independents may not always confront destructive aggression head-on when this is needed.

The clinical *sine qua non* this book sets out to demonstrate is the ability to think pluralistically. The possession of a range of theoretical perspectives on the same clinical issue makes it possible both to shift perspective as one way through an impasse with a particular patient and to adapt one's technique to the needs of different patients. Most importantly, only by engaging in Bion's (1970) 'multiple vertices' can we safeguard ourselves from analytically damaging certainty and righteousness.

NOTES

1. This remark was made when Green was disclaiming his own Lacanianism at a series of talks by French analysts at the Institute of Contemporary Arts in London in spring 2004.
2. Nonetheless, Lacanian analysts do work with a concept of the 'truth' of the impossibility of definitive knowledge owing to the limitations of symbolization and '. . . the irreducible status of the unconscious as a knowledge without a knowing agency' (Nobus 2000: 176). (See also Nobus and Quinn 2005.) Lacan differentiated this from the Cartesian subject of scientific 'truth'. In psycho-analysis, there is a split subject which incorporates both 'I *am* where I am not thinking' and 'I think where I am not' (Fink 1995: 140, his emphasis).
3. For an introduction to the journey of subjectification, the reader should turn to Chapter 3, and for the movement from desire to the drive, Chapter 9. Bion's theories are discussed in Chapter 4, and those of Bollas in Chapter 2.

The aims of analysis and psychic growth

The aims of analysis and criteria for termination of the three schools discussed here almost entirely preclude forms of normative adaptation. As an intrinsic aspect of a gradual shift from structural to process-based models of subjectivity, capacities and growth trajectories may be set in motion and enabled to take hold: where they may lead is another matter. Openness, desirousness, aliveness and flexibility are aspects of these growth processes, qualities emphasized in different ways by all three schools.

Yet the aims of analysis cannot be established purely on a relational basis between analyst and patient, as has been suggested (de Simone 1997). Psychological evolution can proceed both through relationships with others and through the opening and development of inherent or even newly found potentialities. In Lacanian theory, new signifying moments can re-structure experience and metaphor's creative spark can create fresh meanings, to which the subversion of imaginary identifications and restrictive unconscious neurotic organizations paves the way. Contemporary Independents emphasize the routes of intersubjectivity, and those of aliveness and the aesthetic or ecstatic cathexes of experience. Lacanians privilege the traversing of fantasy and the dialectization (or setting free) of desire, and the precipitation of subjectivity and the ability to enjoy one's enjoyment or *jouissance*, whatever that might come to be. Post-Kleinians prioritize depressive concern and aesthetic reciprocity (Meltzer 1988), and post-depressive faith and becoming one's reality (Bion 1970). The means of the analytic method and the aims of analysis can no longer be entirely differentiated.

All three schools specify certain issues in relation to ending. All three, in their different ways, deem the ability to separate from one's objects, mourn one's losses and accept one's lacks to be crucial in ending analysis and getting going in life. Post-Kleinians and Independents warn of the likelihood of a resurgence of symptomatology, and of some of the issues that brought the patient to analysis, in the period prior to ending (Quinodoz 1991, 2001; Murdin 2000). Lacanians aim to promote their analysands' independence throughout so that they will eventually leave of their own accord. Setting a date for termination always brings into sharp focus anxieties and transference concerns remaining to be dealt with.

Jean-Michel Quinodoz, a contemporary Swiss Independent, adds two key concepts related to ending analysis. The first is translated as 'buoyancy' from the French *'portance'*, which means both vertical lift in aerodynamics and hydrodynamics and the maximum load-bearing capacity of a structure (Quinodoz 1991). Quinodoz uses this term to denote both resilience and autonomy, or a patient's increased sense of being able to 'fly with his own wings' (ibid. [1993]: 172). Although buoyancy proceeds from the working through of separation anxiety and the internalization of a good object, it also incorporates an enhanced sense of personal responsibility and a capacity for a sophisticated level of interdependence, which includes the ability to use solitude as replenishment.

Quinodoz (2001) describes tolerance of certain kinds of frightening dreams as evidence of a capacity to bear increased quantities of anxiety, which in itself betokens a greater level of psychic integration.

> For example, you may recall that my patient 'Kevin' (described in Chapters 4, 5 and 8) had terrifyingly persecutory dreams about war zones during the first two years of his therapy. In these dreams he occupied the position of either helpless, beleaguered refugee with no internal allies other than bogus 'helpers' who eventually attacked him, or aggressive fighter pilot. Towards the end of Kevin's therapy, he had a succession of dreams which seemed to repeat these early themes, but with a slightly different twist. In one dream, he was a Kurdish journalist reporting on a conflict between Turkish and Iraqi forces from the safe shelter of a glass dome. In another, he was in the West Bank in Palestine looking at a scene of conflict and trying to work out what was going on.
>
> Whilst it was clear that he was revisiting early conflicts, he assumed a newly authoritative and separate position within them. Interestingly, at the top of the stairs that lead to my consulting room, there is a domed glass skylight. His therapy had given Kevin the capacity to bear looking at his internal conflicts without becoming either victim or aggressor within them.

CONTEMPORARY INDEPENDENT VIEWS ON PSYCHIC GROWTH

The two main thrusts of contemporary Independent thinking about growth and development can be summarized as intersubjectivity (the relational route), and aesthetic or ecstatic cathexes of objects, both human and non-human, as actualizations and openings of potentialities which may have lain previously dormant. Intersubjectivity, or the capacity to recognize difference in another's subjectivity, grounded in Winnicott's (1969) 'use of an object' (discussed in Chapter 2), supplements intrapsychic models of mind and has many implications for development.

As we also saw in Chapter 2, Benjamin (1995) argues the capacity to recognize the mother as a subjective other is a critical stage in infant development. Relating to difference becomes necessary for psychic development, and benign aggression has a central role in enabling this (ibid.). Benjamin extends the uses of intersubjectivity to the acquisition of gendered identity. If we can recognize the differences of and identify with both parents, gender can be based on multiple fluid identifications, freeing us from the confines of fixed, narrow and rigid assimilation into one gender only.

Benjamin's view of the role of intersubjectivity in infant development can serve as a model for continuing development throughout life. The intersubjective space between mother and child lays the foundations of triangular space. Extended to other relationships, including the analytic one, recognition of and relating to difference becomes central to the development of personal subjectivity. Benjamin calls this '. . . the evolving capacity of communicative interaction to digest and transform affect and create self-other awareness' (ibid.: 95). Intersubjectivity privileges the moment of mutual recognition, that there is a completely other point of view to be discovered, as a critical leap forward in development.

Without the bracing re-integrative charge of drive-related aggression, we might become overly concerned or depressive. We might lack the necessary impetus to propel us into adventures of new initiatives, ideas and relationships or to become sufficiently independent as a necessary concomitant of an interdependent position. Without it, we might also have more of a tendency to remain cocooned in a chimera of projective mechanisms, without sufficiently robust contact with and recognition of external reality. With it, the negotiation of external reality becomes part of the growth process. This has profound implications for the expansion of the psychoanalytic frame of reference to include, as developmentally significant, areas such as race and racialization, gender, class and culture. Through intersubjective processes growth becomes, at least potentially, limitless.

Ogden's focus is, as we have seen, more on the clinical applications of the concept of intersubjectivity. His model of the aims and means of the analytic process is also grounded in object usage, but Ogden emphasizes the aliveness aspect, which Winnicott called a 'feeling of real' (Winnicott 1956 [1975]: 304). Ogden claims:

> I believe that every form of psychopathology represents a specific type of limitation of the individual's capacity to be fully alive as a human

being. The goal of analysis from this point of view is larger than the resolution of unconscious intrapsychic conflict, the diminution of symptomatology, the enhancement of reflective subjectivity and self-understanding, and the increase of one's sense of personal agency. Although one's sense of being alive is intimately intertwined with each of the above-mentioned capacities, I believe that the experience of aliveness is a quality that is superordinate to these capacities and must be considered as an aspect of the analytic experience *in its own terms*.

(Ogden 1997 [1999]: 26, his emphases)

Eigen also privileges aliveness as one of the great indicators of growth, and he too links becoming alive and, to a large extent, the discovery of meaning to Winnicott's use of an object:

The new awakening in object usage involves the realization that the other is in some basic way outside one's boundaries, is 'wholly other'. And while this may precipitate disorganization and dismay, it culminates in quickening and enhancing the subject's sense of aliveness. It opens the way for a new kind of freedom, one *because* there is radical otherness, a new realness of self-feeling exactly because the other is now felt as real as well.

(Eigen 1981 [1993]: 112, his emphasis)

Contact with external reality and difference feeds the self and makes profound personal transformation possible, through the dizzying perspective that the self is now also potentially other.

According to these Independent theorists, therefore, aggression, used in the service of the integrative thrust of lived experience, is essential to both feeling alive and real, and also to the discovery and creation of meaning and the ability to use external reality, in whatever form, in the service of the growth, expansion and development of the self. As I said in Chapter 2, Winnicottian object usage is a joy-based account of development, not a guilt-based one. Bollas states unambiguously that the capacity to live creatively is predicated on the ability to use life itself as an object, and by implication with some aggression, or even on occasion necessary ruthlessness (Bollas in Molino (ed.) 1997).

For these processes to be possible, faith is required—according to Eigen (1981, 1998) and Bion (1970). Both use the term in a non-religious sense to denote maximal openness to the potential of difference in new experience. Eigen (1981) expounds on the concept of faith as the necessary attitude to facilitate psychic development. For Eigen, the self is an open expanding system, and only the limits of one's tolerance of openness restrict how far one can develop (Eigen 1998: 71). Eigen privileges the experience of going into the unknown, in the unconscious intuitive knowledge that what is found there will enrich and open the self, even though that may be in unexpected ways which do not always correspond with more conventional views of development.

Faith, for Eigen, comes into being with a gap—a gap which opens as separation processes come underway and is foreclosed if the self chooses to stay enmeshed in projective mechanisms. He posits that faith explodes adaptation and manipulation. He dubs an 'all out, nothing held back' movement of the self as crucial in maintaining high levels of integrity, honesty and realness (Eigen 1981 [1993]: 113). Adaptation to social mores or the expectations of others can sometimes stand in the way of these developments. He continually re-emphasizes that the self grows through paradoxical and not dissociative awareness:

> The vicissitudes of faith involve the struggle not only to know but also to be one's true self, to take up the journey with all that one is and may become, and to encounter through oneself the grounds of one's being. . . . The undertaking itself involves one in continuous re-creation.
>
> (Eigen 1981 [1993]: 127)

Eigen, Bollas and, to a lesser extent, Ogden (2001), are part of an aesthetic tradition (Bollas in Molino (ed.) 1997; Rayner 1990). I argue in Chapter 2 that this could equally be named an ecstatic tradition because of the emphasis on the joyful intensity of cathexes of objects, human and non-human. Milner advanced the idea of an ecstatic cathexis as a beatific moment in which consciousness can suffuse the whole body, which may then become 'clothed with light as if it were a garment' (Milner 1950 [1971]: 157). She claimed such moments were indissoluble from psychic creativity. For Milner, these experiences were linked with a non-defensive concept of idealization, alternating with disillusion in a reciprocity of passion, necessary to creativity, intense relationships and aesthetic appreciation (ibid.). She described:

> A feeling representation of a kind of orgasm, and ecstasy (what Winnicott called an ego-orgasm). The work of art then contains a symbolization of this kind of ecstasy (even an ecstasy of hate) which is achieved by a harmony of form or wholeness, this being an essential part of what beauty is in a work of art.
>
> (Milner (1989). personal communication, in Rayner 1990: 76)

In 'The role of illusion in symbol formation' (1952), Milner argued the link between aesthetic appreciation and children's play, and quoted Berenson:

[T]he aesthetic moment is that fleeting instant, so brief as to be almost timeless, when the spectator is at one with the work of art he is looking at . . . He ceases to be his ordinary self, and the picture or building, statue, landscape, or aesthetic actuality is no longer outside himself. The two become one entity; time and space are abolished and the spectator is possessed by one awareness. When he recovers workaday consciousness it is as if he had been initiated into illuminating, formative mysteries.

(Berenson 1950, quoted in Milner 1952 [1987]: 97)

Milner argued that until 'a recurrent merging of the opposites' was '. . . established necessity was indeed a mechanized god, whose service was not freedom but a colourless slavery' (Milner 1952 [1987]: 101).

These ideas relate to Bollas' (1992) concepts of 'psychic genera' and 'psychic intensities'. Psychic genera, in Bollas' use of the term, constitute nascent unconscious ideas, feelings or self states which through the tolerance of 'generative chaos' mate with resonant objects to constellate 'intense psychic interest' and eventually '. . . a fundamentally new perspective . . . This moment will often feel revelatory . . . it does describe those seminal visions created by unconscious processes pushed by the life instincts, and is an erotics in form' (ibid. [1993]: 88–9). Here, we see the melding of benign aggression, unconscious form and an intense ecstatic/aesthetic meeting with external reality as a fundamental drive to what Bollas describes as idiom, destiny and character.

A brief clinical example of an intersubjective moment, which includes an integration of aggression and an act of freedom in Symington's (1983) sense, comes from the therapy of the patient I call 'Ruth' in Chapter 3. She was furious with me because I was not able to change one of her session times to one she felt would be more convenient for her. She was prone to finding a way of developing grievances and using them to dominate the entire picture of her therapy. In this way, her earlier rebelliously enmeshed relationship with her mother was recapitulated in the transference, and her savagely attacking superego was turned onto me. She berated me continually and at great length for my alleged failure to give her what she needed, claiming that it meant she could not use her therapy properly.

Then she brought a dream: she had gone to the theatre with her sister and a friend, but they had not been given the seats they wanted and she was concerned they would not be able to see the play properly. She went to complain but was told they could not change their seats. The play was starting, so they returned to their original seats. As the curtain rose, she realized that she could see perfectly clearly. A great white pyramid rose up, marvellously complex and intricate, and she gazed at the spectacle in awe. 'Oh', I said, 'My name's White.'

Ruth's aggressive collision with my reality, combined with my non-retaliation and non-collapse, enabled this patient to see her therapy in a dramatically different way, of which she could make far more robust use. This moment was also part of a shift from a complaining and blaming stance, to one in which she could begin to take more responsibility for herself and be more confidently assertive in discerning and following her desires and needs.

These contemporary Independent ideas on the actualization of self and becoming alive through intersubjective encounters and ecstatic cathexes suggest that neither the self nor the 'true self' (Winnicott 1960) can be conceived as a single unified entity. Winnicott, indeed, claimed the true self '. . . does no more than collect together the details of the experience of aliveness' (ibid. [1965]: 148). Bollas (1995) proposes, like Bion (1965) and Lacan (1945, 1957), a dual movement: dispersal and the breaking up of narrative cohesion are as necessary as their coalescence. He thinks we need a functional self with 'an illusion of integration' (Bollas in Molino (ed.) 1997: 6) but that the true self ultimately consists in spontaneous gestures and the erotics of instinctual life. Within the arc of the instinct's source, aim and object:

> [T]here are many lines that fragment and break, in something like a vast symphonic movement which is, in and of itself, a pleasure. It is not the end point . . . not the objects that reduce the excitation, that constitute the pleasure. The pleasure is in the entire movement.
>
> (ibid.: 9)

This leads us on to Lacan's post-1964 theorizations of the *jouissance* of the drive.

LACANIAN APPROACHES TO PSYCHIC EVOLUTION

The Lacanian version of becoming a subject is in part an uncompromising account of discoveries of lack and loss mediated through the Other of language and the social order, and the fantasy of *objet a* (see Chapter 3). We can no longer sustain any illusion of being whole or complete in ourselves.

Until the 1960s, acceptance of castration and lack, the dialectization of desire and the traversing of the fantasied relation to *objet a* were considered the objectives of Lacanian analysis. As long as we could accept symbolic castration as a structural precondition of subjectivity we could enjoy the limited but open-ended freedoms of desire and the creation of meaning through symbolization of our experience. The dialectization of desire keeps close company with the Independent emphasis on the use of an object and aliveness: one is then freed to use and be used by one's objects, human and non-human, in a very personal way and to move between and on from them. The traversing of fantasy and taking responsibility for one's own life constitute a re-incorporation of aggression and mobility of possible object choice which also signal subjective freedom.

However, as from *Seminar XI* (1964a), Lacan shifted his emphasis from desirousness to the drive as one eventual goal of analysis.[1] This coincided with a partial shift of emphasis from linguistics to topology as the template of the unconscious (Nobus 2003). Topology is a pre-geometric structuring of space, which focuses on its forms of connection and separation (Burgoyne 2000b). Unlike three-dimensional Euclidean space and time, topology assumes a rubbery distortable space: a car tyre and a needle are assumed to be topologically identical as they each have one hole (Hill 2002). The most commonly cited example is the map of the London Underground. Contemporary cosmological research relies on topology (Penrose 2004). Lacan (1964a, 1964b) used topological concepts to demonstrate the structural homology of the body, the unconscious and the subject: he focused on their gaps, borders and rims and on an opening and closing movement in which something is lost. One, but by no means the greatest, value of these extraordinary concepts is to throw into high relief the metaphorical nature of all psychoanalytic theory.[2]

This new phase of Lacan's theory did not replace his earlier work but retroactively elaborated it (Verhaeghe 2001). Whilst previously the body was brought into being in symbolic and/or imaginary form, after 1964 the 'real' of the body was understood as organism and drive (in a topological sense) (ibid.). Castration became the secondary elaboration of an original lack: the loss of eternal life at the birth of a sexed being (Lacan 1964a [2004]: 205). One (mythical) consequence becomes 'lamella', a (topological) ultra-thin film of tissue '. . . which moves like the amoeba. It is just a little more complicated. But it goes everywhere' (ibid.: 197). This represents a primordial form of libido, a pure *objet a* (in the sense of lack), '. . . from which the subject, in order to constitute itself, has separated itself off as organ' (ibid.: 103). The mother/child and male/female divides are predicated on this originating loss. Lacan (1972–3) came to distinguish between phallic *jouissance*, in which the subject is divided and limited, and 'feminine' or 'other' *jouissance* which is beyond signification (see also Chapter 3). The partial drive (also internally divided into somatic and psychically elaborated) aims to re-establish something which has been lost, and *jouissance* becomes the driving force in this attempt to return to a previous level (Verhaeghe 2001).

Lacan deemed that his previous formulation of desire, as protection from the Other's *jouissance*, still tied the subject to the Other: desire was predicated on subservience to the Law and inscription within the symbolic Other: 'For desire is a defence (*défense*), a prohibition (*défense*) against going beyond a certain limit in *jouissance*' (Lacan 1960 [2001]: 356). Henceforth new forms of subjective freedom became the opening of windows onto the unconscious and the real, and the *jouissance* of the drive (Lacan 1964a).

Lacan distinguished carefully between the Freudian '*Instinkt*' (instinct) and '*Trieb*' (drive). Both were translated as 'instinct' in the Strachey edition, which led to an unfortunate obliteration of the implications of the new concept of the drive. Whilst instinct refers to an animal's innate predisposition to certain behaviours necessary to survival of the species (eating, hunting, camouflage, reproduction etc.), the drive is a human concept which links the psychic with the somatic (Harari 2004): it transmutes and transcends the biological. Lacan translated *trieb* as both '*pulsion*' (drive) and '*dérive*' (adrift): '. . . my last resort would be "*dérive*" if I were unable to give the bastard term "*pulsion*" the necessary force' (Lacan 1960 [2001]: 334). *Dérive* refers to the unstable, variable nature of the drives. He completely rejected any notion of an organized development of drive-related stages culminating in a genital organization: 'Genital love turns out to be absolutely unassimilable to a unity which is the fruit of an instinctual maturation' (Lacan 1954–5 [1991]: 263).

Lacan (1964a), following Freud (1915c), posited the drives as plural and always partial. He added the scopic and the invocatory to the oral and anal drives with their corresponding partial objects of the gaze[3] and the ear, in addition to the breast and faeces. In Lacanian theory, each drive with its corresponding source, pressure, object and aim (Freud 1915c [2005]: 17) circles around a respective *objet a*. Lacan did not designate the 'phallus' an *objet a* because, as the signifier of lack, its meaning is purely symbolic. Aggression is a necessary aspect of the insistence of all the drives: 'an incoercible, ungovernable agency' (Harari 2004: 197). Because it is unstoppable, it implies motility, like Winnicott's benign aggression.

Lacan theorized the life and death drives as two hypothetical sides of a Moebius strip in which each side inevitably leads into the other: the two are indissociable. He likened libido to an organ or a force field (Lacan 1964b [1995]: 274). 'Man' is the diminished result of the internal divisions produced by the entry into language and the Law, and so is '*l'hommelette*' (manlet or little man) and the aforementioned '*lamella*' (Lacan 1964a, 1964b). A pun on omelette, *l'hommelette* also refers to the theoretical breaking of eggs in Lacan's Copernican revolution.[4] For Lacan, the *lamella* represented '. . . the part of a living being that is lost when that being is produced through the straits of sex' (Lacan 1964b [1995]: 274) and *l'hommelette* '. . . has for guidance but the pure real' (ibid.: 273). The divisive impact of signification therefore produces a reduced subject in the symbolic but also a 'subject in the real' (ibid.: 265) or subject as drive (Fink 1997: 210).

The multiple permutations and combinations of the various and variant drives and their expression are potentially infinite: in this way human individuality is ensured. Lacan likened the drive to a Surrealist *montage* (Lacan 1964a [2004]: 169). A collage of disparate, perhaps jarring, elements guarantees the diversity of human experience. There can never be a uniform goal to human development. What is definitive about the drives is their urgency, and as they can be sublimated, the forms this urgency can take are limitless. The urge to self-expression in writing or painting or music, for example, in the service of the life force is very different from a compulsion, which may be experienced as a nuisance.

Like the unconscious of which it is part, the movement of the drive opens and closes: it encircles its object ('*La pulsion en fait la tour*' (ibid.: 168))[5]. Lacan described its trajectory as an adventure (ibid.: 162). What matters is not what the drive achieves but its process, beyond need and pleasure—into an area of excess, *jouissance* or something more than pleasure which can easily tip into its opposite. The drive's pursuit of *jouissance* correlates with contemporary Independent highlighting of aggression as a necessary aspect of growth. One of the objectives of analysis, for Lacan, became the capacity to enjoy one's enjoyment, whatever form it took. Openings of unconscious processes became the Lacanian ethic, and effectively constitute an '. . . ever more radical depersonalization of the subject' (Muller and Richardson 1982: 416). The subject's continuing development throughout life is inhered in something elemental, albeit mediated through language and the symbolic order.

Kristeva and Irigaray's work supplements the concept of a subject in the drive. In Kristeva's (1974) early work, she extended Lacan's 'real' (merged with the imaginary) into the 'semiotic', a pre-Oedipal, primary-process, drive-related area of early maternal experience, which provides the substance behind and the impetus towards signification.

The semiotic is never entirely subsumed into the symbolic order in language or psychic processes: it supplements and overflows them. It is composed of retroactively conceived experiences of rhythm, energy and kinaesthesia through which children of both sexes feel pleasures, sounds, colours and movements in the body (Grosz 1990). Kristeva sees manifestations of the semiotic in many areas of adult life including some modernist literature, in particular the work of Joyce and Mallarmé (Kristeva 1974), madness, holiness and poetry (Kristeva 1983), and in the experience of pregnancy and maternity (Kristeva 1979). It follows, then, that the subject in the drive might be supposed to include a sensory, kinaesthetic dimension.

This quality of metabolization of experience suggests the aesthetic/ecstatic cathexes of objects of some of today's Independents.

Irigaray also expands Lacanian notions of subjectification, specifically in the way her idea of the possibility of a female imaginary (discussed in Chapter 3) could transform women's ability to represent themselves in language. As Lacanian conceptions of the unconscious preclude any unmediated relationship with the body, Irigaray is trying to intervene in the process of signification itself. Existing language, including psychoanalytic language, is based in a masculine imaginary, she argues (Irigaray 1974, 1977). She wants to develop accounts of subjectivity and knowledge which acknowledge the existence of two sexes, not just one as the excluded and negated of the other (Irigaray 1977, 1984). Her contention—'A man minus the possibility of (re)presenting oneself as a man = a normal woman' (Irigaray 1974 [1985]: 27)—is a more extreme way of putting Lacan's dictum that '. . . woman [as a classifiable set] does not exist' (Lacan 1972–3 [1998]: 7) and constitutes the 'One-missing' ('l'un-en-moins') of man-made language (ibid.: 131). Both Lacan and Irigaray stress that women can only define or represent themselves individually: in masculine discourse, woman is created as other.

Irigaray commandeers the link Lacan forged between the psychical and the linguistic in signifying processes to give some examples of woman's representation of her bodily experience (Irigaray 1977 [1985]: 23–33). Like Kristeva, she affirms the plurality and diversity hidden within normative signification, but Irigaray stresses that woman's experience cannot be reduced to Cartesian dualism or to the single-minded, goal-oriented discourse of 'scientific' rationality. Women's desire, for Irigaray, involves '. . . a different economy more than anything else, one that upsets the linearity of a project, undermines the goal-object of a desire, diffuses the polarization towards a single pleasure, disconcerts fidelity to a single discourse . . .' (ibid.: 29–30). She is critical, at times scathing, about psychoanalysis as a prime example of unselfcritical masculine discourse (ibid.). She aims to enable women to claim some space as women into what has up to now been an implicitly mono-sexual model in language and in psychoanalysis.

Post-1964 Lacanian theorizations of the subject in the drive could include Kristeva and Irigaray's expansion of the potential of subjective experience and self-representation.

A clinical example comes from the therapy of the artist I call 'Claudia', introduced in the previous chapter. Claudia had been depressed to the point that she could not work and needed medication. In Lacanian terms, she would have been classified as a hysteric: her unconscious goal was always to remain the indispensable object of the Other's desire. Her Italian father had left when she was three and her little brother only a baby, and she had assumed the role of her mother's helper at the cost of following her own desire. When she married, she recapitulated this early constellation: she gave of herself to her husband and daughters unstintingly, until she felt empty and resourceless.

After about two years in therapy she began to burst out of her depression in a particularly lively way, with several vivid and colourful dreams whose diffusely sensual and sexual imagery suggested a semiotic body/mind component. Some months later, Claudia brought a dream in which she and I were at an exhibition of Georgia O'Keeffe. I was behind her. Someone commented on a painting that she thought was by Canaletto, that it was by Caravaggio. Then, Georgia O'Keeffe herself appeared and announced: 'Of course it's sexual.'

In the transference, Claudia had regressed to a stage before she was precociously attuned to her mother's depression, and when she could both love and participate in her then sexy mother's exuberance. This early seam of rich sensual experience was maintained and elaborated in Claudia's painting before she became too depressed to work. However, her primordial sense of the feminine had been overlaid with a deep vein of ambivalence and riven with Oedipal conflict. Shortly after her parents' divorce, she found herself in hate-fuelled competition with a glamorous stepmother. This splitting of the Oedipal scenario effectively prevented the gradual transitional integration of a more separate, sexual mother into the semiotically undifferentiated early substratum (cf. Ogden 1987). Claudia had turned against evidence of sexuality or femininity in both herself and others. She had been internally assisted in this process by an introject of a cruel, hypercritical, rejecting father with which her own aggression was confused.

The eruption of early semiotic sexual feeling in the transference brought this conflict to the surface. Over time, she was able to disentangle the strands and sort the ambivalence. Her hypercritical, rejecting paternal superego lost its sting, and much of her aggression could now be withdrawn from this imago and re-incorporated into her own love and life-force. She recovered more of her own desire, and began to transform her image of femininity from a selfless version in which her own needs and feelings were ruthlessly cut off, to a more robust, vigorous, healthily selfish, desiring and expressive version of womanhood.

In Lacanian terms, Claudia had separated from the Other (her masochistic mother who demanded she be similar, and her rejecting father) and traversed the fundamental fantasy in which the Other's desire was all-important. Her own desire had been set in motion, in both sexual and creative ways. She had also begun to follow her drives, incorporating the sensual, semiotic aspects articulated by Kristeva. In addition, she had started to develop some authority as a woman in the form Irigaray shows to be possible—through ownership and expression of her sensuality and sexuality, pre- and post-Oedipal, she strengthened her sense of herself as female.

SOME POST-KLEINIAN THEORIES OF HUMAN DEVELOPMENT

Here, I shall concentrate on those post-Kleinians influenced by Bion. More traditional Kleinians, however significant their expansions of technique (for example, Joseph's work on transference and countertransference discussed in Chapter 7), or conceptualizations of psychopathology (for example, Rosenfeld's theories of destructive narcissism and psychotic states discussed in Chapters 5 and 6), share the assumptions about growth and development in 'On Mental Health' (Klein 1960). Integration of the personality, intro-jection of a benign parental couple, and predominance of depressive processes or the capacity to mourn, were the primary indicators of mental health according to Klein. Whilst no Kleinian would disagree with these as objectives of analysis, Bion and Meltzer added radically new dimensions.

All Kleinians, to some extent, posit fluctuations between paranoid/schizoid and depressive processes in health, with some conceptual variation. One radical version is Britton's (1998) 'Before and after the depressive position: Ps (n) → D (n) → Ps (n+1)' (also mentioned at the end of Chapter 6). Britton introduces the idea of a post-depressive paranoid/schizoid position, which entails the relinquishment of cognitive and moral confidence for incoherence and uncertainty. The depressive position, in this theorization, constitutes 'a point of departure' (ibid.: 74). Drawing from Bion, Britton states: 'Unlike the other positions, D (n + 1) is not a state of mind that is realized, but a hope, based on faith, that future developments will bring coherence and meaning' (ibid.: 81). Grotstein formulates the paranoid/schizoid position as, at best, '. . . a challenging *guardian* of the freshness and vitality of depressive position achievements' (Grotstein 2000b [2003]: 48, his emphasis), and relates Bion's Ps↔D to 'the post-modern notion of *inter-subjectivity*' (ibid.: 46, his emphasis).

Bion's later work

Bion's thinking, as I outlined in Chapter 4, introduced a process-based model of mind and self. His concepts of psychic growth and development can be divided into two phases. The first privileged thought, grounded in emotional experience, as the primary route to development. His later theories of transformations and 'O' were predicated on an ability to think.

In Bion's (1962) earlier work, the all-important attitude was represented by the letter 'K'. K means 'getting to know' rather than holding or having a piece of knowledge: it describes a journey of emotional and intellectual discovery. Later, prefigured in *Transformations* (1965) and fully spelt out in *Attention and Interpretation* (1970), Bion came to think K was less central than what he describes as F or faith, and ultimately than O. His shift in emphasis from K to F as both the analytic attitude and the primary route to development heralded a shift in paradigm in Bion's thinking and outlook: a change from a scientific outlook, grounded in mathematics and geometry, to a mystical view of development, which incorporated the mathematical. Here, Bion parted intellectual company from many Kleinians. To this day, his later work is less clinically influential than his early concepts.

At this stage in his development (Bion was in his seventies), he drew from the work of the early Christian mystics, especially the Spanish John of the Cross, the Gnostics and Meister Eckhart. However, Bion's mysticism was very much in and of this world: it signalled a movement towards ever-greater contact with reality, grounded in a precise attitude towards analysis. These mystics emphasized a path of negation of the behavioural, prescriptive and dogmatic aspects of Christianity in favour of a direct encounter with God. Bion did not believe in God, but he believed humankind was capable of greater encounters with reality than intellectual, moral or doctrinal systems of any persuasion permit. As Bléandonu (1994) points out, Bion's intellectual affinity with a doctrine for which the redemptive aspect of divine incarnation is relatively unimportant is like his view that gratitude and reparation have a secondary role within Kleinian analysis. Like many contemporary Independent theorists and suggestive of Lacan's work after 1964, Bion emphasized contact with 'reality' or O, both internal and external, as the primary route towards development. I shall explore what this means a little later in this chapter.

For Bion, faith is inextricably linked with his concepts of 'reverie' and 'negative capability' (discussed in Chapters 4 and 8), yet it goes far beyond these concepts in its implications. It describes an analytic attitude, which facilitates the quality Bion was increasingly to privilege as the route to learning and growth, that of intuition. Faith is an unsaturated or open concept. Eigen expands:

> [F]aith enhances rather than mutes precision. One's contact with subtle nuances of experience deepens as one develops an appreciative sensibility for what remains out of reach. The very taste of experience gains new meaning. The subject learns the gesture of repeatedly starting from scratch, of living in a wall-less moment and sensing his walls in a way that makes a difference.
>
> (Eigen 1985 [1993]: 219)

These developments are predicated on the ability to process one's experience through *alpha* function and thought.

Bion's (1965) theory of transformations is not primarily a theory of profound personal transformation, although this is one of its extensions and applications. As another empty unsaturated concept, it describes a fundamental human process, applicable in a multitude of areas (see also Chapter 7). By transformation, Bion meant change of form. In psychotherapy we are continually observing and performing transformations. The patient's associations formulated into words are a product of a transformation of thoughts and emotions; these thoughts and emotions refer to events (internal and external, past and present) of which they are in turn transformations (Grinberg *et al.* 1993).

Thought, in Bion's sense, is a continual transformation of emotion and experience, which irrevocably changes the thinker and her perceptions of internal and external reality. Thoughts are in themselves capable of growing and acquiring further meaning, and thereby promoting further personal development and change. Different psychoanalytic theories can be conceptualized as groups of transformations, as can the poetic, artistic, scientific, philosophical and educational fields of knowledge. Each of these intellectual or cultural paradigms is the transformation, in someone's mind, of primary unknowable reality, which Bion designated O.

Bion's earlier model of human development can be summarized as 'transformations in K'. As long as there is sufficient tolerance of frustration and 'no-thing' (cf. Green in Abram (ed.) 2000), and a capacity to recognize emotional truth undistorted by the omnipotent and omniscient mechanisms Bion termed 'lies' or 'propaganda', the personality can continue to develop or to evolve indefinitely through thought. In Bion's later work he changed his emphasis to a more profound theory of radical renewal, that of 'transformations in O' or the grounds of one's being (Bion 1965, 1970). Bion used the term 'O' both as the internal or external starting point in an initial experience or situation, the reality present before it becomes subject to processes of metabolism and understanding, and as the unknown that is reached towards psychically, that stark clarity of encounter with reality which comes when enough knowledge or detail has been discarded, at points of extreme intuition at the highest levels of evolution of mind. The psychoanalytic point of view, or as Bion preferred to call it, the psychoanalytic vertex, is therefore O, the unknown, new, and as yet not evolved.

Transformations in K are 'knowing about growth' (Bion 1965 [1984]: 156). Bion stressed the K into O transformation as a more profound and vivid knowledge of psychic reality. 'Becoming O' is essentially 'becoming what one is', and hence this transformation is feared and resisted and commonly accompanied by 'turbulence': 'turbulence and its sources are part of O' (ibid.: 48). Only those interpretations which transform 'knowing about something' to 'becoming that something' produce change and psychic growth (ibid.: 148–9). Transformations in O always have a disruptive character, which Bion termed 'catastrophic change' (ibid.: 9). They involve the disorganization of the system in place before the change. If the change takes place in a K medium, there is no real catastrophe. For Bion, catastrophic change is usually a profoundly positive phenomenon. It is the evolutionary point of departure for psychic growth, and a radical development in personal emotional progress. Like Winnicott's (1963) 'fear of breakdown', it may initially be felt as disastrous.

If the change is articulated in -K medium, or one which is too intolerant of emotion to allow thought to evolve, it will be experienced as persecution and dealt with through evacuation in some form. If it can be contained, it may be compared to an explosion which transforms a pre-catastrophic moment into a post-catastrophic one, rich in emotions (Bion 1965). As Eigen states: 'Bion points to something inherently explosive in psychic birth processes in themselves' (Eigen 1998: 71). Alberto Meotti (2000) outlines the preparatory circumstances for a transformation in O: a person may not be conscious of its imminence but it may be anticipated in a dream in visual images or even in a waking state, if the mind is sufficiently free of intentions or memories.

An example comes from a patient I call 'William', whom I had been seeing five times a week for about five years some years ago. He had been depressed to the point that he was absolutely convinced that his life would end in suicide. He also felt very stuck and was both accident-prone, often getting knocked off his bicycle, and liable to self-sabotage and getting himself into self-destructive situations such as being scapegoated by his employers. His suicidal feelings and fatalistic pessimism would intensify during breaks from therapy. Diagnostically, he would probably have been described as schizoid—he tended to project huge areas of himself, most particularly his own desires, needs and aggression, into other people.

At this point in his therapy, he seemed to both of us to be more substantial, alive and in his own experience. He was enjoying life more, and seemed more resilient. We agreed that he was probably ready to reduce to four times a week, and set a date several weeks ahead when he would stop coming on Wednesdays. The night before his last Wednesday session, he dreamt that he was walking down a street and saw a bird trapped inside a window. He wanted to go inside and release it but instead he let a man who was holding a great muzzled black dog on a lead go in.

The dog killed the bird, and William was heartbroken to see the pattern of its wings etched in blood on the window. He awoke torn apart by great wracking sobs. His association was to a time when he had been travelling, and some beautiful birds had flown into the bus and been killed by hitting the windows. We knew his black dog from long experience as the self-destructive killjoy part of himself which intervened disastrously when he had the opportunity to do something he much desired. It was composed of his own projected aggression turned against himself in the most deadly fashion. At the point at which William had wanted to begin to fly the nest, he had allowed this self-defeating, self-attacking part of himself to take over again.

In the subsequent few weeks, he lost much of his newly-found ebullience and solidity, but eventually he was able to ask if he could return to being in five times weekly psychotherapy. Now, this kind of request was quite new for William. He was the youngest of a large number of children. By the time of his arrival, his parents' marriage was loveless and unhappy. He had made himself special to his tired mother and more boisterous and demanding siblings by becoming a kind of assistant to them all, and cared for his own split-off needs by tending to others. With me, whom he perceived both transferentially and accurately as also managing a large number of people, he had up to this point been careful, considerate and solicitous, and never made demands which could tax my resources in any way. His previous session frequency had been instigated at my suggestion, but he had gobbled it up nonetheless.

After his return to five times weekly psychotherapy, there followed six months of intensive analytic work on the multiple disguises the projected killer assumed within him, which required ruthless honesty on his part, and mine. Towards the end of this period, during my three-week Easter break, he had quite a different kind of dream from any he had had before. He dreamt that, during the holiday, he'd come to visit my house with a colleague, whom he associated as representing a very bitter, angry part of himself. It was a big clapboard house with a verandah and a swimming pool. (At this point in the recounting of his dream I laughed, and in his dream I laughed too. Never underestimate how well your patients get to know you.) The back garden flooded, and swimming in the floodwater were all kinds of discarded household objects and debris. But the flood remained contained and did not come into the house or damage it. He stayed overnight in my house, but told his companion that they would have to get up very early before my patients arrived. They did get up early, but I was up before them and feeding a crowd of lively, talkative teenagers, sitting around my large table. I took them all, including William and his friend, out on a trailer drawn by a pony.

Then William realized he had left his keys behind. He told his companion that he could not possibly go back to collect them, but, to his surprise, found that he had turned into a helpful, friendly woman, whom he did not recognize, but who assured him that of course it was OK to ask to go back. On their return, they met my partner at the front door, who was holding a spade and who was also friendly and easy-going. I wasn't at all put out by the return to the house. Eventually, we all set off again in the pony and trailer, with all the adolescents on the back—a journey he said was great fun.

This dream was a harbinger of a transformation in O because for the first time in William's life or therapy, he was able to tolerate a gap without his angry resentment and envy being projected into someone else who would then attack him in a disguised way. He was newly able to find the resources within himself to tolerate and deal with his feelings of rage, hostility, deprivation and jealousy, and there was no intensification of his depression. The flood was contained. His angry, bitter companion was transformed into someone he did not recognize, but who helped him to go back and get what he needed, as he had been able to when he asked for his fifth session back. There was a benign but prosaic parental couple.

In my break, he also managed to have a holiday from his relentless victim status. He reached the point at which he felt ready to reduce his session frequency again. This time there was no dream, but a near-fatal catastrophe. He was involved in a diving incident in which he had a panic attack which could have had fatal consequences if he had reacted by trying to surface too quickly. But at the critical moment, he was able to act calmly, rationally and safely, and saved his own life. He chose life, finally. And after that time, he was not only more alive and more real, but newly assertive, confident, capable of overcoming setbacks he would previously have been floored by, and increasingly clear about his own needs and desires. He felt the loss of his fifth session for almost a year afterwards and of course much further analytic work was needed, but he survived my next breaks without crisis and without depression.

With this patient, a near-fatal catastrophe erupted as his old defence structure kicked back at the moment he broke free. It was different from his previous accidents and life crises, from which he had always emerged much the worse. He was born into a much expanded version of himself in a terrifying and painful moment that he occasionally relived in dreams for several months afterwards.

Grotstein (2000a) argues that the concept of O transforms all existing psychoanalytic theories (for example, the pleasure principle, the death instinct, and the paranoid/schizoid and the depressive positions) into psychoanalytic manic defences against the unknown. Arguably, not only

Bion's concepts of faith, transformations and O, but also the developmental thrusts inaugurated by the concept of intersubjectivity, with the aesthetic/ecstatic tradition in contemporary Independent theory, and the precipitation of subjectivity and access to the drive in Lacanian theory, lend radically new dimensions to psychoanalytic thinking about human development.

Postscript: A state regained?

Finally, I would like to remind the reader of one more recent post-Kleinian theorization of growth and development: Meltzer's (1988) concept of 'aesthetic reciprocity' (also discussed in Chapter 4). His idea that the depressive position precedes the paranoid/schizoid position was revolutionary. Meltzer thought that a baby is born into a state of grace, in which she is full of awe and wonder at the mother's beauty and the miraculous nature of the world. Meltzer called this state 'aesthetic reciprocity' as, in his view, the new-born baby manages to hold in tension the pain, delight and desire to possess and control these wonders. But as the delicate balance is difficult to maintain, the baby then lapses into the paranoid/schizoid position, where splitting and the phantasy of omnipotent control replace depressive awe and wonder. This lapse, according to Meltzer, may be precipitated by some form of environmental failure, but it may also occur as all of us struggle to maintain the precarious balance between L (love), K (desire to know) and H (hate). Meltzer called this difficulty 'aesthetic conflict' reminiscent of Blake's (1789) poem 'Infant Joy':

> He who kisses a joy as it flies
> Lives in Eternity's sunrise.
> But he who binds to himself a joy
> Doth the winged life destroy.

NOTES

1. The timing of these conceptual shifts is interesting: Lacan's new metapsychology took off after his self-styled 'excommunication'—after he was finally refused readmittance to the IPA. These new concepts emphasize a greater independence from any form of Other.
2. Lacan, however, claimed that topology was not a metaphor for the structure of the unconscious but the structure itself (Nobus 2003).
3. The 'gaze' as partial object incorporates the dual meaning of the French 'regard': both 'look' and 'being looked at'. It is one of the most widely applied and articulated of Lacan's innovatory concepts, particularly in film studies.

4. Lacan frequently referred to Freud's subversion of the Cartesian subject as a Copernican revolution, as the unconscious overturned any notion of conscious mastery in man's concept of himself.

5. '*La pulsion en fait la tour*' (the drive moves around the object) is also a pun on '*tour*' (trick). Therefore, 'the drive tricks the object' is also implicit in its meaning (Sheridan (trans.) in Lacan 1964a [2004]: 168).

Part III

The future?

Chapter 10

Conclusion

Throughout this book I have outlined exciting advances in psychoanalytic theory today. A gradual shift to process models of mind and self in continual evolution explodes any lingering notions of 'normal' (ideal) states to be achieved through psychoanalytic psychotherapy. The more complex arenas of subjectivity thereby generated render a version of human nature in constant flux and clear the way for further vitalizing developments in the future, if we can learn through difference. The many innovations in technique explored in Chapter 8 open the psychoanalytic process into a dynamic interchange between two engaged subjects in which new and unexpected configurations and developments may emerge.

Such innovations incorporate areas of radical contrast—at times apparent contradiction. Perhaps the most striking difference between Lacanian and post-Kleinian thought lies in the relative weighting given to separation from one's objects. In Lacanian theory, a journey of subjectivity cannot commence without negotiation of several stages of discovery of lack and loss, and separation from the first Other. It cannot continue without the sealing of these gaps and breaks through the traversing of fantasy, the opening of the space of desire and the *jouissance* of the drive. Subjective freedom, a capacity for creativity and individuality are all contingent on the tolerance of lack, incompleteness and existential aloneness achieved through a high degree of internal and external separation from others.[1] Lacan's algebraic *objet a* in itself denotes a motivating lack rather than a reliable internal presence, although without the recognition of the Other of the symbolic world and the unconscious, the subject would remain in a psychotic cocoon.

These differences may not be as absolute as they at first appear: Kleinian depressive concern implies tolerance of loss and lack. However, the Kleinian view emphasizes dependence on one's objects, internal and external, as the route to mental health. Bion, in part, transcends this view, although his theory of mind is predicated on the introjection of maternal containment. The Independents incorporate something of both these positions. Although, as I have argued, their thinking can no longer accurately be described as 'object relational', they still partly rely on a model of securely established internal objects. Nonetheless, Independent views on the aesthetic or ecstatic cathexes of objects and the uses of aggression carry the possibilities of object relating into regions which may be surprising, revelatory and disruptive of the influence of the original parental and even analytic influences. Winnicott's groundbreaking 'use of an object', so thoroughly made use of by today's Independents in expanding the uses of intersubjectivity, reveals the value of difference in radical internal subjective freedom and consolidation of 'true self' movements out into the world. Independent views, therefore, incorporate a dual emphasis on both introjection and separation as the routes to aliveness and creativity.

Attainment of neurotic levels of structure is necessary to achieve separation for all three schools, but growth and aliveness are potentiated through more fluid models of mind. The status of the ego within this shifting state of affairs has become vexed. Is it primarily narcissistic and an essential but limited plank in the establishment of subjective process as Lacanians think, or is it a structural precondition for recognition and negotiation of internal and external reality, still an implicit view within much Kleinian and Independent theory? Bion bypasses considerations of the role of the ego with his model of a mind or self in continual evolution or process. Some Independents hover between '. . . identifying ego health as a factor in analysis and in life' (Bollas 1987: 98) and an implicit devaluation of its role through accentuation of other facets of developmental processes such as the breaking open of identifications through a more adventuring approach to analysis (for example Eigen 1981; Ogden 1994a). Gurewich suggests (in relation to Lacanian theory): '. . . there is no need . . . to make a radical distinction between the ego as the agent of the reality principle and the ego as an object narcissistically invested by the subject' (Gurewich 2003: 193). Even if the role of the ego is not an either/or question, these distinctions do lead to marked differences in analytic approach and therefore require further consideration and debate.

Not only is the emphasis increasingly on a self continually in process, but a self which need not be singular and unified but composed of plural strands of impetus and cathexis. Lacan (1967–8) maintained there was nothing in (Freudian) psychoanalytic theory which could accurately be called a self. His stress on the mobility of desire and the unlimited possible permutations and combinations of the (partial) drives as a Surrealist *montage* highlights a decentred subject and one (or several) that may embark on many possible routes of discovery and actualization. This well-chosen word—'subject'—incorporates the elusive nature of any sense of identity. The subject of the unconscious and the drives is fleeting, variable and never ultimately knowable. Some Independents theorize instinctual drive as plural (Bollas in Molino (ed.) 1997) and models of subjectivity as potentially so (Ogden 1994a, 1997; Bollas 1992, 1995). Bion and Meltzer do not conceive of the self as plural, but their model of mind in evolution through thought and transient contacts with 'O', and the formative value of 'aesthetic reciprocity' like the Independents' aesthetic or ecstatic cathexes of objects, open the possibility of a multiple, plural journey of intense engagements with internal and external sources of enrichment.

Divergences in these three schools' clinical practice abound. The same patient might be diagnosed differently by each, leading to a profound disparity in treatment approach (see Chapter 6). The lack of clinical concepts of narcissism and borderlinity in the Lacanian school, the arguably insufficient attention paid to the structure of perversion in the post-Kleinian group and its differentiation from sexual practice in the Independent school are but a few striking examples. Even within a supposed diagnostic convergence, contrasting clinical practices result in totally different analytic experiences. The use of transference interpretations as the principal mutative instrument (post-Kleinians and sometimes Independents) and the provocation of ambiguity and contradiction in the analysand's discourse to produce new meaning(s) (Lacanians and sometimes Independents) constitute such diametrically opposed approaches as to stretch the meaning of psychoanalysis as a treatment modality to its limits.

Lacan's (1963) 'excommunication' from the IPA and the continued exclusion of the Lacanian school may impoverish the internal resources of psychoanalysis. In Britain at least, Lacanian theory is often absent in clinical training curricula, despite the fact that some leading contemporary theorists have used it to sharpen their theoretical approach, enliven their practice, put existing psychoanalytic shibboleths into question and re-focus on the unconscious. Meadow, for example, emphasizes the North American 'Modern' stress on the analysand's finding the truth of their own desire and 'drive destiny' instead of identifying with an analyst's desire for them. She suggests the Lacanian technique of 'punctuation' can be used to bring emotion into connection with repressed ideas and the excitement attached to the drive-related impulse as opposed to interpretation of defences against it (Meadow 2003: 10–21). Ogden uses Lacanian theory as a point of contrast: Lacan's symbolic third (the Name of the Father), although '. . . creating a space in which the interpreting, self-reflective, symbolizing subject is generated', lacks the intersubjective and transitional dimension of his own 'analytic third' (Ogden 1994a: 64). Bollas (1992, 1995) is fascinated both by the formative power of the Lacanian 'real', waiting to be discovered in the object world, and by the unconscious freedom generated by the associative slide of the signifier.

The recognition of difference as a route to development is theorized differently by all three schools. Winnicott's 'object usage', evolved into multiple forms of intersubjectivity in Independent thought, shows how difference in itself feeds the self as the shock of radical otherness forces an awakening recognition of one's own boundaries and limitations. Irigaray's

(1984) argument for the acknowledgment of sexual difference as a way out of an implicitly monosexual culture could be applied in social and racial arenas, where Lacanian theory is already being used within cultural studies (e.g. Bhabha 1994; Lane (ed.) 1998). Bion grounds the ability to learn in the capacity to metabolize difference (Bion 1962) and his concept of O suggests the apprehension of real alterity to be a very sophisticated accomplishment (Bion 1970).

The elucidation and elaboration of how social, sexual, racial and cultural differences can become an integral part of the psychoanalytic process remains one of the foremost challenges posed to psychoanalysis today. Although some have begun to tackle this task,[2] it is still relatively rare to see a real clinical engagement with these issues. Without this, the danger remains that psychoanalysis and the psychoanalytic psychotherapies may be insulated within a privileged and socially narrow backwater. The reluctance of psychoanalysis to recognize its own internal differences and pluralism as one of its most valuable assets may constitute one source of resistance to this essential project.

Throughout this book, I have argued for an urgent reconsideration of the necessity of psychoanalytic pluralism. The philosophical difficulty—even omnipotence—of an attempt to synthesize paradigms as diverse as the three outlined here need not be further underlined. In Lacanian terms, such an attempt would be 'imaginary'—based on the illusion that external reality can be brought under the domain of one's own narcissistic image. In Independent theory, such a project would be seen as a preference for remaining cocooned in projective/introjective mechanisms and a refusal of the bracing developmental shock of a confrontation with external difference. In Bion's terms, it would be psychotic: the incapacity to engage with 'multiple vertices', or the ability to view the same issue from different perspectives, results in a delusional single-mindedness and certainty. Within Lacanian thought, an attempt to construct a metatheory is also psychotic: Lacan's dictum '. . . there is no Other of the Other' (Lacan 1960 [2001]: 344) refers to the absolute necessity of accepting one's own lack in any authentic engagement with symbolic meaning.

How can these three psychoanalytic paradigms hope to learn from each other if they do not acknowledge and respect their mutual differences? In this book, I have tentatively indicated how this might begin. For the Lacanians, a consideration of issues of containment and perhaps also more attention to affect may be necessary. For the post-Kleinians, a more serious weighting of external reality, humility and tentativeness, and for the Independents a more robust engagement with human destructiveness could strengthen their praxes. The future growth of psychoanalytic theory depends on our honouring the wealth of diversity that lies within it. As Green (2005b) and Wallerstein (2005) suggest, this can only really come about through detailed clinical discussion of respective practices. I hope that, as well as giving a picture of the enormous range of psychoanalytic theory today, this book may act as a spur to the furtherance of comparative cross-paradigmatic discussion.

NOTES

1. Lacan's (1959–60) concept of 'extimacy' (see Chapter 3) and later (post-1964) use of topological concepts render the distinction between internal and external problematic.
2. See, for example, Littlewood and Lipsedge (1982), White (1989), Kareem and Littlewood (1992), O'Connor and Ryan (1993), Dalal (2002), Davids (2003), Maguire (2004).

Bibliography

Wherever possible, references to Freud are given to the most recent editions in Penguin Classics and Penguin Modern Classics. Where the work cited has not yet been published in Penguin Classics (to 2005), reference is given to the Standard Edition (SE) (London: Vintage).

Similarly, wherever there is an official translation of Lacan's text, I quote from and refer to that. Where these are unavailable (to 2005), I refer to the French texts edited by Jacques-Alain Miller (Paris: du Seuil). Where these are unavailable (to 2005), I refer to the unofficial translation by Cormac Gallagher from unedited manuscripts.

Abram, J. (ed.) (2000) *André Green at the Squiggle Foundation*, London and New York: Karnac.

Appignanesi, L. and Forrester, J. (1992) *Freud's Women*, London: Weidenfeld and Nicolson.

Aron, L. and Mitchell, S. A. (eds) (1999) *Relational Psychoanalysis – the emergence of a tradition*, Hillsdale, NJ, and London: Analytic Press.

Arrué, O. (1995) 'Chile' in P. Kutter (ed.) *Psychoanalysis International*, Vol. 2, Stuttgart: Frommann-Holzboog.

Astor, J. (1995) *Michael Fordham – innovations in analytical psychology*, London and New York: Routledge.

Bachelard, G. (1958) trans. Maria Jolas (1964) *The Poetics of Space*, Orion Press; reprinted (1969, 1994) Boston, MA: Beacon Press.

—— (1971) *The Poetics of Reverie*, trans. D. Russell, Boston: Beacon Press.

Bain, A. (1982) *The Baric Experiment: The design of jobs organization for the expression and growth of human capacity*, Tavistock Institute of Human Relations Occasional Paper No. 4.

Balint, M. (1968) *The Basic Fault*, London: Tavistock.

Barthes, R. (1955) *The Semiotic Challenge*, trans. R. Howard, University of California Press, 1995.

Bass, A. (2001) 'It takes one to know one, or whose unconscious is it anyway?', *Psychoanalytic Dialogues*, 11: 683–702.

Bateman, A. (1998) 'Thick and thin-skinned organizations and enactment in borderline and narcissistic disorders', *International Journal of Psychoanalysis*, 79: 13–26.

Bateman, A. and Holmes, J. (1995) *Introduction to Psychoanalysis*, London and New York: Routledge.

Bell, D. (1997) 'Primitive mind of state', in *Psychoanalytic Psychotherapy*, 10: 45–57.

Benjamin, J. (1988) *The Bonds of Love: Psychoanalysis, feminism and the problem of domination*, New York: Pantheon Books; and (1990) London: Virago.

—— (1995) *Like Subjects, Love Objects: Essays on recognition and sexual difference*, New Haven and London: Yale University Press.

—— (1998) *Shadow of the Other – intersubjectivity and gender in psychoanalysis*, New York and London: Routledge.

Benvenuto, B. and Kennedy, R. (1986) *The Works of Jacques Lacan: An introduction*, London: Free Association Books.

Berenson, B. (1950) *Aesthetics and History*, London: Constable.

Bhabha, H. (1994) *The Location of Culture*, London and New York: Routledge.

Bion, W. R. (1957) 'Differentiation of the psychotic from the non-psychotic personalities', *International Journal of Psychoanalysis*, 38: 266–75; reprinted in *Second Thoughts* (1967), London: Heinemann; and also in E. B. Spillius (ed.) (1988) *Melanie Klein Today*, Vol. I, London and New York: Routledge.

—— (1959) 'Attacks on linking', *International Journal of Psychoanalysis*, 40: 308–15; reprinted in *Second Thoughts* (1967), London: Heinemann; and also in E. B. Spillius (ed.) (1988) *Melanie Klein Today*, Vol. I, London and New York: Routledge.

—— (1961) *Experiences in Groups and Other Papers*, London: Tavistock.

—— (1962a) *Learning from Experience*, London: Heinemann; and (1984) London: Karnac.

—— (1962b) 'A theory of thinking', *International Journal of Psychoanalysis*, 43: 306–10; reprinted in *Second Thoughts*, (1967) London: Heinemann, and (1984) London: Karnac; and also in E. B. Spillius (ed.) (1988) *Melanie Klein Today*, Vol. I, London and New York: Routledge.

—— (1963) *Elements of Psychoanalysis*, London: Heinemann; and (1984) London: Karnac.

—— (1965) *Transformations*, London: Heinemann; and (1984) London: Karnac.

—— (1967) *Second Thoughts*, London: Heinemann; and (1984) London: Karnac.

—— (1970) *Attention and Interpretation*, London: Tavistock; and (1984) London: Karnac.

—— (1977) *Two Papers: The grid and the caesura*, Rio de Janeiro: Imago Editora; and (1989) London: Karnac.

—— (1992) *Cogitations*, London: Karnac.

Bion Talamo, P. (1997) 'Bion: A Freudian innovator', *British Journal of Psychotherapy*, 14: 47–59.

Bion Talamo, P., Borgogno, F. and Merciai, S. (eds) (2000) *W.R. Bion: Between past and future*, London and New York: Karnac.

Black, M. J. and Mitchell, S. (1995) *Freud and Beyond – a history of modern psychoanalytic thought*, New York: Basic Books.

Blake, W. (1789) 'Infant joy', in G. Keynes (ed.) (1969) *Blake – Complete Writings*, London, Oxford and New York: Oxford University Press.

—— (1790–3) 'The marriage of heaven and hell', in G. Keynes (ed.) (1969) *Blake – Complete Writings*, London, Oxford and New York: Oxford University Press.

Bléandonu, G. (1994) *Wilfred Bion: His life and works 1897–1979*, trans.

C. Pajaczkowska, London: Free Association Books, and New York: Guilford Press.

Blum, H. P. (1983) 'The position and value of extratransference interpretations', *Journal of the American Psychoanalytic Association*, 31: 587–617.

Bollas, C. (1979) 'The transformational object', *International Journal of Psychoanalysis*, 60: 97–107; reprinted in *The Shadow of the Object* (1987), London: Free Association Books.

—— (1987) *The Shadow of the Object: Psychoanalysis of the unthought known*, London: Free Association Books.

—— (1989) *Forces of Destiny: psychoanalysis and human idiom*, London: Free Association Books.

—— (1992) *Being a Character – psychoanalysis and self experience*, New York: Hill & Wang; and (1993) London and New York: Routledge.

—— (1995) *Cracking Up – the work of unconscious experience*, New York: Hill & Wang; and London: Routledge.

—— (1999) *The Mystery of Things*, London and New York: Routledge.

—— (2000) *Hysteria*, London and New York: Routledge.

—— (2004) *Dark at the End of the Tunnel*, London: Free Association Books.

—— (2005) *I Have Heard the Mermaids Singing*, London: Free Association Books.

Borossa, J. (2001) *Hysteria*, Cambridge: Icon Books, and Maryland: Totem Books.

Bowie, M. (1991) *Lacan*, London: Fontana Modern Masters.

—— (1993) *Psychoanalysis and the Future of Theory*, Oxford: Blackwell.

Bowlby, J. (1969) *Attachment and Loss: Vol. 1. Attachment*, New York: Basic Books.

—— (1973) *Attachment and Loss: Vol. 2. Separation: anxiety and anger*, New York: Basic Books.

—— (1980) *Attachment and Loss: Vol. 3. Loss: sadness and depression*, New York: Basic Books.

Britton, R. (1989) 'The missing link: Parental sexuality in the Oedipus Complex', in R. Britton, M. Feldman and E. O'Shaunessy (eds) *The Oedipus Complex Today*, London: Karnac.

—— (1992) 'The Oedipus situation and the depressive position' in R. Anderson (ed.) *Clinical Lectures on Klein and Bion*, London and New York: Routledge.

—— (1998) *Belief and Imagination: Explorations in psychoanalysis*, London and New York: Routledge.

—— (2003) *Sex, Death and the Superego – experiences in psychoanalysis*, London and New York: Karnac.

Burgoyne, B. (1997) 'Interpretation', in B. Burgoyne and M. Sullivan (eds) *The Klein–Lacan Dialogues*, London: Rebus Press.

—— (ed.) (2000a) *Drawing the Soul: Schemas and models in psychoanalysis*, London: Rebus Press; and (2003) London: Karnac.

—— (2000b) 'Autism and topology', in B. Burgoyne (ed.) *Drawing the Soul*, London: Rebus Press; and (2003) London: Karnac.

—— (2003) 'From the letter to the matheme: Lacan's scientific methods', in J-M. Rabaté (ed.) *The Cambridge Companion to Lacan*, Cambridge: Cambridge University Press.

Butler, J. (1990; 2nd edn 1999) *Gender Trouble: Feminism and the subversion of identity*, London and New York: Routledge.

Campbell, J. (2000) *Arguing with the Phallus: Feminist, queer and post-colonial theory – a psychoanalytic contribution*, London and New York: Zed Books.

Caper, R. (1999) A *Mind of One's Own: A Kleinian view of self and object*, London and New York: Routledge.

Capra, F. (1975) *The Tao of Physics*, London: Wildwood House, and Berkeley, CA: Shambhala; (1976) London: Fontana; and (1983) London: Flamingo.

—— (1982) *The Turning Point: Science, society and the rising culture*, New York: Simon & Schuster, and London: Wildwood House; and (1983) London: Flamingo.

—— (1996) *The Web of Life*, London: HarperCollins.

Casement, P. (1985) *On Learning from the Patient*, London: Tavistock.

—— (1990) *Further Learning from the Patient*, London: Routledge.

—— (2002) *Learning from Mistakes: Beyond dogma in psychoanalysis and psychotherapy*, New York and London: Guilford Press.

Cassese, S. P. (2002) *Introduction to the Work of Donald Meltzer*, London and New York: Karnac.

Castoriadis, C. (1997) *World in Fragments – writings on politics, society, psychoanalysis, and the imagination* (ed. and trans. D. A. Curtis), California: Stanford University Press.

Charraud, N. (2000) 'A calculus of convergence', in B. Burgoyne (ed.) *Drawing the Soul*, London: Rebus Press; and (2003) London: Karnac.

Chasseguet-Smirgel, J. with Luquet-Parat C-J., Grunberger B., McDougall J., Torok M. and David C. (1964) *Female Sexuality – new psychoanalytic views*, (1970) Michigan: University of Michigan Press; and (1985) London: Karnac.

—— (1984) *Creativity and Perversion*, New York: W. W. Norton & Company; and (1985) London: Free Association Books.

—— (1986) *Sexuality and Mind: The role of the father and the mother in the psyche*, New York University Press; reprinted (1989) London: Karnac.

Chodorow, N. (1978) *The Reproduction of Mothering: Psychoanalysis and the sociology of gender*, Berkeley, CA, and London: University of California Press.

Chomsky, N. (1957) *Syntactic Structures*, The Hague: Mouton.

Cohen, M. and Hahn, A. (eds) *Exploring the Work of Donald Meltzer: A festschrift*, London: Karnac.

Coltart, N. (1986) '"Slouching towards Bethlehem . . .", or thinking the unthinkable in psychoanalysis', in Kohon, G. (ed.) *The British School of Psychoanalysis*, London: Free Association Books.

—— (1993) *How to Survive as a Psychotherapist*, London: Sheldon Press.

Costello, S. (2002) *The Pale Criminal: Psychoanalytic perspectives*, London: Karnac.

Dalal, F. (2002) *Race, Colour and the Processes of Racialization – new perspectives from group analysis, psychoanalysis and sociology*, Hove and New York: Brunner-Routledge.

Danneberg, E. (1995) 'Cuba', in P. Kutter (ed.) *Psychoanalysis International*, Vol. 2, Stuttgart: Frommann-Holzboog.

Davids, F. (2003) 'The internal racist', *Bulletin of the British Psychoanalytic Society*, 39: 1–15.

De Simone, G. (1994) *Ending Analysis: Theory and technique*, trans. J. D. Baggott (1997), London: Karnac.

Dor, J. (1985) *Introduction to the Reading of Lacan – the unconscious structured like a language*, J. F. Gurewich with S. Fairfield (eds) (1998), New York: Other Press.
—— (1997) *The Clinical Lacan*, J. F. Gurewich with S. Fairfield (eds), Northvale, NJ, and London: Jason Aronson Inc.
—— (2001) *Structure and Perversions*, trans. S. Fairfield, New York: Other Press.
Egeland, B. and Stroufe, L. A. (1981) 'Developmental sequelae of maltreatment in infancy', in *Developmental Perspectives on Child Maltreatment*, San Francisco: Jossey-Bass.
Eigen, M. (1981) 'The area of faith in Winnicott, Lacan and Bion', *International Journal of Psychoanalysis*, 62: 413–33; reprinted in A. Phillips (ed.) (1993) *The Electrified Tightrope*, Northvale, NJ, and London: Jason Aronson Inc.
—— (1983) 'Dual union or undifferentiation? A critique of Marion Milner's view of the sense of psychic creativeness', *International Review of Psychoanalysis*, 10: 415–28; reprinted in A. Phillips (ed.) (1993) *The Electrified Tightrope*, Northvale, NJ, and London: Jason Aronson Inc.
—— (1985) 'Between catastrophe and faith', *International Journal of Psychoanalysis*, 66: 321–30; reprinted in A. Phillips (ed.) (1993) *The Electrified Tightrope*, Northvale, NJ, and London: Jason Aronson Inc.
—— (1993) A. Phillips (ed.) *The Electrified Tightrope*, New Jersey and London: Jason Aronson Inc.
—— (1998) *The Psychoanalytic Mystic*, London and New York: Free Association Books.
Einstein, A. (1971) *Physics and Beyond: Encounters and conversations*, New York: Harper and Row.
Elliott, A. (1994) *Psychoanalytic Theory – an introduction*, London: Blackwell; 2nd edn (2002) London: Palgrave.
—— (1988; 2nd edn 1999) *Social Theory and Psychoanalysis in Transition – self and society from Freud to Kristeva*, London: Free Association Books.
—— (2001) *Concepts of the Self*, Cambridge: Polity Press, and Malden, MS: Blackwell.
Elliott, A. and Frosh, S. (eds) (1995) *Psychoanalysis in Contexts: Paths between theory and modern culture*, London and New York: Routledge.
Etchegoyen, R. H. (1999) 'Preface', in G. Kohon (ed.) *The Dead Mother*, London and New York: Routledge.
Evans, D. (1996) *An Introductory Dictionary of Lacanian Psychoanalysis*, London and New York: Routledge.
—— (1998) 'From Kantian ethics to mystical experience: An exploration of *jouissance*', in D. Nobus (ed.) *Key Concepts of Lacanian Psychoanalysis*, London: Rebus Press.
Fairbairn, W. R. D. (1952) *Psychoanalytic Studies of the Personality*, London: Tavistock with Routledge and Kegan Paul.
Feldstein, R., Fink, B. and Jaanus, M. (eds) *Reading Seminar XI – Lacan's four fundamental concepts of psychoanalysis*, Albany: State University of New York Press.
Filho, V. F. (1995) 'Brasilia', in P. Kutter (ed.) *Psychoanalysis International*, Vol. 2, Stuttgart: Frommann-Holzboog.
Fink, B. (1995) *The Lacanian Subject – between language and jouissance*, Princeton, NJ, and Chichester: Princeton University Press.

—— (1997) *A Clinical Introduction to Lacanian Psychoanalysis – theory and technique*, Cambridge, MS, and London: Harvard University Press.

—— (1998) 'Translator's notes', in *Encore, The Seminar of Jacques Lacan, Book XX*, New York: W. W. Norton & Company.

—— (2004) *Lacan to the Letter – reading Écrits closely*, Minneapolis and London: University of Minnesota Press.

Fischer, R. and Fischer, E. (1995) 'Russia' in P. Kutter (ed.) *Psychoanalysis International*, Vol. 2, Stuttgart: Frommann-Holzboog.

Fordham, M. (1995) in V. R. Hobdell (ed.), *Freud, Jung, Klein: The fenceless field*, London: Routledge.

Foucault, M. (1977) *Language, Counter-Memory, Practice*, D. Bouchard (ed.), trans. D. Bouchard and S. Simon, Ithaca, NY: Cornell University Press.

Freud, S. (1900) *The Interpretation of Dreams*, SE IV and V, (1953) London: Hogarth; and (2001) London: Vintage.

—— (1905) *Three Essays on the Theory of Sexuality*, SE VII, London: Hogarth; and (2001) London: Vintage.

—— (1909) 'Analysis of a phobia in a five-year-old boy ("Little Hans")', in trans. L. A. Huish (2002) *The 'Wolfman' and Other Cases*, London: Penguin Classics.

—— (1911a) 'Formulations on the two principles of mental functioning', in trans. G. Frankland (2005) *The Unconscious*, London: Penguin Modern Classics.

—— (1911b) *The Schreber Case (Psychoanalytic Remarks on an Autobiographically Described Case of Paranoia (Dementia Paranoides)*, trans. A. Webber (2002), London: Penguin Classics.

—— (1912a) 'On the dynamics of transference', in trans. A. Bance (2002) *Wild Analysis*, London: Penguin Classics.

—— (1912b) 'Advice to doctors on psychoanalytic treatment', in trans. A. Bance (2002) *Wild Analysis*, London: Penguin Classics.

—— (1913) 'On initiating treatment', in trans. A. Bance (2002) *Wild Analysis*, London: Penguin Classics.

—— (1914) 'On the introduction of narcissism', in trans. J. Reddick (2003) *Beyond the Pleasure Principle and Other Writings*, London: Penguin Classics.

—— (1915a) 'Observations on love in transference', in trans. A. Bance (2002) *Wild Analysis*, London: Penguin Classics.

—— (1915b) *The Unconscious*, trans. G. Frankland (2005), London: Penguin Modern Classics.

—— (1915c) 'Drives and their fates', in trans. G. Frankland (2005) *The Unconscious*, London: Penguin Modern Classics.

—— (1917) 'Mourning and melancholia', in trans. S. Whiteside (2005) *On Murder, Mourning and Melancholia*, London: Penguin Modern Classics.

—— (1920) 'Beyond the pleasure principle', in trans. J. Reddick (2003) *Beyond the Pleasure Principle and Other Writings*, London: Penguin Classics.

—— (1923) 'The Ego and the Id', in trans. J. Reddick (2003) *Beyond the Pleasure Principle and Other Writings*, London: Penguin Classics.

—— (1924a) 'Neurosis and psychosis', *SE XIX*, (1961) London: Hogarth; and (2001) London: Vintage.

—— (1924b) 'The dissolution of the Oedipus Complex', *SE XIX*, (1961) London: Hogarth; and (2001) London: Vintage.

—— (1925) 'Negation', in trans. G. Frankland (2005) *The Unconscious*, London: Penguin Modern Classics.

—— (1926) 'Inhibition, symptom, and fear', in trans. J. Reddick (2003) *Beyond the Pleasure Principle*, London: Penguin Classics.

—— (1927) 'Fetishism', in trans. G. Frankland (2005) *The Unconscious*, London: Penguin Modern Classics.

—— (1940) 'The splitting of the ego in defence processes', in trans. G. Frankland (2005) *The Unconscious*, London: Penguin Modern Classics.

Freud, S. with Breuer J. (1893–5) *Studies in Hysteria*, trans. N. Luckhurst (2004), London: Penguin Modern Classics.

Gell-Mann, M. (1994) *The Quark and the Jaguar*, London: Abacus.

Genet, J. (1946) *The Maids and Deathwatch: Two plays*, trans. B. Frechtman (1962), New York: Grove Press.

Gerhardt, S. (2004) *Why Love Matters: How Affection Shapes a Baby's Brain*, Hove and New York: Brunner-Routledge.

Gerlach, A. (1995) 'China', in P. Kutter (ed.) *Psychoanalysis International*, Vol. 2, Stuttgart: Frommann-Holzboog.

Gilligan, C. (1982) *In a Different Voice: Psychological theory and women's development*, Cambridge, MS: Harvard University Press.

Giroud, F. (1990) *Leçons Particulières*, Paris: Fayard.

Glowinski, H., Marks, Z. and Murphy, S. (eds) (2001) *A Compendium of Lacanian Terms*, London: Free Association Books.

Godin, J-G. (1990) *Jacques Lacan, 5, Rue de Lille*, Paris: du Seuil.

Green, A. (1975) 'The analyst, symbolization and absence in the analytic setting', *International Journal of Psychoanalysis*, 56; reprinted in *On Private Madness* (1986) London: Hogarth; and (1997) London: Karnac.

—— (1977a) 'The borderline concept', in P. Hartocollis (ed.) *Borderline Personality Disorders*, New York: International Universities Press; reprinted in *On Private Madness* (1986) London: Hogarth; and (1997) London: Karnac.

—— (1977b) 'Conceptions of affect', *International Journal of Psychoanalysis*, 58; reprinted in *On Private Madness* (1986) London: Hogarth; and (1997) London: Karnac.

—— (1980) 'Passions and their vicissitudes', *Nouvelle Revue de Psychanalyse*, 21; trans. K. Aubertin (1986), in *On Private Madness*, London: Hogarth; and (1997) London: Karnac.

—— (1981) 'Negation and contradiction', in J. Grotstein (ed.) *Do I Dare Disturb the Universe?*, Beverly Hills, CA: Caesura Press, and (1983) London: Karnac; reprinted in *On Private Madness*, (1986) London: Hogarth and (1997) London: Karnac.

—— (1983) 'The dead mother', trans. K. Aubertin (1986), in *On Private Madness* London: Hogarth, and (1997) London: Karnac; and also in trans. A. Weller (2001) *Life Narcissism Death Narcissism*, London: Free Association Books.

—— (1986) *On Private Madness*, London: Hogarth; and (1997) London: Karnac.

—— (1988) *Life Narcissism Death Narcissism*, trans. A. Weller (2001), London and New York: Free Association Books.

—— (1995) 'An interview with André Green', in *New Formations*, 26: 15–35.

—— (1997) *The Chains of Eros – the sexual in psychoanalysis*, trans. L. Thurston (2000), London: Rebus Press; and (2001) London: Karnac.

—— (1998) 'The primordial mind and the work of the negative', *International Journal of Psychoanalysis*, 79: 649–65.

—— (1999a) *The Work of the Negative*, trans. A. Weller, London: Free Association Books.

—— (1999b) 'The greening of psychoanalysis: André Green in dialogues with Gregorio Kohon', in G. Kohon (ed.) *The Dead Mother*, London and New York: Brunner-Routledge.

—— (1999c) *The Fabric of Affect in the Psychoanalytic Discourse*, trans. A. Sheridan, London and New York: Routledge.

—— (2000) 'The intuition of the negative in *Playing and Reality*', in J. Abram (ed.) *André Green at the Squiggle Foundation*, London: Karnac.

—— (2002) *Time in Psychoanalysis*, trans. A. Weller, London: Free Association Books.

—— (2003) *Diachrony in Psychoanalysis*, trans. A. Weller, London: Free Association Books.

—— (2005a) *Key Ideas for a Contemporary Psychoanalysis*, trans. A. Weller, Hove and New York: Routledge.

—— (2005b) 'The illusion of *common ground* and mythical pluralism', *International Journal of Psychoanalysis*, 86: 627–32.

—— (2005c) *Psychoanalysis: A paradigm for clinical thinking*, trans. A. Weller, London: Free Association Books.

Grigg, R. (1998) 'From the mechanism of psychosis to the universal condition of the symptom: On foreclosure', in D. Nobus. (ed.) *Key Concepts of Lacanian Psychoanalysis*, London: Rebus Press.

Grinberg, L. (1990) *The Goals of Psychoanalysis – identification, identity and supervision*, London and New York: Karnac.

Grinberg, L., Sor, D. and Tabak de Bianchedi, E. (1993) *New Introduction to the Work of Bion*, London and Northvale, NJ: Jason Aronson Inc.

Grosskurth, P. (1985) *Melanie Klein*, London: Hodder & Stoughton.

Grosz, E. (1990) *Jacques Lacan – a feminist introduction*, London and New York: Routledge.

Grotstein, J. S. (ed.) (1981) *Do I Dare Disturb the Universe? A memorial to W.R. Bion*, Beverly Hills, CA: Caesura Press; reprinted (1983), London: Karnac.

—— (1993) 'Foreword', in N. Symington, *Narcissism – a new theory*, London: Karnac.

—— (2000a) 'Bion's "transformations in O" and the concept of the "transcendent position"', in P. Bion Talamo, F. Borgogno and S. A. Merciai (eds.), *W.R. Bion: Between past and future*, London and New York: Karnac.

—— (2000b) 'The significance of Bion's concepts of P-S↔D and transformations in O: A reconsideration of the relationship between the paranoid-schizoid and depressive positions – and beyond', in B. Burgoyne (ed.) *Drawing the Soul*, London: Rebus Press, and (2003) London: Karnac.

—— (2002) '"Love is where it finds you": The caprices of the "aleatory object"', in J. Scalia (ed.) *The Vitality of Objects*, London and New York: Continuum.

Grunberger, B. (1989) *New Essays on Narcissism*, trans. D. Macey, London: Free Association Books.

Gunn, D. (2002) *Wool-Gathering or How I Ended Analysis*, Hove and New York: Brunner-Routledge.

Gurewich, J. F. (1999a) 'Who's afraid of Jacques Lacan?', in J. F. Gurewich and M. Tort with S. Fairfield (eds) *Lacan and the New Wave in American Psychoanalysis*, New York: Other Press.

—— (2000) 'The Lacanian clinical field: Series overview', in J. Dor, *Introduction to the Reading of Lacan*, New York: Other Press.

—— (2003) 'A Lacanian approach to the logic of perversion', in J-M. Rabaté (ed.) *The Cambridge Companion to Lacan*, Cambridge and New York: Cambridge University Press.

Gurewich, J. F. and Tort, M. with Fairfield, S. (eds) (1999b) *Lacan and the New Wave in American Psychoanalysis: The subject and the self*, New York: Other Press.

Haber, M. (1992) 'Belgium' in P. Kutter (ed.) *Psychoanalysis International*, Vol. 1, Stuttgart: Frommann-Holzboog.

Habermas, J. (1970) 'A theory of communicative competence', in H. P. Dreitzel (ed.) *Recent Sociology*, no. 2, New York: Macmillan.

Hamilton, V. (1982) *Narcissus and Oedipus – the children of psychoanalysis*, London: Routledge & Kegan Paul; and (1993) London: Karnac.

Hanly, C. (1995) 'Canada' in P. Kutter (ed.) *Psychoanalysis International*, Vol. 2, Stuttgart: Frommann-Holzboog.

Harari, R. (2004) *Lacan's Four Fundamental Concepts of Psychoanalysis: An introduction*, trans. J. Filc, New York: Other Press.

Harmatta, J. and Szönyi, G. (1992) 'Hungary' in P. Kutter (ed.) *Psychoanalysis International*, Vol. 1, Stuttgart: Frommann-Holzboog.

Hegel, G. W. F. (1807) *The Phenomenology of Mind*, trans. J. B. Baillie (1931), London and New York: Macmillan.

Heimann, P. (1950) 'On counter-transference', *International Journal of Psycho-analysis*, 31: 81–4.

Herrigel, E. (1953) *Zen in the Art of Archery*, trans. R. F. C. Hull, London: Routledge & Kegan Paul, and (1985) London: Penguin.

Hill, P. H. F. (2002) *Using Lacanian Clinical Technique – an introduction*, London: Press for the Habilitation of Psychoanalysis.

Hinshelwood, R. D. (1989) *A Dictionary of Kleinian Thought*, London: Free Association Books.

—— (1994) *Clinical Klein*, London: Free Association Books.

Hoggett, P. (1992) *Partisans in an Uncertain World: The psychoanalysis of engagement*, London: Free Association Books.

Holmes, J. (2001) *Narcissism*, Cambridge: Icon Books, and New York: Totem Books.

Husserl, E. (1935) *The Crisis of the European Sciences and Transcendental Phenomenology*, trans. D. Carr, Evanston, IL: Northwestern University Press.

Hyatt Williams, A. (1998) *Cruelty, Violence, and Murder – understanding the criminal mind*, London: Karnac.

Irigaray, L. (1974) *Speculum of the Other Woman*, trans. G. C. Gill (1985), New York: Cornell University Press.

—— (1977) *This Sex Which Is Not One*, trans. C. Porter with C. Burke (1985), New York: Cornell University Press.

—— (1984) *Éthique de la Différence Sexuelle*, Paris: Minuit.

—— (1985) *To Speak is Never Neutral*, trans. G. Schwab (2002), London and New York: Continuum.

Isaacs, S. (1952) 'The nature and function of phantasy', in J. Riviere (ed.) *Developments in Psychoanalysis*, London: Hogarth.

Joseph, B. (1978) 'Different types of anxiety and their handling in the analytic situation', *International Journal of Psychoanalysis*, 59: 223–28; reprinted in *Psychic Equilibrium and Psychic Change* (1989), London and New York: Routledge.

—— (1985) 'Transference: the total situation', *International Journal of Psychoanalysis*, 66: 447–54; reprinted in M. Feldman and E. B. Spillius (eds) (1989) *Psychic Equilibrium and Psychic Change*, London and New York: Routledge.

—— (1989) *Psychic Equilibrium and Psychic Change*, London and New York: Routledge.

Joyce, J. (1916) *Portrait of the Artist as a Young Man*, London: Grafton Books, 1987.

—— (1929) *Ulysses*, Harmondsworth: Penguin, 1986.

—— (1939) *Finnegan's Wake*, London: Penguin Classics, 1999.

Kakar, S. (1995) 'India' in P. Kutter (ed.) *Psychoanalysis International*, Vol. 2, Stuttgart: Frommann-Holzboog.

Kareem, J. and Littlewood, R. (eds) (1992) *Intercultural Therapy – themes, interpretations and practice*, London: Blackwell Science.

Keats, J. (1817) 'Letter to George and Thomas Keats', in M. B. Forman (ed.) *Letters*, London: Oxford University Press, 1948.

Kernberg, O. (1975) *Borderline Conditions and Pathological Narcissism*, Northvale, NJ, and London: Jason Aronson Inc.

—— (1986a) 'Factors in the psychoanalytic treatment of narcissistic personalities', in A. P. Morrison (ed.) *Essential Papers on Narcissism*, New York and London: New York University Press.

—— (1986b) 'Further contributions to the treatment of narcissistic personalities', in A. P. Morrison (ed.) *Essential Papers on Narcissism*, New York and London: New York University Press.

—— (2004) *Aggressivity, Narcissism and Self-Destructiveness in the Psychotherapeutic Relationship*, New Haven, CT: Yale University Press.

Khan, M. M. R. (1963) 'The concept of cumulative trauma', *The Psychoanalytic Study of the Child*, 18; reprinted in *The Privacy of the Self* (1974) London: Hogarth, and (1996) London: Karnac.

—— (1964) 'Ego-distortion, cumulative trauma and the role of reconstruction in the analytic situation', *International Journal of Psychoanalysis*, 45; reprinted in (1974) *The Privacy of the Self*, London: Hogarth; and (1996) London: Karnac.

—— (1969) 'Vicissitudes of being, knowing and experiencing in the analytic situation', *British Journal of Medical Psychology*, 42; reprinted in (1974) *The Privacy of the Self*, London: Hogarth, and (1996) London: Karnac.

—— (1974) *The Privacy of the Self*, London: Hogarth; reprinted (1996) London: Karnac.

—— (1979) *Alienation in Perversions*, London: Hogarth; reprinted (1989) London: Karnac.

—— (1983) *Hidden Selves: Between theory and practice in psychoanalysis*, London: Hogarth; and (1989) London: Karnac.

Klein, M. (1928) 'Early stages of the Oedipus conflict', in (1975a) *Love, Guilt and Reparation and Other Works 1921–1945*, London: Hogarth, and Toronto: Clarke, Irwin & Co.

—— (1935) 'A contribution to the psychogenesis of manic-depressive states', in (1975a) *Love, Guilt and Reparation and Other Works 1921–1945*, London: Hogarth, and Toronto: Clarke, Irwin & Co.

—— (1945) 'The Oedipus Complex in the light of early anxieties', in (1975a) *Love, Guilt and Reparation and Other Works 1921–1945*, London: Hogarth, and Toronto: Clarke, Irwin & Co.

—— (1946) 'Notes on some schizoid mechanisms', in (1975b) *Envy and Gratitude and Other Works 1946–63*, London: Hogarth.

—— (1952a) 'Some theoretical conclusions regarding the emotional life of the infant', in (1975b) *Envy and Gratitude and Other Works 1946–1963*, London: Hogarth.

—— (1952b) 'The origins of transference', in (1975b) *Envy and Gratitude and Other Works 1946–1963*, London: Hogarth.

—— (1955) 'On identification', in (1975b) *Envy and Gratitude and Other Works 1946–1963*, London: Hogarth.

—— (1957) 'Envy and gratitude', in (1975b) *Envy and Gratitude and Other Works 1946–1963*, London: Hogarth.

—— (1960) 'On mental health', in (1975b) *Envy and Gratitude and Other Works 1946–1963*, London: Hogarth.

—— (1975a) *Love, Guilt and Reparation, and Other Works 1921–1945*, London: Hogarth, and Toronto: Clarke, Irwin & Co.

—— (1975b) *Envy and Gratitude and Other Works 1946–1963*, London: Hogarth.

Klein, S. (1981) 'Autistic phenomena in neurotic patients', *International Journal of Psychoanalysis*, 61: 395–402; reprinted in J. S. Grotstein (ed.) *Do I Dare Disturb the Universe?*, Beverly Hills: Caesura Press; and (1983) London: Karnac.

Kohon, G. (ed.) (1986) *The British School of Psychoanalysis: The Independent tradition*, London: Free Association Books.

Kohut, H. (1971) *The Analysis of the Self*, Madison, CT: International Universities Press.

—— (1977) *The Restoration of the Self*, New York: International Universities Press.

Kovel, J. (1970) *White Racism – a psychohistory*, New York: Pantheon Books; (1984) New York: Columbia University Press; and (1988b) London: Free Association Books.

—— (1988a) *The Radical Spirit – essays on psychoanalysis and society*, London: Free Association Books.

Kris, E. (1951) 'Ego psychology and interpretation in psychoanalytic therapy', *Psychoanalytic Quarterly*, XX: 15–30.

Kristeva, J. (1974) 'Revolution in poetic language', in T. Moi (ed.) (1986) *The Kristeva Reader*, Oxford: Blackwell.

—— (1979) 'Women's time', in T. Moi (ed.) (1986) *The Kristeva Reader*, Oxford: Blackwell.

—— (1980a) *Desire in Language: A semiotic approach to literature and art*, trans. T. Gora, New York: Columbia University Press.

—— (1980b) *Powers of Horror*, trans. L. S. Roudiez (1982), New York and Chichester: Columbia University Press.

—— (1983) *Tales of Love*, trans. L. S. Roudiez (1987), New York and Chichester: Columbia University Press.

—— (1993) *New Maladies of the Soul*, trans. R. Guberman (1995), New York and Chichester: Columbia University Press.

—— (1996) *The Sense and Non-Sense of Revolt – the powers and limits of psychoanalysis*, trans. J. Herman (2000), New York and Chichester: Columbia University Press.

Kurzweil, E. (1989) *The Freudians: A comparative perspective*, New Haven, CT: Yale University Press; and (1998) Brunswick, NJ: Transaction Publishers.

Kutter, P. (ed.) (1992) *Psychoanalysis International: A guide to psychoanalysis throughout the world. Vol. 1: Europe*, Stuttgart: Frommann-Holzboog.

Kutter, P. (ed.) (1995) *Psychoanalysis International: A guide to psychoanalysis throughout the world. Vol. 2: America, Asia, Australia, further European countries*, Stuttgart: Frommann-Holzboog.

Lacan, J. (1932) *De la Psychose Paranoïaque dans ses Rapports avec la Personnalité*, (1975) Paris: du Seuil.

—— (1945) 'Le temps logique et l'assertion de certitude anticipée: un nouveau sophisme', in *Écrits I* (1966a; 1st pocket edn 1970; 2nd pocket edn 1999), Paris: du Seuil.

—— (1946) 'Propos sur la causalité psychique', in *Écrits I* (1966a; 1st pocket edn 1970; 2nd pocket edn 1999) Paris: du Seuil.

—— (1948) 'Aggressivity in psychoanalysis', in trans. A. Sheridan (1977), *Écrits: A selection*, London: Tavistock; (1989) London: Routledge; and also (2001) Routledge Classics.

—— (1949) 'The mirror stage as formative of the function of the *I* as revealed in psychoanalytic experience', in trans. A. Sheridan (1977), *Écrits: A selection*, London: Tavistock; (1989) London: Routledge; and also (2001) Routledge Classics.

—— (1952) 'Intervention on transference', in J. Mitchell and J. Rose (eds), trans. J. Rose (1982), *Jacques Lacan and the École Freudienne*, London: Macmillan.

—— (1953) 'The function and field of speech and language in psychoanalysis' (the 'Rome discourse'), in trans. A. Sheridan (1977), *Écrits: A selection*, London: Tavistock; (1989) London: Routledge; and also (2001) Routledge Classics.

—— (1953–4) *The Seminar of Jacques Lacan, book I: Freud's Papers on Technique*, J-A. Miller (ed.), trans. J. Forrester, (1988) Cambridge University Press, and (1991) New York and London: W. W. Norton & Company.

—— (1954) 'Réponse au commentaire de Jean Hyppolite sur la "Verneinung" de Freud', in *Écrits I* (1966a; 1st pocket edn 1970; 2nd pocket edn 1999) Paris: du Seuil.

—— (1954–5) *The Seminar of Jacques Lacan, book II: The Ego in Freud's Theory and in the Technique of Psychoanalysis*, J-A. Miller (ed.), trans. S. Tomaselli, (1988) Cambridge University Press; and (1991) New York and London: W. W. Norton & Company.

—— (1955–6) *The Seminar of Jacques Lacan, book III: The Psychoses*, J-A. Miller (ed.), trans. R. Grigg (1993), New York: W.W. Norton & Company, and London: Routledge.

—— (1956–7) *Le Séminaire, livre IV, La Relation d'Objet*, J-A. Miller (ed.), (1994) Paris: du Seuil.

—— (1957) 'The agency of the letter in the unconscious or reason since Freud', in trans. A. Sheridan (1977), *Écrits: A selection*, London: Tavistock; (1989) London: Routledge; and also (2001) Routledge Classics.

—— (1957–8a) *Le Séminaire, livre V, Les Formations de l'Inconscient*, J-A. Miller (ed.), (1998) Paris: du Seuil.

—— (1957–8b) 'On a question preliminary to any treatment of psychosis' in *Écrits: A selection*, trans. A. Sheridan (1977), London: Tavistock; (1989) London: Routledge; and also (2001) Routledge Classics.

—— (1958a) 'The direction of the treatment and the principles of its power' in *Écrits: A selection*, trans. A. Sheridan (1977), London: Tavistock; (1989) London: Routledge; and also (2001) Routledge Classics.

—— (1958b) 'The signification of the phallus', in trans. A. Sheridan (1977), *Écrits: A selection*, London: Tavistock; (1989) London: Routledge; and also (2001) Routledge Classics.

—— (1958c) 'Guiding remarks for a congress on feminine sexuality', in J. Mitchell and J. Rose (eds), trans. J. Rose (1982) *Jacques Lacan and the École Freudienne*, London: Macmillan.

—— (1958–9) The Seminar of Jacques Lacan, book VI, *Desire and its Interpretation*, trans. C. Gallagher, Private Publication.

—— (1959–60) *The Seminar of Jacques Lacan, book VII, The Ethics of Psychoanalysis*, J-A. Miller (ed.), trans. D. Porter (1992), New York: W. W. Norton & Company, and London: Routledge.

—— (1960) 'The subversion of the subject and the dialectic of desire in the Freudian unconscious', in *Écrits: A selection*, trans. A. Sheridan (1977), London: Tavistock; (1989) London: Routledge; and also (2001) Routledge Classics.

—— (1960–1) *Le Séminaire, livre VIII, Le Transfert*, J-A. Miller (ed.) , (1991) Paris: du Seuil.

—— (1961–2) *The Seminar of Jacques Lacan, book IX, Identification*, trans. C. Gallagher, Private Publication.

—— (1962–3) *Le Séminaire, livre X, L'Angoisse*, J-A. Miller (ed.), (2004) Paris: du Seuil.

—— (1964a) *The Four Fundamental Concepts of Psychoanalysis*, [Seminar XI], J-A. Miller (ed.), trans. Alan Sheridan (1977) London: Hogarth; reprinted (2004) London and New York: Karnac.

—— (1964b) 'Position of the Unconscious', trans. B. Fink, in R. Feldstein, B. Fink and M. Jaanus (eds) (1995) *Reading Seminar XI*, Albany: State University of New York Press.

—— (1964–5) *The Seminar of Jacques Lacan, book XII, Crucial Problems for Psychoanalysis*, trans. C. Gallagher, Private Publication.

—— (1966a) *Écrits I*, Paris: du Seuil; (1970) 1st pocket edn; and (1999) 2nd pocket edn.

—— (1966b) *Écrits II*, Paris: du Seuil; (1971) 1st pocket edn; and (1999) 2nd pocket edn.

—— (1967) 'Place, origine et fin de mon enseignement', in *Mon Enseignement*, Paris: du Seuil, 2005.

—— (1967–8) *The Seminar of Jacques Lacan, book XV, The Psychoanalytic Act*, trans. C. Gallagher, Private Publication.

—— (1969–70) *Le Séminaire, livre XVII, L'Envers de la Psychanalyse*, J-A. Miller (ed.), (1991) Paris: du Seuil.

—— (1972–3) *The Seminar of Jacques Lacan, book XX, On Feminine Sexuality – the Limits of Love and Knowledge*, J-A. Miller (ed.), trans. B. Fink (1998), New York: W. W. Norton & Company.

—— (1975–6) *Le Séminaire, livre XXIII. Le Sinthome*, J-A. Miller (ed.), (2005) Paris: du Seuil.

Laing, R.D. (1961) *Self and Others*, London: Tavistock; (1969) New York: Pantheon; and (1971) Harmondsworth: Penguin.

Laing, R.D. and Esterson, A. (1964) *Sanity, Madness and the Family*, London: Tavistock; and (1970) Harmondsworth: Penguin.

Lane, C. (ed.) (1998) *The Psychoanalysis of Race*, New York: Columbia University Press.

Langer, M. (1989) *From Vienna to Managua – journey of a psychoanalyst*, trans. M. Hooks, London: Free Association Books.

—— (2000) *Motherhood and Sexuality*, trans. N. C. Hollander, New York: Other Press.

Lasch, C. (1979) *The Culture of Narcissism*, New York: W. W. Norton & Company; and (1980) London: Abacus.

Lévi-Strauss, C. (1949) *The Elementary Structures of Kinship*, Boston: Beacon Press, 1969.

Libbrecht, K. (2001) 'Imaginary', in H. Glowinski, Z. M. Marks and S. Murphy (eds) *A Compendium of Lacanian Terms*, London: Free Association Books.

Limentani, A. (1979) 'The significance of transsexualism', in *International Review of Psychoanalysis*, 6: 379–99.

Littlewood, R. and Lipsedge, M. (1982) *Aliens and Alienists – ethnic minorities and psychiatry*, Harmondsworth: Penguin.

Lopez-Corvo, R. E. (2003) *The Dictionary of the Work of W. R. Bion*, London: Karnac.

Lowenthal, U. and Cohen, Y. (1992) 'Israel' in P. Kutter (ed.) *Psychoanalysis International*, Vol. 1, Stuttgart: Frommann-Holzboog.

Lunacek, M. (1995) 'Slovenia' in P. Kutter (ed.) *Psychoanalysis International*, Vol. 2, Stuttgart: Frommann-Holzboog.

Maguire, M. (1995; 2nd edn 2004) *Men, Women, Passion and Power – gender issues in psychotherapy*, London and New York: Routledge.

Mahler, M., Pine, F. and Bergman, A. (1975) *The Psychological Birth of the Human Infant – symbiosis and individuation*, London: Hutchinson; and (1985) London: Karnac.

Mann, D. (1999) 'Erotic narratives in psychoanalytic practice', in D. Mann (ed.) *Erotic Transference and Countertransference: Clinical practice in psychotherapy*, London and New York: Routledge.

Martin, R. T. (1995) 'Australia' in P. Kutter (ed.) *Psychoanalysis International*, Vol. 2, Stuttgart: Frommann-Holzboog.

Marty, P. and de M'uzan, M. (1963b) 'La pensée opératoire', in *Revue Française de Psychanalyse*, 27: 1345–56.

Marty, P., de M'uzan, M. and David, C. (1963a) *L'Investigation Psychosomatique*, Paris: Presses Universitaires de France.

McDougall, J. (1978) *Plea for a Measure of Abnormality*, (1980) Madison, CT: International Universities Press; and (1990) London: Free Association Books.

—— (1982) *Theatres of the Mind: Truth and illusion on the psychoanalytic stage*, (1985) New York: Basic Books; and (1986) London: Free Association Books.

—— (1989) *Theatres of the Body: A psychoanalytic approach to psychosomatic illness*, London: Free Association Books.

—— (1995) *The Many Faces of Eros – a psychoanalytic exploration of human sexuality*, London: Free Association Books.

Meadow, P. W. (2003) *The New Psychoanalysis*, New York and Oxford: Rowman & Littlefield.

Meltzer, D. (1966) 'The relation of anal masturbation to projective identification', *International Journal of Psychoanalysis*, 47: 335–42; reprinted in E. B. Spillius (ed.) (1988) *Melanie Klein Today*, Vol. I, London and New York: Routledge.

—— (1967) *The Psychoanalytical Process*, Perthshire: Clunie Press.

—— (1968) 'Terror, persecution and dread', *International Journal of Psychoanalysis*, 49; reprinted in (1973) *Sexual States of Mind*, Perthshire: Clunie Press.

—— (1973) *Sexual States of Mind*, Perthshire: Clunie Press.

—— (1978) *The Kleinian Development*, Perthshire: Clunie Press.

—— (1984) *Dream Life*, Perthshire: Clunie Press.

—— (1986) *Studies in Extended Metapsychology – clinical applications of Bion's ideas*, Perthshire: Clunie Press.

—— (1992) *The Claustrum: An investigation of claustrophobic phenomena*, Perthshire: Clunie Press.

—— (1994) *Sincerity and Other Works*, A. Hahn (ed.), London: Karnac.

—— (2000) 'A review of my writings', in M. Cohen and A. Hahn (eds) *Exploring the Work of Donald Meltzer*, London: Karnac.

Meltzer, D. with Williams, M. H. (1988) *The Apprehension of Beauty: The role of aesthetic conflict in development, art and violence*, Perthshire: Clunie Press.

Meotti, A. (2000) 'A dreamlike vision', in P. Bion Talamo, F. Borgogno and S. A. Merciai (eds.), *W. R. Bion: Between past and future*, London and New York: Karnac.

Metz, C. (1982) *The Imaginary Signifier: Psychoanalysis and cinema*, London: Macmillan.

Miller, E. (1993) *From Dependency to Autonomy – studies in organization and change*, London: Free Association Books.

Miller, J-A. (1995) 'Context and concepts', in R. Feldstein, B. Fink and M. Jaanus (eds) *Reading Seminar XI*, Albany: State University of New York Press.

—— (1996) 'On perversion', in R. Feldstein, B. Fink and M. Jaanus (eds.) *Reading Seminars I and II*, Albany: State University of New York Press.

Millot, C. (1979) *Horsexe: Essay on transsexuality*, trans. K. Hylton (1990), New York: Autonomedia.

Milner, M. (1950) *On Not Being Able to Paint*, London: Heinemann; and (1971) Heinemann Educational.

—— (1952) 'The role of illusion in symbol formation', in M. Klein, P. Heimann and R. E. Money-Kyrle (eds) (1955) *New Directions in Psychoanalysis*, London: Tavistock, and (1985) London: Karnac; reprinted in *The Suppressed Madness of Sane Men* (1987), London and New York: Tavistock.

—— (1956) 'The sense in nonsense (Freud and Blake's Job)', in *The Suppressed Madness of Sane Men* (1987), London and New York: Tavistock.

—— (1957) 'The ordering of chaos', in *The Suppressed Madness of Sane Men* (1987), London and New York: Tavistock.

—— (1969) *The Hands of the Living God – an account of a psycho-analytic treatment*, London: Hogarth; Toronto: Clarke, Irwin & Co.

—— (1987) *The Suppressed Madness of Sane Men – forty-four years of exploring psychoanalysis*, London and New York: Tavistock.

Minsky, R. (1996) *Psychoanalysis and Gender – an introductory reader*, London and New York: Routledge.

Mitchell, J. (2000) *Mad Men and Medusas*, London: Allen Lane and New York: Basic Books.

—— (2003) *Siblings*, Cambridge: Polity Press.

Mitchell, S. A. (1997) *Influence and Autonomy in Psychoanalysis*, Hillsdale, NJ: The Analytic Press.

Molino, A. (ed.) (1997) *Freely Associated: Encounters in psychoanalysis with Christopher Bollas, Joyce McDougall, Michael Eigen, Adam Phillips, Nina Coltart*, London and New York: Free Association Books.

Molino, A. and Ware, C. (2001) *Where Id Was – challenging normalisation in psychoanalysis*, London and New York: Continuum.

Mollon, P. (1993) *The Fragile Self – the structure of narcissistic disturbance and its therapy*, London and Northvale, NJ: Jason Aronson Inc.

Morrison, A. P. (ed.) (1986) *Essential Papers on Narcissism*, New York and London: New York University Press.

Muller, J. and Richardson, W. (1982) *Lacan and Language: A reader's guide to Écrits*, New York: International Universities Press.

Muñoz, M. L. and Grinberg, R. (1992) 'Spain' in P. Kutter (ed.) *Psychoanalysis International*, Vol. 1, Stuttgart: Frommann-Holzboog.

Murdin, L. (2000) *How Much is Enough? Endings in psychotherapy and counselling*, London and New York: Routledge.

Nasio, J-D. (1990) *Hysteria: The splendid child of psychoanalysis*, trans. S. Fairfield (ed.) (1997), Northvale, NJ, and London: Jason Aronson Inc.

—— (1992) *Five Lessons on the Psychoanalytic Theory of Jacques Lacan*, trans. D. Pettigrew and F. Raffoul (1998), Albany: State University of New York Press.

—— (2002) *Un Psychanalyste sur le Divan*, Paris: Éditions Payot et Rivages.

Nemiah, J. (1978) 'Alexithymia and psychosomatic illness', *Journal of Continuing Education in Psychiatry*, 25–37.

Ng, M. L. (1985) 'Psychoanalysis for the Chinese – applicable or not applicable?', in *International Review of Psychoanalysis*, 12: 449–60.

Nobus, D. (ed.) (1998) *Key Concepts of Lacanian Psychoanalysis*, London: Rebus Press.

—— (2000) *Jacques Lacan and the Freudian Practice of Psychoanalysis*, London and Philadelphia, PA: Routledge.

—— (2003) 'Lacan's science of the subject: between linguistics and topology', in J-M. Rabaté (ed.) *The Cambridge Companion to Lacan*, Cambridge: Cambridge University Press.

—— (2004) 'The punning of reason', *Angelaki, Journal of the Theoretical*

Humanities, Vol. 9, no.1, 189–201; and in Nobus, D. and Quinn, M. (2005) *Knowing Nothing Staying Stupid*, Hove and New York: Routledge.

Novelletto, A. (1992) 'Italy' in P. Kutter (ed.) *Psychoanalysis International*, Vol. 1, Stuttgart: Frommann-Holzboog.

Obholzer, A. and Roberts, V. Z. (eds) (1994) *The Unconscious at Work – individual and organizational stress in the human services*, London and New York: Routledge.

O'Connor, N. and Ryan, J. (1993) *Wild Desires and Mistaken Identities*, London: Virago; (1994) New York: Columbia University Press; and (2004) London: Karnac.

Ogden, T. H. (1982) *Projective Identification and Psychotherapeutic Technique*, Northvale, NJ: Jason Aronson Inc.; and (1992) London: Karnac.

—— (1986) *The Matrix of the Mind – object relations and the psychoanalytic dialogue*, Northvale, NJ, and London: Jason Aronson Inc.

—— (1987) 'The transitional Oedipal relationship in female development', *International Journal of Psychoanalysis*, 68: 485–98; reprinted in *The Primitive Edge of Experience* (1989), Northvale, NJ: Jason Aronson Inc.; and London: Karnac.

—— (1989a) *The Primitive Edge of Experience*, Northvale, NJ: Jason Aronson Inc.; and London: Karnac.

—— (1989b) 'The threshold of the male Oedipus Complex', *The Bulletin of the Menninger Clinic*, 53: 394–413; reprinted in *The Primitive Edge of Experience* (1989), Northvale, NJ: Jason Aronson Inc. and London: Karnac.

—— (1994a) *Subjects of Analysis*, London: Karnac.

—— (1994b) 'The concept of interpretive action', *Psychoanalytic Quarterly*, 63; reprinted in *Subjects of Analysis* (1994a), London: Karnac.

—— (1994c) 'The analytic third: Working with intersubjective clinical facts', *International Journal of Psychoanalysis*, 75: 3–20; reprinted in *Subjects of Analysis* (1994a), London: Karnac.

—— (1995) 'Analysing forms of aliveness and deadness of the transference countertransference', *International Journal of Psychoanalysis*, 76: 695–709; reprinted in *Reverie and Interpretation*, (1997) Northvale, NJ: Jason Aronson Inc. and (1999) London: Karnac.

—— (1996) 'The perverse subject of analysis', *Journal of The American Psychoanalytic Association*, 44: 1121–46; reprinted in *Reverie and Interpretation* (1997) Northvale, NJ: Jason Aronson Inc. and (1999) London: Karnac.

—— (1997) *Reverie and Interpretation: Sensing something human*, Northvale, NJ: Jason Aronson Inc; and (1999) London: Karnac.

—— (2001) *Conversations at the Frontier of Dreaming*, Northvale, NJ: Jason Aronson Inc. and London: Karnac.

—— (2004) 'An introduction to the reading of Bion', in *International Journal of Psychoanalysis*, 85: 285–300; reprinted in (2005) *The Art of Psychoanalysis*, London and New York: Routledge.

—— (2005) *The Art of Psychoanalysis – dreaming undreamt dreams and interrupted cries*, Hove and New York: Routledge.

Okonogi, K. (1995) 'Japan' in P. Kutter (ed.) *Psychoanalysis International*, Vol. 2, Stuttgart: Frommann-Holzboog.

O'Shaunessy, E. (1992) 'Psychosis: Not thinking in a bizarre world', in R. Anderson (ed.) *Clinical Lectures on Klein and Bion*, London and New York: Routledge.

Pajaczkowska, C. (2000) *Perversion*, Cambridge: Icon Books and New York: Totem Books.

Pawlak, K. and Sokolik, Z. (1992) 'Poland' in P. Kutter (ed.) *Psychoanalysis International*, Vol. 1, Stuttgart: Frommann-Holzboog.

Penrose, R. (2004) *The Road to Reality: A complete guide to the physical universe*, London: BCA.

Phillips, A. (1988) *Winnicott*, London: Fontana Press.

—— (1993) *On Kissing, Tickling and Being Bored*, London: Faber and Faber.

—— (1994) *On Flirtation*, London: Faber and Faber.

—— (1995) *Terrors and Experts*, London: Faber and Faber.

—— (1998) *The Beast in the Nursery*, London: Faber and Faber.

—— (2000) *Promises Promises*, London: Faber and Faber.

—— (2001) *Houdini's Box – the art of escape*, New York: Vintage Books.

—— (2002) *Equals*, New York: Basic Books.

—— (2005) *Going Sane*, London: Hamish Hamilton.

Pierrakos, M. (2004) *La "Tapeuse" de Lacan*, Paris: L'Harmattan.

Quinn, M. and Nobus, D. (2005) *Knowing Nothing, Staying Stupid: Elements for a psychoanalytic epistemology*, London and New York: Brunner-Routledge.

Quinodoz, J-M. (1991) *The Taming of Solitude: Separation anxiety in psycho-analysis*, trans. P. Slotkin (1993), London and New York: Routledge.

—— (2001) *Dreams That Turn Over a Page: Paradoxical dreams in psychoanalysis*, trans. P. Slotkin (2002), Hove and New York: Brunner-Routledge.

Rabaté, J-M. (ed.) (2003a) *The Cambridge Companion to Lacan*, Cambridge: Cambridge University Press.

—— (2003b) 'Lacan's turn to Freud', in J-M. Rabaté (ed.) *The Cambridge Companion to Lacan*, Cambridge: Cambridge University Press.

Racker, H. (1968) *Transference and Countertransference*, London: Hogarth Press; and (1982) London: Karnac.

Ramon, S., Castillo, H. and Morant, N. (2001) 'Experiencing personality disorder: A participative research', in *International Journal of Social Psychiatry*, 47, 4: 1–15.

Raphael-Leff, J. (1992) 'Mother of Ajase and Jocasta', paper presented to the Tokyo Meeting of Infant Psychiatry.

Rayner, E. (1990) *The Independent Mind in British Psychoanalysis*, London: Free Association Books.

Reich, A. (1960) 'Further remarks on counter-transference', *International Journal of Psycho-analysis*, 41: 389–95.

Reid, S. (1990) 'The importance of beauty in the psychoanalytic experience', *Journal of Child Psychotherapy*, Vol. 16, no. 1: 29–52.

Rey, J. H. (1979) 'Schizoid phenomena in the borderline', J. Le Boit and A. Capponi (eds) *Advances in the Psychotherapy of the Borderline Patient*, New York: Jason Aronson Inc.; reprinted in E. B. Spillius (ed.) (1988) *Melanie Klein Today*, Vol. I, London and New York: Routledge.

—— (1994) *Universals of Psychoanalysis in the Treatment of Psychotic and Borderline States*, London: Free Association Books.

Rey, P. (1989) *Une Saison chez Lacan*, Paris: Robert Laffont.

Richards, B. (ed.) (1984) *Capitalism and Infancy – essays on psychoanalysis and politics*, London: Free Association Books, and Atlantic Highlands, NJ: Humanities Press.

Rimbaud, A. (1871) 'À Georges Izambard', in *Letters and Other Documents*, in *Collected Poems*, trans. O. Bernard (1962), Harmondsworth: Penguin.

—— (1873) 'Mauvais Sang', in *Une Saison en Enfer*, in *Collected Poems*, trans. O. Bernard (1962) Harmondsworth: Penguin.

Riviere, J. (1929) 'Womanliness as a masquerade', *International Journal of Psychoanalysis*, 9: 303–13; reprinted in A. Hughes (ed.) (1991) *The Inner World and Joan Riviere*, London and New York: Karnac.

—— (1936) 'A contribution to the analysis of the negative therapeutic reaction', in A. Hughes (ed.) (1991) *The Inner World and Joan Riviere*, London and New York: Karnac.

—— (1952) 'General introduction to Melanie Klein, Paula Heimann, Susan Isaacs, and Joan Riviere', *Developments in Psycho-Analysis*; reprinted in A. Hughes (ed.) (1991) *The Inner World and Joan Riviere*, London and New York: Karnac.

Roberts, G. (1992) 'The origins of delusion', *British Journal of Psychiatry*, 161: 298–308.

Rodriguez, L. (2001) 'Desire', in H. Glowinski, Z. M. Marks and S. Murphy (eds) *A Compendium of Lacanian Terms*, London: Free Association Books.

Rose, J. (1986) *Sexuality in the Field of Vision*, London: Verso.

Rose, J. and Mitchell, J. (1982) *Jacques Lacan and the École Freudienne – feminine sexuality*, trans. J. Rose, London: Macmillan.

Rosenfeld, H. A. (1952a) 'Notes on the psycho-analysis of the superego conflict in an acute schizophrenic patient', in *Psychotic States*, London: Maresfield, 1965.

—— (1952b) 'Transference-phenomena and transference-analysis in an acute catatonic schizophrenic patient', in *Psychotic States*, London: Maresfield, 1965.

—— (1965) *Psychotic States – a psychoanalytical approach*, London: Hogarth; and (1982) London: Karnac.

—— (1971) 'A clinical approach to the psychoanalytic theory of the life and death instincts: An investigation into the aggressive aspects of narcissism', *International Journal of Psychoanalysis*, 52, 169–78; and also in E. B. Spillius (ed.) (1988) *Melanie Klein Today*, Vol. I, London and New York: Routledge.

—— (1978) 'Notes on the psychopathology and psychoanalytic treatment of some borderline patients', *International Journal of Psychoanalysis*, 53: 215–21.

—— (1987) *Impasse and Interpretation: Therapeutic and anti-therapeutic factors in the psychoanalytic treatment of psychotic, borderline and neurotic patients*, London: Tavistock; and (1988) London and New York: Routledge.

Roudinesco, E. (1982) *Jacques Lacan & Co. – a history of psychoanalysis in France 1925–1985*, trans. J. Mehlman (1986), London: Free Association Books.

—— (1993) *Jacques Lacan – an outline of a life and a history of a system of thought*, trans. B. Bray (1997), New York: Columbia, and Cambridge: Polity.

Rutter, M. and Madge, N. (1976) *Cycles of Disadvantage: A review of research*, London: Heinemann.

Ryle, A. (1995) 'Psychoanalysis, cognitive-analytic therapy, mind and self', *British Journal of Psychotherapy*, 11: 568–74.

Ryle, G. (1949) *The Concept of Mind*, Chicago: University of Chicago Press.

Samuels, A. (1985) *Jung and the Post-Jungians*, London and New York: Routledge & Kegan Paul.

Sandler, J. and Sandler, A-M. (1998) *Internal Objects Revisited*, London: Karnac.

Sandor, V. (1995) 'Romania' in P. Kutter (ed.) *Psychoanalysis International*, Vol. 2, Stuttgart: Frommann-Holzboog.

Saussure, F. de (1966) *Course in General Linguistics*, trans. W. Baskin, New York: McGraw-Hill.

Sayers, J. (1991) *Mothering Psychoanalysis: Hélène Deutsch, Karen Horney, Anna Freud, Melanie Klein*, London: Hamish Hamilton; and (1992) London: Penguin.

—— (2000) *Kleinians – psychoanalysis inside out*, Cambridge: Polity Press; and Malden, MS: Blackwell.

Scalia, J. (ed.) (2002) *The Vitality of Objects: Exploring the work of Christopher Bollas*, London and New York: Continuum.

Schafer, R. (1976) *A New Language for Psychoanalysis*, New Haven, CT: Yale University Press.

—— (1981) *Narrative Actions in Psychoanalysis: Narratives of space and narratives of time*, Worcester, MA: Clark University Press.

—— (1983) *The Analytic Attitude*, New York: Basic Books.

—— (1992) *Retelling a Life: Narration and dialogue in psychoanalysis*, New York: Basic Books.

—— (1997a) *Tradition and Change in Psychoanalysis*, London: Karnac.

—— (ed.) (1997b) *The Contemporary Kleinians of London*, Madison, CT: International Universities Press.

Schneiderman, S. (ed.) (1980) *How Lacan's Ideas are Used in Clinical Practice*, Northfield, NJ, and London: Jason Aronson Inc.

—— (1983) *Jacques Lacan – the death of an intellectual hero*, London and Cambridge, MS: Harvard University Press.

Searles, H. (1958) 'The schizophrenic's vulnerability to the therapist's unconscious processes', *Journal of Nervous and Mental Disease*, 127: 247–62; reprinted in *Collected Papers on Schizophrenia and Related Subjects* (1965), London: Hogarth; and (1986a) London: Karnac.

—— (1959a) 'The effort to drive the other person crazy – an element in the aetiology and psychotherapy of schizophrenia', *British Journal of Medical Psychology*, 32: 1–18; reprinted in *Collected Papers on Schizophrenia* (1965), London: Hogarth; and (1986a) London: Karnac.

—— (1959b) 'Oedipal love in the countertransference', *International Journal of Psychoanalysis*, 40: 180–90; reprinted in *Collected Papers on Schizophrenia* (1965), London: Hogarth; and in (1986a) London: Karnac.

—— (1962) 'Scorn, disillusionment and adoration in the psychotherapy of schizophrenia', in *Collected Papers on Schizophrenia*, (1965) London: Hogarth; and (1986a) London: Karnac.

—— (1963) 'Transference psychosis in the psychotherapy of chronic schizophrenia', *International Journal of Psychoanalysis*, 44: 249–81; reprinted in *Collected Papers on Schizophrenia* (1965) London: Hogarth; and (1986a) London: Karnac.

—— (1965) *Collected Papers on Schizophrenia and Related Subjects*, London: Hogarth; and (1986a) London: Karnac.

—— (1973) 'Concerning therapeutic symbiosis: The patient as symbiotic therapist, the phase of ambivalent symbiosis, and the role of jealousy in the fragmented ego', in *The Annual of Psychoanalysis*, Vol. 1, New York: Quadrangle; reprinted in *Countertransference and Related Subjects* (1979), Madison, CT: International Universities Press.

—— (1979) *Countertransference and Related Subjects*, Madison, CT: International Universities Press.

—— (1986b) *My Work with Borderline Patients*, Northvale, NJ: Jason Aronson Inc.

Segal, H. (1950) 'Some aspects of the analysis of a schizophrenic', *International Journal of Psychoanalysis*, 31: 268–78; reprinted in *The Work of Hanna Segal* (1981), Northvale, NJ: Jason Aronson Inc.; and also in E. B. Spillius (ed.) (1988) *Melanie Klein Today*, Vol. II, London and New York: Routledge.

—— (1957) 'Notes on symbol formation', *International Journal of Psychoanalysis*, 38: 391–7; reprinted in E. B. Spillius (ed.) (1988) *Melanie Klein Today*, vol. I, London and New York: Routledge.

—— (1973) *Introduction to the Work of Melanie Klein*, London: Hogarth; and (1988) London: Karnac.

—— (1979) *Klein*, London: Fontana Modern Masters.

—— (1981) *The Work of Hanna Segal: A Kleinian approach to clinical practice*, Northvale, NJ: Jason Aronson Inc.; and (1986) London: Free Association Books.

—— (1987) 'Silence is the real crime', *International Review of Psychoanalysis*, 14: 3–19.

—— (1997) *Psychoanalysis, Literature and War: Papers 1972–1995*, London and New York: Routledge.

Segal, J. (1985) *Phantasy in Everyday Life – a psychoanalytical approach to understanding ourselves*, Harmondsworth: Penguin.

Self, W. (2002) *Dorian*, London: Viking; and (2003) London: Penguin.

Shamdasani, S. and Munchow, M. (eds) (1994) *Speculations after Freud – psychoanalysis, philosophy and culture*, London and New York: Routledge.

Shepherdson, C. (2000) *Vital Signs – nature, culture, psychoanalysis*, New York and London: Routledge.

Sheridan A. (1977) 'Translator's Note', in *Jacques Lacan – Écrits: A selection*, London: Tavistock; (1989) London: Routledge; and also (2001) Routledge Classics.

Showalter, E. (1985) *Hystories: Hysterical epidemics and modern culture*, London: Picador.

Siegel, A. M. (1996) *Heinz Kohut and the Psychology of the Self*, London and New York: Routledge.

Soler, C. (1996) 'Hysteria and obsession', in R. Feldstein, B. Fink and M. Jaanus (eds) *Reading Seminars I and II*, New York: State University of New York Press.

Spence, D. (1982) *Narrative Truth and Historical Truth: Meaning and interpretation in psychoanalysis*, New York: Norton.

Spillius, E. B. (ed.) (1988a) *Melanie Klein Today: Developments in theory and practice, Volume I: Mainly theory*, London: Routledge.

—— (ed.) (1988b) *Melanie Klein Today: Developments in theory and practice, Volume II: Mainly practice*, London: Routledge.

Spotnitz, H. (1976) *Psychotherapy of Preoedipal Conditions*, New York: Jason Aronson Inc.

—— (1985) *Modern Psychoanalysis of the Schizophrenic Patient*, Northvale, NJ: Jason Aronson Inc.

Stacey, R. D. (1996) *Complexity and Creativity in Organizations*, San Francisco: Berrett-Koehler.

Stallybrass, P. and White, A. (1986) 'Bourgeois hysteria and the carnivalesque', in *The Politics and Poetics of Transgression*, London: Methuen.

Steiner, J. (1985) 'Turning a blind eye: the cover-up for Oedipus', *International Review of Psychoanalysis*, 12: 161–172.

—— (1993) *Psychic Retreats: Pathological organizations in psychotic, neurotic and borderline patients*, London and New York: Routledge.

Steiner, J. and Britton, R. (1994) 'Interpretation: Selected fact or overvalued idea?' *International Journal of Psychoanalysis*, 75: 1069–78.

Stern, D. (1985) *The Interpersonal World of the Infant: A view from psychoanalysis and developmental psychology*, New York: Basic Books.

Stewart, H. (1989) 'Technique at the basic fault regression', *International Journal of Psychoanalysis*, 66: 221–30.

—— (1992) *Psychic Experience and Problems of Technique*, London and New York: Tavistock/Routledge.

Stolorow, R., Brandschaft, B. and Atwood, G. (1987) *Psychoanalytic Treatment: An intersubjective approach*, Hillsdale, NJ: Analytic Press.

Strachey, J. (1934) 'The nature of the therapeutic action of psychoanalysis', *International Journal of Psychoanalysis*, 15: 127–59.

Sullivan, M. and Burgoyne, B. (eds) (1997) *The Klein–Lacan Dialogues*, London: Rebus Press.

Symington, J. and Symington, N. (1996) *The Clinical Thinking of Wilfred Bion*, London and New York: Routledge.

Symington, N. (1983) 'The analyst's act of freedom as agent of therapeutic change', *International Journal of Psychoanalysis*, 10: 283–91; reprinted in G. Kohon (ed.) (1986) *The British School of Psychoanalysis – the Independent tradition*, London: Free Association Books.

—— (1986) *The Analytic Experience – lectures from the Tavistock*, London: Free Association Books.

—— (1993) *Narcissism – a new theory*, London: Karnac.

—— (1994) *Emotion and Spirit*, London: Karnac.

—— (2001) *The Spirit of Sanity*, London and New York: Karnac.

Thurston, L. (1996) '*sinthome*' in D. Evans, *An Introductory Dictionary of Lacanian Psychoanalysis*, New York and London: Routledge.

Tomov, T. and Atanassov, N. (1995) 'Bulgaria' in *Psychoanalysis International*, Vol. 2, Stuttgart: Frommann-Holzboog.

Tort, M. (1999) 'The subject and the self: Conclusions', in J. F. Gurewich, M. Tort and S. Fairfield (eds) *Lacan and the New Wave in American Psychoanalysis*, New York: Other Press.

Trevarthen, C. (1980) 'Communication and cooperation in early infancy: A description of primary intersubjectivity', in M. Bullowa (ed.) *Before Speech: The beginning of interpersonal communication*, New York: Cambridge University Press.

Turquet, P. (1974) 'Leadership: The individual and the group', in A. D. Colman and M. H. Geller (eds) *Group Relations Reader 2*, Washington, DC: A. K. Rice Institute Series 2, 1985.

Tustin, F. (1972) *Autism and Childhood Psychosis*, London: Hogarth; and (1995) London: Karnac.

—— (1981) *Autistic States in Children*, London: Routledge.

—— (1990) *The Protective Shell in Children and Adults*, London: Karnac.

Tynan, K. (1989) *Profiles*, London: Nick Hern Books.

Van Haute, P. (2002) *Against Adaptation: Lacan's 'subversion' of the subject*, trans. P. Crowe and M. Vankerk, New York: Other Press.

Vellacott, P. (1971) *Sophocles and Oedipus: A study of Oedipus Tyrannus with a new Translation*, London: Macmillan.

Verhaeghe, P. (2001) *Beyond Gender – from subject to drive*, New York: Other Press.

Vico, G. (1744) *The New Science of Giambattista Vico*, Cornell: Cornell University Press, 1984.

Waddell, M. and Williams, G. (1991) 'Reflections on perverse states of mind', in *Free Associations*, 22: 203–13.

Waldrop, M. M. (1992) *Complexity: The emerging science at the edge of order and chaos*, New York: Simon & Schuster.

Wallerstein, R. (2005) 'Will psychoanalytic pluralism be an enduring state of our discipline?', *International Journal of Psychoanalysis*, 86: 623–6.

White, J. (1989) 'Racism and psychosis: Whose madness is it anyway?', paper presented at 'Psychoanalysis and the Public Sphere' conference, University of East London, September 1989.

—— (2002) 'On "learning" and "learning about": W. R. Bion's theory of thinking and educational praxis', in D. Barford (ed.), *The Ship of Thought: Essays on psychoanalysis and learning*, London: Karnac.

White, J., Berry, D., Dalton, J., Napthine, G., Prendeville, B. and Roberts, J. (2001) 'Holding and treating severe disturbance in the NHS: The containment of borderline personality disorders in a therapeutic environment', *British Journal of Psychotherapy*, 18 (1): 89–105.

Whitford, M. (ed.) (1991a) *The Irigaray Reader*, Oxford and Malden, MS: Blackwell.

Whitford. M. (1991b) *Luce Irigaray – philosophy in the feminine*, London and New York: Routledge.

Wilde, O. (1891) *The Picture of Dorian Gray*, London: Ward, Lock & Co.; (1949) London: Penguin; and reprinted (1985) Penguin Classics.

Wilden, A. (1968) *The Language of the Self – the function of language in psychoanalysis by Jacques Lacan*, Baltimore, MD and London: Johns Hopkins University Press.

Williams, G. (2000) 'Reflections on "aesthetic reciprocity"', in M. Cohen and A. Hahn (eds) *Exploring the Work of Donald Meltzer*, London: Karnac.

Winnicott, D. W. (1945) 'Primitive emotional development', in (1975) *Through Paediatrics to Psychoanalysis*, London: Hogarth.

—— (1947) 'Further thoughts on babies as persons', in (1967) *The Child, The Family and the Outside World*, Harmondsworth: Penguin.

—— (1950) 'Aggression in relation to emotional development', in (1975) *Through Paediatrics to Psychoanalysis*, London: Hogarth.

—— (1951) 'Transitional objects and transitional phenomena', in (1975) *Through Paediatrics to Psychoanalysis*, London: Hogarth.

—— (1954a) Review of 'Aggression and its interpretation', *British Medical Journal*, 76: 1362–4.

—— (1954b) 'Metapsychological and clinical aspects of regression within the psycho-analytical set-up', in (1975) *Through Paediatrics to Psychoanalysis*, London: Hogarth.

—— (1956) 'Primary maternal preoccupation', in (1975) *Through Paediatrics to Psychoanalysis*, London: Hogarth.

—— (1958b) 'The capacity to be alone', in (1965) *The Maturational Processes and the Facilitating Environment*, London: Hogarth Press.

—— (1960) 'Ego distortion in terms of true and false self', in (1965) *The Maturational Processes and the Facilitating Environment*, London: Hogarth.

—— (1962) 'Ego integration in child development', in (1965) *The Maturational Processes and the Facilitating Environment*, London: Hogarth.

—— (1963) 'Fear of breakdown', in C. Winnicott, R. Shepherd and M. Davis (eds) (1989) *Psychoanalytic Explorations*, London: Karnac.

—— (1965) *The Maturational Processes and the Facilitating Environment*, London: Hogarth Press.

—— (1967) 'The location of cultural experience', *International Journal of Psychoanalysis*, 48; and in *Playing and Reality*, (1971) London: Tavistock; and (1974) Harmondsworth: Penguin.

—— (1968) 'Comments on my paper "The use of an object"', in C. Winnicott, R. Shepherd and M. Davis (eds) (1989) *Psychoanalytic Explorations*, London: Karnac.

—— (1969) 'The use of an object and relating through identifications', in *Playing and Reality* (1971) London: Tavistock; and (1974) Harmondsworth: Penguin.

—— (1971) *Playing and Reality*, London: Tavistock, and (1974) Harmondsworth: Penguin.

Wright, E. (ed.) (1992) *Feminism and Psychoanalysis – a critical dictionary*, Oxford, UK and Cambridge, MS: Basil Blackwell.

—— (2000) *Lacan and Postfeminism*, Cambridge: Icon Books; and New York: Totem Books.

Young, R. (1991) 'Psychoanalysis and political literary theories', in J. Donald (ed.) *Psychoanalysis and Literary Theory – thresholds*, London: Macmillan.

Index